Human Resource Management
in the Asia Pacific Region

STUDIES IN ASIA PACIFIC BUSINESS
ISSN 1369-7153
General Editors:
Robert Fitzgerald, Chris Rowley and Paul Stewart

Greater China: Political Economy, Inward Investment
and Business Culture
Edited by Chris Rowley and Mark Lewis

Beyond Japanese Management: The End of Modern Times?
Edited by Paul Stewart

Management in China: The Experience of Foreign Businesses
Edited by Roger Strange

Of Related Interest

The Competitive Advantages of Far Eastern Business
Edited by Robert Fitzgerald

The State and Economic Development: Lessons from the Far East
Edited by Robert Fitzgerald

DEDICATION

For Clive Rowley

A worker with undimmed pride in his labour:
a shining light for us all

HUMAN RESOURCE MANAGEMENT IN THE ASIA PACIFIC REGION: CONVERGENCE QUESTIONED

edited by
CHRIS ROWLEY

Routledge
Taylor & Francis Group

LONDON AND NEW YORK

First published in 1998 in Great Britain by
FRANK CASS AND COMPANY LIMITED

Published 2021 by Routledge
2 Park Square, Milton Park, Abingdon, Oxon OX14 4RN
605 Third Avenue, New York, NY 10017

*Routledge is an imprint of the Taylor & Francis Group,
an informa business*

Copyright © 1998 by Taylor & Francis.

British Library Cataloguing in Publication Data
Human resource management in the Asia-Pacific region:
convergence questioned
1. Personnel management – Pacific area
I. Rowley, Chris, 1959-
658.3'0091823

ISBN 0 7146 4849 3 (hbk)
ISBN 0 7146 4407 2 (pbk)
ISSN 1369-7153 (book series)

Library of Congress Cataloguing-in-Publication Data
Human resource management in the Asia-Pacific region:
convergence questioned / edited by Chris Rowley.
     p. cm. – (Studies in Asia Pacific business)
     "This group of studies first appeared in a Special Issue
of Asia Pacific Business Review, Vol. 3, No. 4 (Summer
1997)" – Verso t.p.
     ISBN 0-7146-4849-3. – ISBN 0-7146-4407-2
     1. Personnel management –Asia. 2. Personnel management
– Pacific Area. I. Rowley, Chris, 1959-   . II. Series.
HF5549.2.A75H86 1998
658.3'0095–DC21   97-42862
                                                              CIP

ISBN 13: 978-0-7146-4407-3 (pbk)
ISBN 13: 978-0-7146-4849-1 (hbk)

This group of studies first appeared in a Special Issue of
Asia Pacific Business Review (ISSN 1360-2381), Vol.3, No.4 (Summer 1997)
[Human Resource Management in the Asia Pacific Region: Convergence Questioned]

Contents

Introduction: Comparisons and Perspectives on HRM in the Asia Pacific

CHRIS ROWLEY

The focus of this volume – human resource management (HRM) across the Asia Pacific region – while important and salient, is complex and problematic. Yet, a cacophony of commentators have distilled complex developments into simple mantras. These include: 'an organization's employees are its greatest assets' and require careful nurturing, often blindly taken as HRM; the 'Pacific Age' is upon us, and Asia provides a paragon of practices around which companies searching for 'success' and the 'one best way' can converge. Thus, business success, it is often baldly asserted, stems from 'human resources' and their management. While such fashionable nostrums are not new, their profile has been given extra prominence by a phalanx of processes and practices. Competitiveness based on location, capital and even technology was seen as eroding. Many organizations floundered in the early 1980s and 1990s, while economies were increasingly exposed to international trade, competition and capital flows, privatization and marketization, and declining state sectors. An Asian focus emerged with the economic success of Japan (producing a large 'learning from Japan' literature, see *inter alia*, Ouchi, 1981), and then 'Tigers' and 'Dragons'. The spread of factory 'transplants' (with its biological metaphor of foreign practices accepted by host bodies) and usage of the term 'Japanization' (despite debate over its meaning) occurred. Belief in the rejuvenating elixir of 'new' production concepts (such Total Quality Management, Just In Time, Lean Production) and competing by quality and service also grew.

Within all of these developments the management of seemingly ruthlessly efficient workers and white collar professionals was identified as integral and something to try to replicate. Thus, ideas were popularized concerning the need to cultivate closer and more positive relations with employees (Peters and Waterman, 1984), with human resources painted as key to 'progressive', profitable and growing companies (Kanter, 1984) and a vital foundation for corporate success (Kay, 1994). These factors were 'supercharged' by increasingly speedy and powerful communications and technology transference, seemingly allowing 'best practice' to be copied across a 'borderless globe'. At the same time, 'Across the world, HRM has spread its wings and its international pretensions have expanded as so-called globalization has gathered pace' (Warner, 1996:189). There was a

Chris Rowley, Royal Holloway, University of London.

growing awareness of HRM in the global arena and greater understanding of its international dimensions (see, *inter alia*, Dowling and Schuler, 1990). Indeed, approximation to full employment led many Asian countries themselves to take an interest in HRM '... as a prescription for obtaining workforce commitment to increasing productivity' (Leggett and Bamber, 1996:9).

However, much of the above not only implies identifiable, homogeneous and, of course, transferable systems, but is cliche-ridden and contentious. For example, often the quickest way to boost organizational performance (if only in the short term) is simply to downsize rather than engage in sophisticated, long term and expensive people management. There is also a 'darker side' to Asian management practice (see Kamata, 1982; Parker and Slaughter, 1988, for early examples; Stewart, 1996 for others). Such dissenting voices have been reinforced by slowing Asian economic growth and other developments eroding the 'attractiveness' of the model. These include the 1996–97 labour disputes in Korea[1] (Bae *et al.*, 1997); the costs and erosion of key employment practices and economic difficulties in Japan (see Nakamoto, 1997), with stagnant exports and currency and financial sector problems in Thailand and elsewhere (Smith and Sheriden, 1997).

Nevertheless, there remains an enduring fascination with the clarion calls for HRM, universalistic 'best practice' and the Asia Pacific region, and this collection will examine these themes. Such a search often 'casts no shadow', but the picture is frequently more blurred and mixed. Shifts towards HRM are often equivocal and restricted to some practices. Trends may represent more of a converging recognition of the relevance of employees to economic success and types of competition. HRM retains, both between and within locations, its messy diversity. This is partly due, on the one hand, to HRM's '... own cultural base' (Warner, 1996:192) and on the other, to the specific political, socio-economic, cultural and institutional locational milieu.

MAIN THEMES

This collection covers HRM in a selection of varied locations in the Asia Pacific region. The purpose was broad and demanding: to both locate HRM in its wider historical and socio-economic and political contexts, as well as to provide diverse 'real life' examples across a mix of variously developed locations. As HRM is a large topic and attracts diversified opinions, guidelines for contributors, while not overly prescriptive, were designed to ensure some themes, synthesis and overall purpose for the volume.

Contributors were asked to compare and note parallels and contrasts, both within the Asia Pacific and with allusions to the West. Several theoretical and empirical perspectives are raised, and authors were asked to bear in mind the following issues, as HRM does not exist in a vacuum but interacts with wider environments, structures and cultures. First, basic details, such as social, economic, employment and legal matters, political involvement in the economy, the structure of capital and finance, the production. Second, the 'distinctiveness' of HRM practice, such as personnel management (PM), and if any changes are pragmatic responses to opportunities and constraints in environments rather than a coherent, 'new' employment philosophy. Third, the extent of imitation/adaptation of Western conceptions of HRM in various organizations, such as indigenous firms, small and medium-sized enterprises (SMEs), state-owned enterprises (SOEs), joint ventures and multinational enterprises (MNEs). Fourth, the relative value in HRM of explanatory approaches such as convergence, contingency, culture and institutional. In short, not just culturalist, but also more 'structuralist' evidence for HRM (see, *inter alia*, Storey, 1995) were to be explored to locate HRM developments across the Asia Pacific.

KEY ISSUES

An immediate issue in this analysis concerns spatial locations, utilized not because they are somehow 'watertight', but for ease. Much comparison uses the idea of 'national models' as the basic unit of analysis, focusing on macro-institutional features as key dimensions. This is based on assumptions that: national borders are synonymous with market scope; differences across states are more pronounced and salient than variations within; certain national institutional arrangements are more effective than others at adapting to changing political-economic circumstances (Locke, 1995). Yet characterizations of national 'systems', even ones presented as relatively homogeneous, are contested. For instance, 'conventional wisdom' concerning Japan's key employment practices, such as its 'three pillars' of permanent jobs, seniority pay, and enterprise unions (see, *inter alia*, Abegglen, 1958; Dore, 1974) is seen as: stylized (Sako, 1997); a caricature (Price, 1997); partial and ignoring practices such as day labour employment (Fowler, 1996); and eroding (Dawkins, 1997). For example, there has been some weaking of uniform pay systems, as at Matsushita; increasing merit pay, as at Sony, Honda and Mitsubishi; share option schemes at Daiwa Securities, Orix and Toyota (ibid.). Furthermore, diverse employment practices within nations have proliferated and appear to be increasing, weakening national systems (see Locke, 1995; Verma *et al.*, 1995; Katz, 1997). Nevertheless, enterprises remain influenced by national level arrangements and patterns among key actors and history, as seen in the development of Soviet-influenced PM in China (see Kaple, 1994).

A further issue concerns the geographical and organizational coverage of the collection (see Table 1). Many locations are not included (see Rowley, 1996 for those commonly covered in this field), while single chapters *per* location are necessarily broad brush. Also, those included are at different stages of economic development. Following Leggett and Bamber (1996), the locations in this volume can be categorized as: (a) Developed: Japan; (b) Newly Industrialized Economies: First Tier – Singapore, Hong Kong, Korea, Taiwan; Second Tier – Thailand, China;[2] (c)

Beginning Phase: the Philippines. Furthermore, within these locations, a wide and disparate mix of organizations, and descriptions and terms, are used (see Table 1).

TABLE 1
LOCATIONS AND EXAMPLES OF ORGANIZATIONS COVERED

Location: Type:	C	HK	J	K	P	S	Ta	Th
Indigenous: FOEs								✓
Small				✓		✓	✓	
Large		✓	✓	✓	✓	✓	✓	
SOEs	✓	✓			✓		✓	✓
MNEs: Foreign						✓		
Western								✓
American				✓			✓	✓
Japanese		✓		✓			✓	✓
European				✓			✓	
Chinese		✓						
JVs:	✓					✓	✓	✓

Key:
C:	China
HK:	Hong Kong
J:	Japan
K:	Korea
P:	Philippines
S:	Singapore
Ta:	Taiwan
Th:	Thailand
FOEs:	family owned enterprises
SOEs:	state owned enterprises
MNEs:	multinational enterprises
JVs:	joint ventures
✓:	noted (see individual contributions in this volume for greater details concerning size, sectors, ownership, and so on)

Another issue concerns the variety of methods to examine HRM. These are variously utilized in this volume, presenting potential usage and comparability constraints. First, large scale data sets and secondary analysis provide information, for example, about trends from national labour force surveys. Such data has the advantage of being representative and longitudinal. However, it is difficult to establish causality, and care is needed in making direct comparisons between data designed and collected across countries (or times within one country), as 'definitions' are generated by differing historical and ideological suppositions and conceptions. Neither are surveys always available for independent secondary analysis, for example, Singapore's labour force and Japan's Ministry of Labour surveys.[3] Second, questionnaires produce standardized data at relatively limited cost. Yet, only superficial evidence is obtained, and research questions are pre-determined, so that unexpected findings are difficult to integrate, and ethnocentrism (that is, questions relevant to Western audiences meaning little in Asian contexts) can occur (see Sparrow *et al.* 1994). Third, case studies, involving in-depth interviews, observational methods and ethnographies provide data at closer levels, revealing unforeseen issues, and rationales. However, such methods are comparatively expensive, and require extensive knowledge of the society and its language to fully interpret findings, which remain difficult to generalize.

In sum, a diverse range of methods is available to conduct comparative research, and some are utilized in this collection. These impact on results, as does over-reliance on one-sided interviews, questionnaires and surveys of individuals (often management) with personal stakes, for example, in projecting 'success' and 'contented' employees, and concerning 'loaded', value-laden issues, such as 'flexibility'.

Another problem for this volume is the amorphous and contested nature of HRM itself (as a concept, model and theory, see Noon, 1992) and the variety of its meanings and possible 'distinctiveness' from PM. A few broad brush points are worth noting. Classic American views use a HRM 'territory map' (Beer *et al.* 1984), including policy choices, outcomes and long term consequences; or a HRM 'cycle' (Fombrun *et al.* 1984) composed of selection, rewards, appraisal, development and performance. From the UK, Guest's (1987) framework has HRM policies (organization/job design; recruitment, selection and socialization; appraisal, training and development; reward systems; and communication) feeding into outcomes (strategic integration; commitment; flexibility/adaptability; quality) and organizational success. Storey (1987) makes the now popular distinction between 'soft' and 'hard' HRM. Other models and frameworks now exist, but are beyond this piece. Interestingly, Storey (1992:24) outlines four views on HRM. First, it can be a synonym of PM, '...a guileless substitution ...', or a more modern form. Second, it could indicate that various techniques of PM are/ought to be used in a more integrated way. Third, it can be a more business-oriented and business-integrated approach to guiding labour management, with an emphasis on the concept of 'resource'. Fourth, it can contain some extra ingredients, such as commitment.

HRM is often naively linked to 'progressive' practices, enjoying a root metaphor selling 'hope' rather than 'despair' (Dunn, 1990). Yet, HRM should not be rendered down to simplistic associations with 'enlightened' and 'sophisticated' policies; this is so even in its Asian contexts. It can be seen in the problems for workforces in Japanese corporations in a variety of locations (see Garrahan and Stewart, 1992; various contributors to Babson, 1995; Green and Yanarella, 1996; Stewart, 1996). Korean and Taiwanese firms use harsh, authoritarian labour regimes in China, with applicants screened for strength, stamina, military-style obedience and readiness for enforced overtime and long hours (Chan, 1996). There are labour abuses in Vietnam (*Free Labour World*, 1997) and 'authoritarian capitalism' in Singapore (Lingle, 1997). Often practices are a far cry from the ideas of 'empowered', 'respected' and 'resourceful' employees.

This leads onto difficulties in actually distinguishing, quantifying and measuring HRM's impacts. There is also the issue of its commonly argued 'success', not just because of counterfactuals, but association does not imply causality, and whether HRM produces successful organizations or whether it is profitable firms that can afford to employ HRM in the first place. A related issue concerns 'levels' of existence of HRM. For instance, if HRM is a 'package' of ideas and practices, which ones are included, is there an irreducible minimum, and what level and strength of practices have to be in place? (Storey, 1992). A temporal perspective is also required – does HRM need to exist over a period of time? We will not become too engrossed in these endless debates, or make a fetish of definition, as a wealth of literature already exists in this area (see, *inter alia*, Storey, 1995; Blyton and Turnbull, 1992; Sisson, 1994; Legge, 1995; Towers, 1996).

Such problems as the above, visible even with more homogeneous studies, are exacerbated in spatially diverse collections (some with sharp internal cultural, ethnic and religious distinctions) of authors with varied backgrounds and assumptions. Usefully, Warner (in this volume[4]) reviews the differences between Western and Eastern notions of people management, while Benson and Debroux delineate Western HRM and Japanese employment practices, and Bae comprehensively outlines the underpinnings of Confucianism in relation to work matters. Importantly: 'Often the use of HRM notions could pay more attention to local contexts' (Warner, 1996:194). Indeed, varying differences and 'family resemblances' across 16 HRM characteristics have been teased out to produce different country models: Western traditional industrial relations (IR); Western HRM (large MNEs, often US owned); Japanese (large corporations); and Chinese (large SOEs) (ibid.).[5]

The above indicates that HRM is not monolithic in its meanings, aspects or implications. Nevertheless, despite some drawbacks, HRM is broadly, even if somewhat simplistically, conceived as involving the policies and practices in the management of employment.

MAKING COMPARISONS

We are still often faced with comparing disparate information on HRM. One aid here are versions of a framework presented by Storey (1992) and Duberley and Walley (1995) initially distilled by Warner in his contribution

TABLE 2
COMPARING PM WITH HRM

	PM	HRM
1. Rules	defined	flexible
2. Behaviour	norms/customs/practice	values/mission
3. Managerial roles	monitoring	nuturing
4. Key managers	personnel/IR specialist	general/line managers
5. Personnel selection	separated	integrated
6. Payment systems	job evaluation	performance related
7. Work conditions	separate negotiation	harmonized
8. Labour–management	collective	individual contracts
9. Job design	division of labour	teamwork
10. In-house training	distinct	ongoing

Sources: based on Storey (1992), Duberley and Walley (1995)

here and utilized in many of the volume's contributions. This contrasts various employment elements (see Table 2) under 'typical' HRM and PM regimes.

Yet, as Warner (1996:189) perceptively warns, many authors seem to believe that a mixture of national HRM pieces constitutes an international mix '... although there may be no over-arching conceptual framework'. For Verma *et al.* (1995), the need to locate both the role of national institutions and the micro-level in comparisons led to a common analytical framework to assess Asia Pacific employment. A set of five HRM practices was used to provide 'windows' through which to examine changes: nature of work organization; skill formation; compensation systems (structure and level); employment security and staffing; and corporate governance. Comparisons of HRM dimensions are used to varying extents in this collection, as shown in Table 3. Some of these, notably training and remuneration, are also common across many of the locational studies.

Another way to view comparisons in the Asia Pacific is in the Jennings *et al.* (1995) framework. This is outlined in Table 4, with the present collection's locations amended where appropriate by the contributors. Moore and Jennnings (1995) assert that the relationship between external and internal labour markets (whose interface is critically influenced by the state and organized labour) is associated with features of a firm's HRM system, the degree of bureaucratization and professionalization of HRM. Characteristics of HRM systems (supply and demand for labour and dynamism of external labour markets, direct and indirect effects of the state, labour organization, and culture) are each associated with the complexity, formalization and centralization of internal labour markets within medium/large organizations. The relationship between the two types of labour market is, in turn, associated with the features (degree of bureaucratization and professionalization of human resource personnel) of the firm's HRM system.

Finally, what must also be recognized, and remembered, is the role

TABLE 3
SELECTED HRM PRACTICES UTILIZED WITHIN LOCATIONS

China
(Warner)
- rewards
- social insurance
- trade unions
- workers congresses

Japan
(Benson and Debroux)
- employment security
- compensation
- recruitment
- training
- promotion
- role of personnel department
- equal employment opportunities
- trade unions

Korea
(Bae)
- work systems
- human resource flow:
  • recruitment and selection
  • promotion
  • termination and retirement
- training and development
- performance appraisal and reward systems

The Philippines
(Amante)
- skills development
- compensation practices
- determination of work rules
- labour co-operation schemes

Singapore
(Yuen)
- trade union organization
- employment relations
- wage settlement
- training and development
- social insurance

Taiwan
(Chen)
- staffing
- training and development
- compensation
- participation
- security

Thailand
(Lawler et al.)
- human resource strategic planning
- staffing
- compensation
- training and development

within HRM of critical and external forces. Often literature in this area is not just ahistorical and descriptive, but also prescriptive, and reads as if HRM can be simply management guru-created and managerially-directed (as implied by the obsession with 'strategic HRM'). Yet, key among influencing variables is the role of labour and the state (along with organizational economic performance and business strategies, often external to the HRM function[6]). These are seen within the locational studies that follow.

TABLE 4
INSTITUTIONAL AND POLICY FEATURES OF ASIA PACIFIC HRM

Location:	C	HK	J	K	P	S	Ta	Th
External Labour Market:								
Surplus unskilled labour	H	L	M	L	H	L	L	M
Surplus skilled labour	L	L	L	L	Mi	L	L	L
Volatile market	M	H	H	H	M	H	H	M
Direct state involvement	Md	L	L	H	M	H	H	M
Indirect state involvement	Mi	M	M	M	L	M	M	L
Labour organization	M	L	M	H*	Ld	M	M	M
Cultural diversity	L	M	L	L	M	M	L	L
Labour firm presence	H	M	Li	H	H	L	M	M
Internal Labour Market:								
Complexity	M	M	H	H	L	M	M	M
Formalization	L	L	Li	M	M	M	M	M
Centralization	L	L	M	M	L	M	M	L
Firm's HRM System:								
Bureaucratized	Li	Li	M	Mi	Md	M***	Mi	M
Professionalized	L	Mi	Li	Li**	Li	Mi	Mi	L

Key:
C: China
HK: Hong Kong
J: Japan
K: Korea
P: Philippines
S: Singapore
Ta: Taiwan
Th: Thailand

H: High
M: Medium
L: Low
i: Increasing
d: Decreasing

Specific author points:
* But union density is low and has been decreasing continually
** For indgenous firms, while 'Mi' for foreign subsidiaries
*** Trend is complex: while the HRM system for small and medium sized firms are becoming more formalized, the systems in some MNEs, high tech firms and firms that have gone regional have become more flexible/less bureaucratic.

Source: Adopted from Jennings *et al.* (1995), with amendments by current contributors.

PERSPECTIVES ON DIFFERENCES

Several theories accounting for differences across countries can be applied to HRM.[7] Broadly, these emphasize the structural characteristics of organizations (convergence and contingency theory) or cultural factors (ideational and institutional approaches) (see Rowley and Lewis, 1996). Many of the contributors provide data and insights on these approaches.

Convergence theorists (see, *inter alia*, Kerr *et al.*, 1962) assumed that processes of industrialization and spreading technology would move countries towards similarities. However, such views over-simplified developments and over-emphasized technology's impacts, while failing to see the instabilities created for Western capitalist societies by interest group activity on the operation of the market mechanism and the challenges and demands of organized labour (Goldthorpe, 1985). Furthermore, not only does convergence require something identifiable to converge around, but temporal factors (such as starting points, speed of change), along with comparison judgements, are important (see Locke, 1995). For example, Chan (1995) notes compatibilities between certain legacies of Maoist socialism in SOEs and the Japanese model of management, including support for 'companymen' (sic), paternalism, workers responding to appreciation and not regarding relations with management as necessarily conflictual (see also Ng and Warner, 1998, on this point). Likewise, units and levels of analysis can become blurred – is it convergence at international (Asia Pacific locations moving towards each other or the West; Western locations moving towards the Asia Pacific), national, sectoral, enterprise, production system, workplace, HRM policy or practice levels? Are trends to be across or within the units? As Lipietz (1995:345) concludes, '...there already exists a large variety of industrial relations even within advanced capitalist countries. Moreover, in these very countries, the divergences are increasing ...'

Another way to look at variations is via contingency theory. This recognizes that working practices are affected by differences in technology (Woodward, 1965), operating environments (Lawrence and Lorsch, 1967), and so on. However, as these contingent factors still impose a 'rational logic' of administration and organization, such approaches fail to understand that the way ideas and practices are interpreted and implemented varies between and within countries.

This sort of complexity, and the uncertainties produced, often allow both support and refutation of convergence. Thus, Locke (1995) suggests that four common patterns are emerging across advanced industrial countries: an enterprise focus (as locus of HRM decision making and strategy); increased flexibility (in work organization and labour deployment); growing importance of skill development; and declining union membership. Yet, Locke goes on to argue that common trends are sometimes deceiving, given that not all countries began at the same starting point and, crucially, seemingly similar practices and arrangements have significantly *different meanings* across national contexts. Therefore, he sees national variations in: work organization, types and diffusion; job mobility, staffing and employment security; compensation; human resources and firm governance. Similarly, Sparrow *et al.* (1994) conclude that there is HRM convergence (across 15 characteristics and 12 countries), but then add that there is still some clear divergence.[8] Even within a single sector, telecommunications, inter- and intra-nationally convergence and divergence can be indicated (see Katz, 1997). Similarly, work on the steel industry (Hasegawa, 1996) shows convergence, with Britain following Japan in some developments (production systems), but also the reverse, of Japan following Britain (in corporate structures).

Yet, Kerr (1983) argued that the convergence thesis remained valid. Furthermore, universalistic-type themes remain, for example, in such seemingly all conquering paradigms as 'excellence' (Peters and Waterman, 1984) and 'lean production' (Womack et al., 1990). Variants have also emerged. Some argue that organizational techniques and practices are so powerful they can be lifted out of their (Japanese) context and transferred and do not adapt to environments, but transform environments to meet their needs (Florida and Kenney, 1996). Others believe that forces for convergence across (but divergence within) countries are now more likely to overwhelm national differences (MacDuffie, 1995). Others see convergence around intensified Taylorism of 'management by stress', oppressive work organization such as team concepts, and shopfloor resistance and conflict (Parker and Slaughter, 1988). Indeed, more locationally-related research on the subsidiaries of large US pharmaceutical MNEs in Malaysia and Taiwan shows workplace relations approximating a neo-Taylorist ideal type (Frenkel, 1995). Some credence to convergence, at least in IR policy and outcomes, is provided by work on the Philippines (Kuruvilla, 1995) and on similarities in conflict resolution and conciliation practices between Hong Kong and Singapore (Kirkbride et al. 1991).

The second broad grouping is a cultural one (see Rowley and Lewis, 1996). Much has been made of differences in culture, emphasizing groups' values and attitudes (see Hofstede, 1980) and the collective orientation of neo-Confucianism. One only has to watch the movie 'Gung Ho' (1986) to see cultures xenophobically portrayed in a US car plant taken over by the Japanese. Wilkinson (1994) details a new culturalist perspective, focusing on the characteristics of entrepreneurialism, business organization and work ethics in relation to pre-modern belief systems – usually Confucianism – which continued into the modern period.

However, can all differences be explained in terms of people's attitudes? Japanese, Korean and Taiwanese MNEs have established Western operations using 'native' workers, as have Western firms in China, Singapore, the Philippines, and so on. Other problems include: post-hoc rationalization; gross assumptions about causal links; racism; and absence of historical understanding (ibid.). Similarly, there are limits on a crudely perceived 'common' culture, with sharp differences between some Asia locations and even within societies strongly influenced by neo-Confucian ethical codes (ibid.). This can be seen in different management styles across Asia (Luce, 1995): some operations in China are incompatible with Confucian images and underlying beliefs as they are based on military discipline, unquestioning loyalty and authoritarianism in Chinese, Korean and Taiwanese management (Chan, 1996) and the varied operation of performance appraisals across Hong Kong, Taiwan and Singapore (Paik et *al.* 1996). A further difficulty concerns changing values over time. For example, as more Western individualist ideas gain popularity in Japan (see Benson and Debroux), and Chinese, Japanese, American and European cultural imports spread into Thailand (Phongpaichit and Baker, 1997), will 'traditional' working practices be affected? Values on their own are not enough, they need to be rooted in society's social and economic structure. Culture includes not only the values held by individuals, but also the relations between people at work and in their families, as well as the structure of the firm and society (Whitehill, 1991). Views taking account of these broader factors are often referred to as institutional approaches.

The institutional perspective emphasizes the social and economic institutions supporting the continuation of traditional values and practices (Whitley, 1992). For example, financial, unionization and consultative practices have been seen as key to Japanese success. For others, systemic separate aspects need locating in specific societal contexts, such as the structure and nature of educational and training systems and business organization (Maurice *et al.*, 1986). Wilkinson (1994) notes institutionalist views, with their sensitivity to historically and geographically specific social formations, focusing on organizational forms in pre-modern cultures, but with culture defined more broadly as a set of social arrangements and patterns of behaviour. Such views in the Asia Pacific include business familism (such as conglomerates) and overseas Chinese family networks. However, drawbacks to such approaches include: explaining 'the modern' predominantly in terms of the pre-modern; determinism; *post-hoc* rationalization (ibid.); presenting a static national industrial 'order', with no account of how change comes about; failing to recognize that divergent and contradictory ranges of practices exist within societies; and under-emphasizing the state's role.

Nevertheless, national institutions and arrangements and traditions continue to be important in shaping HRM (see Locke, 1995; Verma *et al.*, 1995). As Elger and Smith (1994) perceptively point out, 'societal specificity' continues to be reproduced and preserved by agencies such as societal arrangements and institutions. Indeed, 'national uniqueness' is created by socio-economic settlements between social agencies and institutions operating on a national terrain. In particular, institutional arrangements between capital and labour, state-firm relations, inter-capital relations, and distinctive factory regimes within particular societies, which are less the consequence of cultural legacies than of socio-political action, are important (ibid.).

Locationally and topically-related work includes Moore and Jennings (1995), who use a neo-institutionalist theory, which focuses on the ways in which behaviours, technology and structure in organizations come into being, become accepted and then are widely used in different organizational and national settings. This involves the 'institutionalization process' through which innovations become recognized, formalized and then legitimized in society (via mimicry, peer pressure, direct coercion). This recognizes that diffused, institutionalized elements were originally embedded in a set of meanings created by the employment relationship in which they developed, and underscores the role of local culture and historical conditions. Thus, political/structural and cultural/societal configurations in countries produce different HRM systems. Similarly, by stressing the roles of actors, Wilkinson (1994) provides an account which he argues is not deterministic and does not suggest 'iron laws', so that outcomes are the result of choices to be made in the light of, but never wholly determined by, either world economic developments or local cultural affinities. Hence, these choices will be the outcome of indeterminate and complex political processes (ibid.).

In sum, the various views put forward to account for HRM differences are open to empirical and theoretical questioning (see Rowley and Lewis, 1996), and analysis can often be a case of 'weighing' trends, such as towards convergence and divergence.

CONTRIBUTIONS

The contributors to the volume are presented in simple locational alphabetical order. Warner provides a conceptual framework linking market, legislation and human resource policy determination, reviewing contemporary trends in HRM in China and tracing the impact of the 1990s economic reforms on the employment system in joint ventures and SOEs. He uses data from a late-1995 field study of enterprises: Bejing Jeep, Guoxing Electronics, Schindler Elevators, Peony TV, Beijing Transformers and Beijing Pharmaceutical. This detailed and perceptive analysis concludes that there may be some growing, albeit limited, HRM overlap between these organizations.

Ng and Poon discuss the implications of business re-adjustment and advances in Hong Kong as its economy restructures into a 'post-industrial' centre for tertiary services. This process of de-industrialization and re-commercialization is basically market-driven, rather than state-engineered (but with impetus from China's economic transformation and reunification moves). Their comprehensive work includes the following cases: Cathay Pacific Airways; China Light and Power; varied types of retailers; a commercial trading house; a tourist agency; and a local bank. It shows that reforms are often benchmarked against Western practices of flexibility and competitiveness in quality service. These have key HRM implications as they emphasize staff performance and labour cost savings. Interestingly, rationalization has not always eroded job security due to an 'Oriental importance' placed upon trust and commitment between employer and employee as a common prescription of HRM.

According to Benson and Debroux, the rise of the Western concept of HRM parallels the global success of Japanese enterprises in which internal labour markets and stable relations between all stakeholders was emphasized. Their analysis includes reviews of surveys as well as cases of a wide variety of sizes (employing 70–80,000) and type of firms in electronics, instrumentation, cosmetics and distribution. They conclude that there are some peripheral changes taking place in HRM, but that this is within the overall structure of 'traditional' Japanese management. This 'gradualism' has important implications for HRM adoption as its context and configuration is 'the essence'.

HRM in Korea in the context of macro environments, recent trends, and an international and comparative framework is covered by Bae. He outlines a model of environmental and organizational factors and HRM strategy composed of: macro environment (economic, political, social and cultural, labour market); organizational factors; characteristics of HRM systems; and goals. His work includes interviews, a questionnaire survey, and several diverse cases: a large (over 3,000 employees) firm in electronics and communications (Korean); and smaller (350–450 employees) firms in electronics (Korean and Japanese), chemicals (American), and pharmaceuticals (European). His sophisticated analysis shows that traditional seniority-based HRM systems with job stability have been challenged by moves towards ability and performance based systems with more flexibility. Therefore, two major HRM issues are: seniority versus performance; stability versus flexibility.

Amante analyses the motives and trends in HRM convergence and divergence in the Philippines arising from openness to inward investment and competition. His work includes cases of a very wide variety of sizes (600–28,500 employees) and types of organization in: food and beverage manufacturing (San Miguel); energy distribution (Manila Electric Company); oil and gas refining and domestic distribution (Caltex Philippines); airways (Philippine Airlines); telecommunications (Philippines Long Distance Telephone Company); banking (Philippine National Bank); and car batteries (Ramcar). He argues that some benchmarking of HRM practices brings about convergence, but these occur within entrenched local work practices and sensitivity to local cultural values, producing a mixed approach.

The three stages of Singapore's economic development as the context from which HRM emerged are outlined by Yuen. The government attracted MNEs to provide capital, technology, management experience and access to international markets, for attainment of its goals of industrialization and economic development. The state, therefore, delivered a disciplined, hard-working and trained labour force. Local practices, as well as trends for convergence and divergence, are discussed.

Chen examines the development of Taiwan's employment structure, labour market, employment legislation and HRM functions. The work includes a questionnaire of 52 Taiwanese-owned, and Japanese, US, Australian, German, Dutch subsidiaries and joint ventures. He also notes that SMEs traditionally lacked distinct HRM functions, while SOEs and large private enterprises gradually established their HRM systems and learned techniques from foreign-owned companies. Employee participation and job security are identified as major challenges for HRM.

Changing HRM practices, especially over the past decade when Thailand underwent substantial economic growth, are explored by Lawler *et al*. They examine practices in traditional family-owned enterprises (of over 100 employees) as well as the 'professionalization' of HRM in large scale, publicly-held Thai companies. They also consider the nature of HRM in subsidiaries of Western (from America, Europe, Australia, New Zealand) and Japanese MNEs. A mixed picture on HRM emerges from their perceptive, detailed and nuanced analysis.

There remains an undiminished business and academic interest in learning about the way HRM is practiced in different places, particularly in the Asia Pacific region. This is despite the problems involved in comparative analysis, and weakening Asian economic performance and the 'darker' side to its management. Importantly, comparative research reveals as much about your own practices as it can about those in other countries, while the ability for managers to use HRM, strategically or otherwise, has to be understood in terms of the opportunities and constraints within a particular society. In short, casting a wider perspective leads to questioning of what might otherwise be assumed as a 'natural' state of affairs, or 'only way', even if to management's ire.

It can further be seen from the above discussion that the exploration of the relative importance of ideas such as convergence, contingency and universalism versus culture and institutions shows their complexity and constraints. Problems remain in terms of units of analysis and mixed trends forcing some sort of 'weighing' of developments, relative movements and even subjective judgement. Despite this, ideas of convergence, even if in some disguise, and belief in universalistic solutions remain popular. This is all too often a mistake – looking to somehow import 'best practice' HRM is a chimera, exacerbated by the 'pick 'n' mix' selection approaches often made by management. Given that the internal contradictions and tensions within HRM (such as flexibility versus commitment, team work versus individualism) are also painted over, the scramble for some all-solving panacea – HRM – is short-sighted and based on caricatures of the employment relationship and ignorance of management's avaricious nature.

ACKNOWLEDGEMENTS

Thanks to Alan Felstead, Pat McGovern and Rod Martin for comments on an earlier draft of this. Also, many thanks to Malcolm Warner for his swift, insightful and unstinting help in the selection and organization of this collection. Thanks to Rosemary Wong for her helpful, efficient and ungrudging secretarial support in the latter stages of amending this collection. The usual disclaimers apply.

NOTES

1. Korea is taken as shorthand for South Korea.
2. China is taken as shorthand for the People's Republic of China.
3. Thanks to Alan Felstead for this point.
4. From this point on, unreferenced authors' names refer to their works in this volume.

5. Yet, as is noted and is obvious, such models remain somewhat restricted and unrepresentative of all organizations (especially small and medium enterprises, family-owned firms, joint ventures, and so on) in a particular location.
6. Thanks to Rod Martin for this point.
7. Much of the following sections on approaches build on the introduction provided by O'Reilly and Peccei (1995).
8. Also, this work is based on secondary analysis of a questionnaire whose sample can be questioned, not least on its pre-selection, respondent and size biases.

REFERENCES

Abegglen, James (1958) *The Japanese Factory: Aspects of its Social Organization*. Glencoe, Ill: Free Press.
Babson, Steve (ed.) (1995) *Lean Work: Empowerment and Exploitation in the Global Auto Industry*. Detroit, MI: Wayne State University Press.
Bae, Jongseok, Chris Rowley, D.H. Kim and John Lawler (1997) 'Korean Industrial Relations at the Crossroads: The Recent Labour Troubles', *Asia Pacific Business Review*, Vol.3, No.3, pp.148–160.
Beer, Michael, B. Spector, P.R Lawrence; D. Quinn Mills and R.E. Walton (1984) *Managing Human Assets*. New York: NY: Free Press.
Blyton, Paul and Pete Turnbull (eds) (1992) *Reassessing Human Resource Management*. London: Sage.
Chan, Anita (1995) 'The Emerging Patterns of Industrial Relations in China and the Rise of Two New Labor Movements', *China Information*, Vol.IX, No.4, pp.36–59.
Chan, Anita (1996) 'Boot Camp at the Shoe Factory', *Washington Post (Outlook Section)*, 3 November, pp.1–4.
Dawkins, William (1997) 'Old Structure Ends in Tiers', *Financial Times*, 9 May, p.9.
Dore, Ronald (1974) *British Factory–Japanese Factory: The Origins of National Diversity in Industrial Relations*. London: Allen and Unwin.
Dowling, Peter and Randall Schuler (1990) *International Dimensions of HRM*. Boston, MA: PWS-Kent.
Duberely, Joanne and Paul Walley (1995) 'Assessing the Adoption of HRM by Small and Medium-Sized Manufacturing Organisations', *International Human Resource Management Journal*, Vol.6, No.4, pp.891–909.
Dunn, Stephen (1990) 'Root Metaphor in the Old and New Industrial Relations', *British Journal of Industrial Relaions*, Vol.28, No.1, pp.1–31.
Elger, Tony and Chris Smith (1994) 'Global Japanization? Convergence and Competition in the Organization of the Labour Process' in Tony Elger and Chris Smith (eds) *Global Japanisation? The Transnational Transformation of the Labour Process*. London: Routledge, pp.31–59.
Florida, Richard and Martin Kenney (1996) 'Japanese Automotive Transplants and the Transformation of the Japanese Production System' in Frederic C. Deyo (ed.) *Social Reconstructions of the World Automobile Industry*. London: Macmillan, pp.51–83.
Fombrun, Charles J., N.M. Tichy and M.A. Devanna (eds) (1984) *Strategic Human Resource Management*. New York, NY: John Wiley.
Fowler, Edward (1996) *San'ya Blues: Laboring Life in Contemporary Tokyo*. Ithaca, NY: Cornell University Press.
Free Labour World (1997) 'Social Awareness Reawakens', March, p.5.
Frenkel, Stephen (1995) 'Workplace Relations in the Global Corporation: A Comparative Analysis in Malaysia and Taiwan' in Stephen Frenkel and Jeffrey Harrod (eds) (1995) *Industrialization and Labor Relations: Contemporary Research in Seven Countries*. Ithaca, NY: ILR Press, pp.179–215.
Garrahan, Philip and Paul Stewart (1992) *The Nissan Enigma: Flexibility at Work in a Local Economy*. London: Mansell.
Goldthorpe, John (1985) 'The End of Convergence: Corporatism and Dualist Tendencies in Modern Western Societies' in Bryan Roberts; Ruth Finnegan and Duncan Gallie (eds) *New Approaches to Economic Life – Economic Restructuring: Unemployment and the Social Division of Labour*. Manchester: Manchester University Press.
Green, William C. and Ernest J. Yanarella (eds) (1996) *North American Auto Unions in Crisis: Lean Production as Contested Terrain*. Albany, NY: State University of New York Press.
Guest, David (1987) 'Human Resource Management and Industrial Relations', *Journal of Management Studies*, Vol.24, No.5, pp.302–21.

Hasegawa, Harukiyo (1996) *The Steel Industry in Japan: A Comparison with Britain*. London: Routledge.
Hofstede, Geert (1980), *Culture's Consequences: International Differences in Work-Related Values*. London: Sage.
Jennings, P. Devereaux and Larry F. Moore (1995) 'Introduction and Theoretical Rationale' in Larry F. Moore and P. Devereaux Jennings (eds) *Human Resource Management On The Pacific Rim: Institutions, Practices and Attitudes*. Berlin: de Gruyter, pp. 7–27.
Jennings, P. Devereaux; Dianne Cyr and Larry, F. Moore (1995) 'Human Resource Management on the Pacific Rim: An Integration', in Larry F. Moore and P. Devereaux Jennings (eds) *Human Resource Management on the Pacific Rim: Institutions, Practices And Attitudes*. Berlin: de Gruyter, pp.351–79.
Kamata, Satoshi (1982) *Japan in the Passing Lane: An Insider's Account of Life in a Japanese Auto Factory*. Great Britain: Allen and Unwin.
Kanter, Rosabeth Moss (1984) *The Change Masters: Corporate Entrepreneurs at Work*. London: Allen & Unwin.
Kaple, Deborah (1994) *Dream of a Red Factory: The Legacy of High Stalinism in China*. Oxford: Oxford University Press.
Katz, Harry C. (1997) 'Introduction' in Harry C Katz (ed.) *Telecommunications: Restructuring Work and Employment Relations Worldwide*. Ithaca, NY: ILR Press.
Kay, John A. (1994) *The Foundations of Corporate Success: Why Firms Succeed*. Oxford: Oxford University Press.
Kerr, Clark (1983) *The Future of Industrial Societies: Convergence or Continuing Diversity?* Cambridge, MA: Harvard University Press.
Kerr, Clark; John T. Dunlop; Frederick H. Harbison and Charles A. Myers (1962) *Industrialism And Industrial Man*. London: Heinemann.
Kirkbride, Paul, Andy Lai and Chris Leggett (1991) 'Perceptions of Labour Concilliation in Hong Kong and Singapore' in Chris Brewster and Shaun Tyson (eds) *International Companies in Human Resource Management*. London: Pitman, pp.103–213.
Komata, Satoshi (1982) *Japan in the Passing Lane*. London: Urwin.
Kuruvilla, Sarosh C. (1995) 'Economic Development Strategies, IR Policies and Workplace IR/HR Practices in Southeast Asia' in Kirsten Wever and Lowell Turner (eds) *The Comparative Political Economy of Industrial Relations*. Ithaca, NY: ILR, pp.115–50.
Lawrence, Paul R. and Jay W. Lorsch (1967) *Organisation And Environment*. Cambridge, MA: Harvard Univesity Press.
Legge, Karen (1995) *HRM: Rhetorics and Realities*. London: Macmillan.
Leggett, Chris and Greg Bamber (1996) 'Asia–Pacific Tiers of Change', *Human Resource Management Journal*, Vol.6, No.2, pp.7–19.
Lingle, Christopher (1997) *Singapore's Authoritarian Capitalism*. Faifax, VI: The Locke Institure.
Lipietz, Alain (1995) 'Capital–Labour Relations at the Dawn of the Twenty-First Century' in Juliet Schor and Jong-Il You (eds) *Capital, The State and Labour: A Global Perspective*. Aldershot: Edward Elgar, pp.345–372.
Locke, Richard M. (1995) 'The Transformation of Industrial Relations? A Cross-National Review', in Kirsten Wever and Lowell Turner (eds), *The Comparative Political Economy of Industrial Relations*. Ithaca, NY: ILR, pp.9–31.
Luce, Richard (1995) 'South East Asia: Singularly Different', *Financial Times*, 4 December, p.2.
MacDuffie, John Paul (1995) 'International Trends in Work Organization in the Auto Industry: Nation-Level vs. Company-Level Perspectives' in Kirsten Wever and Lowell Turner (eds) *The Comparative Political Economy of Industrial Relations*. Ithaca, NY: ILR, pp.71–113.
Maurice, Marc; Francois Sellier, and Jean-Jacques Silvestre (1986) *The Social Foundations of Industrial Power*. Cambridge, MA: MIT Press.
Moore, Larry F. and P. Devereaux Jennings (eds) (1995) *Human Resource Management on the Pacific Rim: Institutions, Practices And Attitudes*. Berlin: de Gruyter.
Nakamoto, Michiyo (1997) 'Death of the Salaryman', *Financial Times*, 17 May, p.1.
Ng Sek Hong and Malcolm Warner (1998). *China's Trade Unions and Management*. London: Macmillan (in press).
Noon, Mike (1992), 'HRM: A Map, Model,or Theory', in Paul Blyton and Pete Turnbull (eds), *Reassessing Human Resource Management*. London: Sage, pp.16–32.
O'Reilly, Jackie and R. Peccei (1995) *Human Resource Management Subject Guide*. London: University of London.
Ouchi, William (1981) *Theory Z: How American Business can meet the Japanese Challenge*.

Reading, MA.: Addison-Wesley.

Paik, Yongsuk, Charles Vance and Daniel Stage (1996) 'The Extent of Divergence in Human Resource Practice Across Three Chinese National Cultures, Hong Kong, Taiwan and Singapore', *Human Resource Management Journal*, Vol.6, No.2, pp.20–31.

Parker, Mike and Jane Slaughter (1988) *Crossing Sides: Unions and the Team Concept*. Boston, MA: South End Press.

Peters, Thomas and Robert Waterman (1982) *In Search of Excellence: Lessons from America's Best Run Companies*. London: Harper & Row.

Phongpaichit, Pasuk and Chris Baker (1997) *Thailand's Boom!* Chiang Mai, Thailand: Silkworm Books.

Porter, Michael (1985) *Competitive Advantage: Creating & Sustaining Superior Performance*. New York, NY: Free Press.

Price, John (1997) *Japan Works: Power and Paradox in Postwar Industrial Relations*. Ithaca, NY: Cornell University Press.

Rowley, Chris (1996) 'Taming The Tigers?: HRM in the Far East', *Asia Pacific Business Review*, Vol.3, No.2, pp.84.

Rowley, Chris and Mark Lewis (1996) 'Greater China At The Crossroads? Convergence, Culture and Competitiveness', *Asia Pacific Business Review*, Vol.3, No.3, pp.1–22.

Sako, Mari (1997) 'Introduction: Forces for Homogeneity and Diversity in the Japanese Industrial Relations System' in Mari Sako and Hiroki Sato (eds) *Japanese Labour and Management in Transition: Diversity, Flexibility and Participation*. London: Routledge, pp.1–24.

Sisson, Keith (1994) 'Personnel Management: Paradigms, Practice and Prospects' in Keith Sisson (2nd ed.) *Personnel Management: A Comprehensive Guide to Theory and Practice*. Oxford: Blackwell, pp.3–50.

Smith, David and Michael Sheridan (1997) 'Asia's Tiger Economies Start to Lose Their Bite', *The Sunday Times*, 12 January, p.4:9.

Sparrow, Paul, Randall S. Schuler, and Susan E . Jackson (1994) 'Convergence or Divergence: Human Resource Management Practices and Policies for Competitive Advantage Worldwide', *International Journal of Human Resource Management*, Vol.5, No.2, pp.267–99.

Stewart, Paul (ed.) (1996) *Beyond Japanese Management: The End of Modern Times?* Frank Cass: London.

Storey, John (1987) *Developments in the Management of Human Resources*. Warwick Papers in Industrial Relations, No.17, University of Warwick.

Storey, John (1992) *Developments in the Management of Human Resources*. Oxford: Blackwell.

Towers, Brian (1996) *The Handbook of HRM*. Second edition. Oxford: Blackwell.

Verma, Anil, Thomas, A. Kochan and Richard, D. Lansbury (1995) 'Employment Relations in an Era of Global Markets: A Conceptual Framework Chapter' in Anil Verma; Thomas A. Kochan and Richard D. Lansbury (eds) (1995) *Employment Relations in the Growing Asian Economies*. London: Routledge, pp.1–26.

Warner, Malcolm (1996) 'Culture, Organisations and Human Resources: Global Versus Less Global HRM Decision Making Models' in Pieter J. D. Drenth; Paul L. Koopman and Bernhard Wilpert (eds) *Organizational Decision-Making Under Different Economic and Political Conditions*. Amsterdam: North-Holland, pp.189–95.

Whitehill, Arthur (1981) *Japanese Management*. London: Routledge.

Whitely, Richard (1992), *European Business Systems*. London: Sage.

Wilkinson, Barry (1994) *Labour and Industry in the Asia-Pacific: Lessons From Newly-Industrialized Countries*. Berlin: de Gruyter.

Womack, James; Daniel Jones and Daniel Roos (1990) *The Machine that Changed the World*. New York: Rawson Associates.

Woodward, Joan (1965) *Industrial Organisation*. Oxford: Oxford University Press.

China's HRM in Transition: Towards Relative Convergence?

MALCOLM WARNER

The People's Republic of China (PRC) is now on its way to becoming the economic 'super-power' of the coming decades, according to International Monetary Fund estimates. On a purchasing-power parity basis, the Chinese economy by the 1990s already accounted for around six per cent of world output, making it third behind the US and Japan (IMF, 1993: 117). As Lardy (1994: 7) points out, 'China's role in the world economy has already far surpassed that played by the Soviet Union and the Communist states of Eastern Europe'.

Since the reforms introduced by Deng Xiaoping in 1978, China's economy has grown by leaps and bounds. In recent years, its growth-rate has been one of the largest ever recorded in modern times. It has averaged over nine per cent over the last decade (with real output almost quadrupling) and over the last five years has ranged between eight per cent (1991) and 13.8 per cent (1993). In 1994, it fell but was still as high as 11.9 per cent (see Table 1). Living standards have also increased substantially in real terms since 1978, with an improvement in diet, particularly a higher consumption of protein. Huge new consumer-goods industries emerged in the 1980s, with the 'first wave' of goods such as bicycles, fridges, television sets, washing machines and so on, with a 'second wave' of motor vehicles, motor cycles, and video recorders in its wake in the 1990s. Housing space per head also considerably expanded (see Nolan, 1995: 12).

Over the same period, Chinese industry and its management has been transformed. Enterprises in the state sector ('owned by the whole people' in the official jargon) had long been the mainstay of Chinese industry (see Warner, 1986; 1992). They were, and are still, mainly found in large industrial cities like Beijing, Dalian, Shanghai, Shenyang, Wuhan and so on. Large and medium sized state-owned enterprises (SOEs) in this sector used to produce the bulk of total gross value of industrial output, nearly 80 per cent in 1978; now they produce under 40 per cent of this total, although still growing in absolute terms. Employing over 100 million workers in all by the end of 1994, SOEs were widely regarded as inefficient and overmanned. As many as 40 per cent were allegedly 'in the red'. Such large firms had the full stereotypical apparatus of Chinese labour–management relations under the 'iron rice bowl' system, providing jobs for life and 'cradle to the grave' welfare and with almost-complete worker-unionization, at least on paper.

Malcolm Warner, University of Cambridge

Today, the non-state-owned sector, comprising urban collectives, town and village industries, joint ventures (JVs), wholly foreign-funded firms and privately-owned enterprises produces the largest part of China's industrial output and employs more workers than the SOEs. The share of collectively-owned enterprises (that is, public locally-owned firms) in this output rose from 22 per cent in 1978 to over 35 per cent by 1994. The private sector grew to over five per cent; with foreign-funded firms (including JVs) producing over a quarter of exports (Lardy, 1994: 112). Since 1978, over 200,000 JV and similar agreements have been signed, of which around half have been implemented. Such developments offer a potentially valuable source of technology-transfer (see Chen, 1996).

TABLE 1
SELECTED CHINESE MACRO-ECONOMIC STATISTICS

	1989	1990	1991	1992	1993	1994	1995
GDP* per capita	449.10	387.4	406.09	483.00	599.01	522.19	650.12
GDP (real % growth rates)	4.30	3.90	8.00	13.20	13.80	11.90	9.70
Population (millions)	1139.20	1153.00	1170.10	1183.60	1196.40	1209.34	1122.40
Inflation (% change)	16.32	1.30	5.08	8.58	18.00	24.20	14.80
Exports **	51.86	61.27	70.45	80.52	90.97	119.82	155.77
Imports **	58.44	52.52	62.57	76.35	103.09	114.56	132.89
Current Account Balance **	−4.48	11.89	3.02	5.81	−12.40	7.20	14.00

Key:
*   in current US dollar prices, unadjusted for purchasing-power parity
**   in billions of US dollars at current prices

Sources: Various (State Statistical Year Book, World Bank, Country-Risk Reports, etc.)

As a recent account puts it:

> The primary Chinese motivations for entering into industrial joint ventures are the acquisition of advanced technology, foreign exchange and management expertise. While there are many vehicles for the transfer of technology such as licensing, coproduction, subcontracting, the equity joint venture is popular because it allows the foreign partner to realise its major objective, ie to participate in the Chinese market while maintaining some control over business activities (ibid.: 223).

Formerly, the management of Chinese industry was dominated by the SOE model and was a by-product of the command-economy, the norm in the pre-reform era. Today, the 'iron rice bowl' is being slowly phased out even in the state sector and is clearly not *de rigueur* in most of the non-state sector, especially in JVs. Instead, a labour-market is slowly emerging with more flexible characteristics, such as labour contracts, reward systems and the like (see Warner, 1995; 1996).

As China set out in the mid-1980s to create factor-markets, the relationship between the demand and supply of labour changed dramatically. The PRC has a productive population close to over 650 million (its size being equal to the population in the productive age group, multiplied by the participation rate). Minami (1994: 204) employs the international standard of those over 15 years old (rather than the Chinese benchmark of 16). The PRC could not have had a 'labour market' (by definition) in its Maoist past because in a 'socialist society', labour could *not* be a 'commodity' and therefore *not* bought or sold (Gao, 1994). Labour was formerly allocated and wages determined by state bodies (see Takahara, 1992). The wage system was reformed in the mid-1980s, but it was only from the early 1990s that significant change occurred *vis-à-vis* matching-up rewards with skills, training, effort and productivity.

To sum up, the Chinese labour–management system is currently in a state of transition. It is as yet a 'hybrid' creature, half-way between the old-style Maoist model and a market-driven one, but which has not currently fully evolved either on Western or East Asian lines (on comparisons with Japan, see Chan, 1995). We now go on to discuss Western *versus* Chinese concepts of human resource management (HRM), in order to more clearly see how the system is developing.

WESTERN VERSUS CHINESE CONCEPTS OF HRM

Western Concepts

Western notions of 'people-management' tend to differ from Asian ones. Such variation is not surprising given the range of cultures encountered and cross-cultural factors that are operative across the continents. North American or European ways of dealing with people in the workplace have often been contrasted with, say, the Japanese model. When we come to discuss how such issues are managed in the West, as Child (1994:157) points out, we can at least identify a core-set of practices:

> Although definitions of personnel management and human resource management vary considerably, modern Western thinking tends to be predicated upon assumptions such as the primary contributions of competent and motivated people to a firm's success, the compatibility of individual and corporate interests, the importance of developing a corporate culture which is in tune with top management's strategy for the firm, and the responsibility of senior management rather than employees' own representative bodies for determining personnel practices.

This author then goes on to argue that Western HRM places great importance not only on systematic recruitment but also on selection, training and development procedures (involving socialization into the corporate culture) emphasizing motivation through involvement in work organization, appraisal and incentive schemes (ibid.). As a description, Child's version is, however, rather broad. There are clear difficulties in pinning down the characteristics of HRM (Legge 1989). Some see it as different from personnel management 'by virtue of its integration with business and other strategies' (Thomason, 1991: 3); while others look upon it as synonymous with specific practices (Guest, 1987, for instance). Even so, both approaches may be combined and some of a possible set of practices could be linked to strategy. As a result, a coherent framework can be developed (see Storey, 1992) which consists of a plausible model, even if its description of HRM may be regarded as 'an idealized future state' (Duberley and Walley, 1995: 893). A list of component factors derived from such a model help us distinguish more clearly the gradation between personnel management and HRM, according to this view.

Chinese Concepts

China had itself developed a 'distinctive' model of personnel management, since 1949 at least, as hinted at earlier (see Warner, 1993; 1995). Its origin lay in the Soviet industrial model which it adopted after the 'Liberation' so-called (see Kaple, 1994). It was for many decades, from the late 1940s to the early 1980s, the predominant mode for most Chinese enterprises which were, at the time, run by the state.

The (Western) notion of HRM is normally not present in Chinese enterprises. At best, HRM 'with Chinese characteristics' is the most appropriate term to be used, mostly in JVs to date (see Warner, 1995: 145ff). Within Chinese enterprises, particularly the state-owned variety, administrative functions are organized differently and are organized into several sections, such as personnel, labour, salaries and training, departments. As Child (1994:157–158) argues:

> Other tasks, such as personnel appointments, communication with workers and political education, are mostly undertaken or supervised by the enterprise party organization. Western human resource management practices are also alien to the Chinese scene, even in Chinese companies outside the PRC.

A further distinction must be made here *vis-à-vis* different categories of Chinese firms. First, there are many Chinese SOEs which are relatively unreformed and still retain many characteristics of the old system. Next, there are those which have been relatively reformed and have abandoned the 'iron rice bowl' system. Third, there are non-state owned firms, such as JVs, which have taken on many Western personnel procedures which might be seen, partially at least, as recognizably HRM-style strategies and practices.

FIGURE 1
CONCEPTUAL FRAMEWORK: THE MARKET, LEGISLATION
AND HR POLICY-DETERMINATION

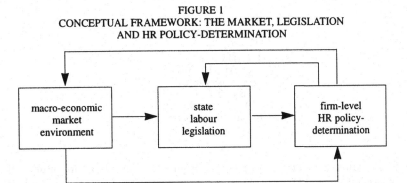

A Possible Model

Up to the early 1980s, state planning and government human resource (HR) policies determined behaviour at the level of the typical Chinese firm (see, for example, a recent account by Verma and Yan, 1995). After the economic reforms were introduced, the market became a growing influence on state HR policies, the two in turn affecting what happened at enterprise level. In Figure 1, we present the relationships between the variables involved with feedback-loops. In the model, market factors influence state labour legislation which in turn affects the firm's HR policies (the term HRM is deliberately avoided here) but what happens at the micro-level (if replicated in a number of firms) may affect both the macro-economic level and the state labour law level. If firms, for example, by making workers redundant do improve factor efficiency, then it feeds back into the market-level. The net result of micro-level labour market actions affects the broader labour market and possibly legally-enforceable employment insurance provision. We would strongly argue that the above model now best helps explain how Chinese enterprise behaviour works. In the next section we examine to what degree the increasing influence of the market has affected HR policies in both JVs and SOEs, assuming for the moment that the former would be most likely to have changed.

THE FIELD STUDY

The Sample

The main data reported in this analysis relates to an empirical study of Chinese enterprises: three JVs and three SOEs, all located in the Beijing area, which are compared and contrasted in terms of labour relations and HR policies and practices (see Table 2). The study to be discussed was carried out in the winter of 1995 and therefore covers the latest phase of the enterprise reforms and the most recently implemented Labour Law (see Child, 1995; Warner, 1996). The firms cover the following sectors: electronic components, lifts, motor vehicles, pharmaceuticals, transformers

TABLE 2
CASE STUDIES DERIVED FROM THE ENTERPRISES SELECTED
(SHORT-NAME AS USED IN THE TEXT)

1. Beijing Jeep
2. Guoxing Electronics
3. Schindler Elevators
4. Peony TV
5. Beijing Transformers
6. Beijing Pharmaceuticals

and television sets. They range in size from medium to large in number of workers employed. The choice of enterprises to be investigated was based partly on their range of industrial products, agreement regarding accessibility and availability of managerial personnel, and partly on existing links with previous research projects (see Child, 1994: 3–4). The selection of a comparative case study approach was seen as appropriate to the problem at hand in the sample. The term 'sample' is used in a pragmatic context and is in no way intended to convey statistical representativeness of the firms chosen for study, although it is hoped that they will in many ways be typical of large JVs and SOEs in the Chinese economy.

DESCRIPTION OF THE COMPANIES SELECTED

Case No.1: Beijing Jeep
Beijing Jeep Corporation has been described as 'the first major manufacturing joint venture' launched in China in 1983 following the Open Door policy (see Mann, 1989: 25; Aiello, 1991: 47). The original partners were the Beijing Automotive Works and the American Motor Corporation (AMC), but the latter was taken over by the Chrysler Corporation in 1987. The official start-up date was 1984, with the Chinese side taking 61.75 per cent and the US side 38.25 per cent. The contracted period for the arrangement is 20 years. It produced in the region of 100,000 vehicles by the end of 1995. Beijing Jeep at that time employed over 7,000 employees.

Case No.2: Guoxing Electronics
Beijing Guoxing Electronics Corporation, part of the Feida Group, was a JV set up in 1988 by the Beijing Honda Electric Appliance Corporation, China International Trust and Investment Corporation, and Hong Kong Xiaoteji Corporation. It was thus a hybrid Hong Kong/Japanese JV, producing heads for recorders, transformers, switches, coils, crystals and so on. It employed over 1,100 employees.

Case No.3: Schindler Elevators
China-Schindler Elevator Company was set up in 1980 in Beijing and claims to be not just the only major Swiss investment, but also the first JV in the machine industry. It has been judged one of the 'Top Ten Joint

Ventures in China' for eight consecutive years. Its cumulative production since the JV was founded has been over 20,000 units. It employed over 1,500 workers in Beijing (as well as another 1,800 in Shanghai).

Case No.4: Peony TV

The Beijing Peony Electronics Corporation was a SOE set up in 1973, originally as the Beijing TV factory. We will from now on refer to it as Peony TV for short. The Group was in a list of the top 100 corporations in China, with a long-standing technological collaboration with the Japanese multinational corporation, Matsushita. It produced over one million colour TV sets a year in 1995, as well as computer monitors, telecommunications equipment and large accessory die-sets for colour TV sets, instruments, meters and automatic production equipment. It employed over 6,300 workers and staff.

Case No.5: Beijing Transformers

Beijing Transformer Works was one of the early wave of industrial factories set up in the 1950s. It became a SOE in 1956 and largely makes convector equipment such as transformers, silicon rectifiers and silicon elements. It differed from the Shanghai Transformer Corporation in that it produces middle-size transformers rather than the former's line of large ones. There were over 2,300 employees on site.

Case No.6: Beijing Pharmaceuticals

The Beijing Fourth Pharmaceutical Works was under the aegis of the Beijing General Pharmaceutical Corporation. It made over 150 products with active substances used being synthetic or Chinese herbal medicine or a combination of both. It also produced high-grade dietetic preparations, in the dosage forms of injections, tablets, oral liquids, syrups and capsules. It employed over 1,000 workers and staff.

LABOUR–MANAGEMENT IN THE SELECTED ENTERPRISES

Since the mid-1980s, Chinese enterprises had slowly begun to abandon the 'iron rice bowl' involving 'jobs-for-life' and 'cradle-to-grave' welfare coverage for their employees (see Korzec, 1992; Leung, 1993; Kaple, 1994; Warner, 1995). Since 1986, JVs and SOEs had begun to introduce labour contracts for new employees. By 1992, this procedure was extended in pilot-enterprises to *all* eligible employees and in 1995 within a wide range of SOEs (*China Daily/Business Weekly*, 1995).

Rewards

Related to the above reforms was a move towards performance-related reward systems (Warner, 1995). Previously, Chinese enterprises had an egalitarian wage-payment system with a flat reward structure (see Takahara, 1992). Since the mid-1980s, a change occurred with material rewards becoming more predominant. Both JVs and SOEs studied here had moved to a performance-based rewards system after the 1986 and 1992 reforms, notwithstanding the recent extensions. Wages varied greatly between the two sub-sets in 1994. Beijing Jeep paid the most per month at over 1,000 Ren Min Bi (RMB) the national unit of currency – approximately 8.5 to the US dollar at the time of the investigation in November 1995 (1,500 by 1995) – followed by Schindler Elevators at over 700 RMB (1,000 in 1995) and Guoxing Electronics at 550 RMB (680 in 1995). The highest paying SOE, Peony TV, overlapped with the latter two at over 700 RMB (750 in 1975) with Beijing Transformers at over 550 RMB (600 in 1995) and Beijing Pharmaceuticals at over 450 RMB (500 in 1995) (see Table 4). The minimum wage in the city in late 1995 was 200 RMB per month.

Social Insurance

Social insurance, after the 1992 'three systems' reforms (*san gaige*) followed a common pattern in that both JVs and SOEs all departed from previous 'iron rice bowl' practice, albeit with some variance. By 1994, the Beijing Municipal Government had introduced unemployment benefit reforms, as had many other provinces (see Taylor, 1996: 45). Reforms of medical care were also launched in over 50 cities (*Beijing Review*, 1996). In Beijing Jeep, for example, medical benefits were related to age and seniority; with the company paying the bulk of the costs, with the worker having to cover five, ten or 15 per cent depending on their years of service. If injured or killed, the firm paid 100 per cent of the costs involved. Retirement for men was at 60 years, and women at 50 years. The company paid an average 1,000 RMB per year contributions, for a pension of 50 per cent of average earnings, which was around 70 per cent of the basic wage. Guoxing Electronics paid 400 RMB per year for medical expenses but if the costs exceeded this, covered 80 per cent, and in severe injury cases paid the whole sum. The company paid 22.5 per cent of each worker's wages to the government pension scheme, with the individual contributing 3.3 per cent. Schindler Elevators paid all medical costs incurred, with no individual worker contribution. They were preparing a contributory pension plan, but the details had not yet been finalized.

In the SOE sub-set, the social insurance arrangements were as follows. Beijing Peony TV contributed 19 per cent of the wage-level to the medical scheme and expected the worker to pay five per cent. The retirement contribution by the firm was six per cent above the level of the government scheme, resulting in a pension of 36 per cent of salary, which was around 400 RMB per month. Beijing Transformers paid 30 per cent of the total wage-level for medical insurance with workers contributing 12 per cent. In Beijing Pharmaceuticals, 80–90 per cent of wages was paid by the company for medical insurance, with the worker providing the rest. Pensions depended on wage levels, ranging from 70–90 per cent of basic wages.

Trade Unions

Although their role is currently in flux (see Warner, 1995; Ng and Warner, 1998) the trade unions (belonging to the official All-China Federation of Trade Unions – ACFTU) remained *prima facie* strong in both JVs and SOEs. Some foreign-funded firms do not have unions in their plants at all (*Xinhua News Agency*, cited by *Reuters*, 1994). However, JVs in larger cities may have a greater degree of union representation. In terms of union membership, Beijing Jeep claimed 95 per cent (with management claiming in interviews that there was an 'active membership') as did Guoxing Electronics ('a mainly social function for the union') with Schindler Elevator claiming 100 per cent ('a comprehensive union role'). In the SOE sub-set, Peony TV ('wide-ranging union activities') claimed somewhat lower union membership at 80–85 per cent, but Beijing Transformers ('an integral role') at 95 per cent and Beijing Pharmaceuticals at 100 per cent ('a mainly welfare role') remained 'solid' union-territory.

Workers' Congresses

All the firms studied had ongoing Workers' Congresses, formally representative bodies which had be reconstituted in workplaces in the early 1980s by Deng Xiaoping to balance the increased powers given to management (see Chan, 1993; Warner, 1995; Ng and Warner, 1998), whether JVs or SOEs. In the former sub-set, those in Beijing Jeep and Guoxing Electronics each met once a year, with Schindler Elevators meeting twice a year. In the latter sub-set, Beijing Peony TV met once a year, as did Beijing Transformers. However, Beijing Pharmaceuticals convened its Congress twice a year. *Ad hoc* sessions could be called, if necessary, in all cases. In the case of JVs, their role was merely said to be mostly 'consultative' and they normally did not take part in managerial decision-making in the SOEs. They met largely as a formality to discuss the previous year's company performance and the plan for the next one. White (1995) has suggested that the role of worker representative bodies among other competing approaches 'has waxed and waned' (1995: 21). Only a very small number (around seven per cent) of workers he interviewed thought the unions' activities were directed to representing their 'views' and 'interests' and a majority thought the Workers' Congress either did not or was 'irrelevant' (19.1 per cent and 41.5 per cent respectively) in his survey (1995: 23–25). The evidence from the present study of JVs and SOEs would appear to confirm the marginality of Workers' Congresses in both sub-sets since the hand of management has been strengthened in the latest phase of enterprise reforms.

ANALYSIS OF HRM PRACTICES IN SELECTED CHINESE
ENTERPRISES

A Framework

Following a recent study (Duberley and Walley 1995), a framework was
distilled in order to go on to analyse the degree to which specific HRM
practices were applicable to the JVs and SOEs respectively. It consisted of
ten dimensions that we thought relatively relevant to the Chinese context
and applying to the following: rules, behaviour, managerial roles, key
managers, selection, pay, conditions, labour–management, job design and
training. Each dimension was defined with respect to personnel
management/industrial relations (IR) on the one hand and HRM on the
other. For example, 'rules' in the enterprise were seen as 'defined' for the
former and 'flexible' for the latter. The list of ten dimensions is set out in
Table 3.

TABLE 3
COMPARING PERSONNEL/IR WITH HRM

DIMENSIONS	PERSONNEL/IR	HRM
1. Rules	Defined	Flexible
2. Behaviour	Norms/Customs/Practice	Values/Mission
3. Managerial roles	Monitoring	Nurturing
4. Key managers	Personnel/IR specialist	General/line managers
5. Personnel Selection	Separated	Integrated
6. Payment Systems	Job evbaluation	Performance related
7. Work Conditions	Separate negotiation	Harmonized
8. Labour-Management	Collective	Individual contracts
9. Job Design	Division of labour	Teamwork
10. In-house Training	Distinct	Ongoing

Sources: Adapted from Storey 91992); Duberley and Walley (1995).

Applying the Framework to Chinese Enterprises

Next, the six Chinese enterprises studies were scored *vis-à-vis* each
dimension as either having all ($\checkmark$), some (%) or none (x) of the
characteristics set out in the earlier table. It was of course a subjective
judgement but firmly based on the data collected for the respective
enterprises. As Duberley and Walley (1995: 897) had similarly stressed, 'the
ticks, crosses and percentage marks ... (were) ... not simply the usual
record of respondents' replies to surveys, they ... (were) ... the researchers'
own judgement based on multiple sources of information'. Interviews with
managers, union officials and workers, plus an analysis of written
documents and procedures, were used to make the judgements.

TABLE 4
PERSONNEL/IR VERSUS HRM IN THE CHINESE SAMPLE

Dimensions	FIRMS					
	JVs			SOEs		
	1 Jeep	2 Elect.	3 Elev.	4 TV	5 Transf.	6 Pharm.
1. Rules	✓	x	✓	✓	x	x
2. Behaviour	✓	x	%	%	x	x
3. Managerial Roles	✓	%	%	%	x	x
4. Key Managers	✓	%	✓	✓	x	x
5. Personnel Selection	✓	%	✓	✓	x	x
6. Payment Systems	✓	✓	✓	✓	✓	✓
7. Work Conditions	✓	x	✓	✓	x	x
8. Labour-Management	✓	✓	✓	✓	✓	✓
9. Job Design	✓	%	✓	✓	%	%
10. In-house Training	✓	%	✓	✓	x	x

Key:
✓ all
% some
x none

Sources: Adapted from Storey (1992); Duberley and Walley (1995).

Results

The results of the analysis set out in Table 4 show that only in *three* case studies (1, 3 and 4) were most items listed scored positively as HRM-style practices, namely Beijing Jeep, Schindler Elevators and Peony TV. While two of these are JVs, the last is still an SOE. By contrast, case 3 (the JV) scored patchily, but had fewer negative scores than cases 5 and 6 (the other SOEs). The main implication of these findings is that there may now be a degree of overlap between the two sub-sets of enterprises selected, which may be found in larger JVs and SOEs in major urban conurbations. The results, therefore, perhaps call for a modest reconsideration of the present writer's earlier evaluation (Warner, 1995). We may as a consequence move on to the next section, where we discuss a possible progression from past *divergence* to future *convergence*.

DISCUSSION

Divergence

In the early days of the economic reforms, there was a visible degree of divergence between the SOE managerial goals on the one hand and those of the JVs on the other, as exemplified in the early experience of the first major manufacturing JV, namely Beijing Jeep in the mid-1980s. The following account sets out the cultural differences between the Chinese and American labour–management models:

> The Chinese and Americans had been trying to coexist and adapt to one another, but it wasn't easy. Both sides found that cultural differences were even greater than either had expected before the joint venture opened its doors ... In theory the Chinese workday began at 8.30 am and ended at 5.30 pm, but in practice production started later, stopped for a long lunch and ended early, perhaps an hour and a half before closing time (Mann, 1989: 199).

It was not easy for expatriate managers in JVs to come to terms with the 'iron rice bowl' employment system and the workers who had grown up within it. The two mind-sets were therefore 'worlds apart' in the mid- to late 1980s. Chinese 'labour-service companies' provided the manpower and took care of labour–management on behalf of the foreign JV managers who confined their activities to technical matters. This practice was known as the 'segregation model', with all personnel matters left to the Chinese side (Taylor, 1996: 86).

Relative Divergence

The next stage was one of relative divergence which was arrived at when Western (and Asian) management practices became more widely diffused. However, several foreign experts (for example, Pearson, 1991: 221) still saw a significant gap between what JV management aspired to, and what Chinese custom and practice offered. Even so, foreign personnel practices, especially freedom to hire and fire workers and to offer more materialistic rewards systems (ibid.), became more acceptable to the Chinese economic reformers, who began to see their benefits to the Chinese economy. These areas could increasingly be placed outside the hands of the Chinese authorities (Child, 1994: 260).

Relative Convergence

The two models began to relatively converge, it may be argued, when the 1992 enterprise reforms (and their 1995 extension) heralded the demise of the 'iron rice bowl', as earlier described. If fully-flexible labour markets on Western lines still seem rather distant, many HR policies in China had clearly changed (see Easterby-Smith *et al.*, 1994), even if HRM in its strictest sense was not specifically evident in most of the enterprises visited as late as 1995, with the possible exception of Beijing Jeep. Many workers now do have fixed-term contracts; reward-systems have been reformed; and training has been expanded for both workers and managers (see Warner, 1996). Even so, formerly protected workers have been resistant to change, and seasoned observers will remain sceptical about reforming entrenched personnel practices in the short- to medium-term. Over 30 million employees are now said to be covered by the new wage system, which was introduced as part of the 'three systems' reforms as noted above, by mid-1995 (*Beijing Review*, 1995). Before long, it should effectively cover all of China's large and medium-sized SOEs. We have seen how the JV and SOE sub-sets described earlier now have a degree of overlap, with Peony TV beginning to look more like a JV in its management approach, for example, although with some earlier JVs still retaining older SOE-related characteristics, as opposed to those set up since the early 1990s. Organizational inertia may hold back many SOEs and not a few JVs.

The evidence presented here thus, we believe, supports the view that we are witnessing the emergence of a more complex, *hybrid* management model as 'marketization' advances and as enterprise autonomy increases. The implementation of the 1994 Labour Law (on 1 January 1995) covering the whole range of enterprises in China may be seen both as a response to such trends, as well as a further spur to a greater degree of coherence in the labour–management system, at least on paper (see Josephs, 1995; Feinerman, 1996; Ng and Warner, 1998; Warner, 1997). The progress towards a fully integrated HRM system may, however, remain slow.

Convergence

Convergence in the strictest sense, between the respective categories of JVs and SOEs, is as yet far in the distance and remains an 'ideal type', which would require them all to become self-standing corporate entities. This development would be a positive step to complete the overlap between the non-state and state sectors, leading to the creation of an integrated HRM system for all Chinese industrial enterprises. As yet, we are not at this stage but it is perhaps conceivable as the final step in the logic of modernization.

CONCLUDING REMARKS

To sum up, this contribution has attempted to look at the changing face of HRM in China by analysing a matched pair of sub-sets, one JVs and the other SOEs. It has concluded that out of four possible 'scenarios' concerning degrees of divergence and convergence, the third one of 'relative convergence' is possibly the most appropriate, at least for the larger and more 'go-ahead' SOEs. Clearly, more extensive research needs to be done in this domain, but it is hoped that this study on a limited scale has helped to more closely define and then to more precisely measure HRM in Chinese enterprises.

ACKNOWLEDGEMENT

The field-work reported here is based on research in Beijing carried out in Winter 1995 which was sponsored by the British Council exchange-scheme, whose generous support was appreciated. I must acknowledge the contribution of colleagues at Tsinghua University who acted as interpreters and translators during the visits to enterprises.

REFERENCES

Aiello, Paul (1991) 'Building a Joint Venture in China: The Case of Chrysler and the Beijing Jeep Corporation', *Journal of General Management*, Vol.17, No.2, pp.47–64.
Beijing Review (1995), 28 August, pp.4–5.
Beijing Review (1996), 29 April, p.5.
Chan, Anita (1993) 'Revolution or Corporatism? Workers and Trade Unions in Post-Mao China', *Australian Journal of Chinese Affairs*, No.29, pp.31–61.
Chan, Anita (1995) 'Chinese Enterprise Reform: Convergence with the Japanese Model? *Industrial and Corporate Change*, Vol.4, No.2, pp.449–70.
China Daily/Business Weekly (1995) 26 November, p.8.
Chen, Min (1996) *Managing International Technology Transfer.* London: International Thomson Business Press.
Child, John (1994) *Chinese Management During the Age of Reform.* Cambridge: Cambridge University Press.
Duberley, Joanne and Paul Walley (1995) 'Assessing the Adoption of HRM by Small and Medium-sized Manufacturing Organizations', *International Journal of Human Resource Management*, Vol.6, No.4, pp.891–909.
Easterby-Smith, Martin, Danusia Malina and Yuan Lu (1994) 'How Culture Sensitive is HRM? A Comparative Analysis of Practice in Chinese and UK Companies', *Working Paper*, Management School, University of Lancaster, England.
Feinerman, James V. (1996) 'The Past and Future of Labour Law in China' in George K. Schoepfle (ed.) *Changes in China's Labour Market: Implications for the Future.* Washington, DC: US Department of Labor.
Gao, Shangquan (1994) 'Market Economy and the Labor Force Market', *Beijing Review*, 3 January, pp.14–16.
Guest, David (1987) 'Human Resource Management and Industrial Relations', *Journal of Management Studies*, Vol. 24, No. 5, pp.302–21.
IMF (1993) *World Economic Outlook.* Washington, DC: International Monetary Fund.
Josephs, Hilary K. (1995) 'Labor Law in a "Socialist Market Economy": The Case of China', *Columbia Journal of Transnational Law*, Vol.33, No.3, pp.561–81.
Kaple, Deborah (1994) *Dream of a Red Factory: The Legacy of High Stalinism in China.* Oxford: Oxford University Press.
Korzec, Michael (1992) *Labour and the Failure of Reform in China.* London: Macmillan.
Lardy, Nicholas (1994) *China and the World Economy.* Washington, DC: Institute for International Economics.
Legge, Karen (1989) 'Human Resources Management: A Critical Analysis', in John Storey (ed.) *New Perspectives on Human Resource Management.* London: Routledge, pp.19–41.
Leung, Winnie Y. (1993) 'Stalinist Unions under Market Socialism', *Working Paper*, Department of Political Science, University of Hong Kong.
Mann, Jin (1989) *Beijing Jeep.* New York: Simon and Schuster.
Minami, Ryoshin (1994) *The Economic Development of China: A Comparison with the Japanese Experience.* London: Macmillan.
Ng Sek Hong and Malcolm Warner (1998) *Trade Unions and Management in China.* London: Macmillan, in press.
Nolan, Peter (1995) *China's Rise, Russia's Fall: Politics, Economics and Planning in the Transition from Stalinism.* London: Macmillan.
Pearson, Margaret M. (1991) *Joint Ventures in the People's Republic of China: The Control of Foreign Direct Investment Under Socialism.* Princeton: Princeton University Press.
SSB (State Statistical Bureau) *Statistical Outline of China (Zhongguo Tongji Zhaiyao).* Beijing: China Statistical Press, various years.
Storey, John (1992) *Developments in the Management of Human Resources.* Oxford: Blackwell.
Takahara, Aakio (1992) *The Politics of Wage Policy in Post-Revolutionary China.* London: Macmillan.
Taylor, Robert (1996) *Greater China and Japan: Prospects for an Economic Partnership in Asia.* London: Routledge.
Thomason, George (1991) 'The Management of Personnel', *Personnel Review*, Vol.20, No.1, pp.3–10.
Verma, Anil and Yan Zhiming (1995) 'The Changing Face of HRM in China: Opportunities, Problems and Strategies' in Anil Verma; Thomas A. Kochan, and Russell D. Lansbury (eds) *Employment Relations in the Growing Asian Economies.* London: Routledge, pp.315–35.

Warner, Malcolm (1986) 'Managing Human Resources in China', *Organization Studies*, Vol.7, No.4, pp.353–66.
Warner, Malcolm (1992) *How Chinese Managers Learn: Management and Industrial Training in the PRC*. London: Macmillan.
Warner, Malcolm (1993) 'Human Resource Management "With Chinese Characteristics"?', *International Journal of Human Resource Management*, Vol.4, No.1, pp.45–65.
Warner, Malcolm (1995) *The Management of Human Resources in Chinese Industry*. London: Macmillan.
Warner, Malcolm (1996) 'Beyond the Iron Rice Bowl: Comprehensive Labour Reform in State-owned Enterprises in North-East China' in David H. Brown and Robin Porter (eds) *Management Issues in China: Domestic Enterprises*. London: Routledge, pp.214–36.
Warner, Malcolm (1997) 'Chinese Enterprise Reform, Human Resources and the 1995 Labour Law', *International Journal of Human Resource Management* (in press).
White, Gordon (1995) 'Chinese Trade Unions in the Transition from Socialism', *Working Paper*, Institute of Development Studies, University of Sussex, May.
Xinhua News Agency (1994), cited by *Reuters*, 10 May.

Economic Restructuring and HRM in Hong Kong

NG SEK HONG and CAROLYN POON

In this study, the authors investigate the role performed by human resources in contributing to the restructuring of business and the economy of Hong Kong; and vice versa, the human resource implications of this process in the workplace. The observations and conclusions are provisional at best, since the case study method is the principal instrument adopted. Moreover, the authors' limited resources have effectively precluded the collection of data by territory-wide surveys to allow broader scope for generalizations. Nevertheless, these studies, all focused upon 'lead' cases of business reforms among key industries in Hong Kong, lend indicative clues, albeit preliminary, as to how Hong Kong's economy and its labour market are shifting amidst the global and trendy process of 'restructuring' and the implications for human resource management (HRM) and its policies and practices.

INDUSTRIALIZATION AND DE-INDUSTRIALIZATION

Hong Kong's economic transformation has been cyclical and market-led, thereby different from other Asian newly industrialized economies (NIEs), where planned intervention by the state is more visible (Maeda and Ng, 1996: 177–92; Verma, 1995b: 351–55). Basically, this city economy commenced as an *entrepot* shortly after its colonization by Britain in 1841 (ceded by China under the Treaty of Nanking). Its nexus of business activities was in the pre-war period, 'commercial' in nature, and associated with mercantile and maritime trade, backed by shipping and other harbour service/port facilities. It persisted as a city port until the mid-1940s. Both its economy and society seemed to have betrayed a 'transient' theme, as the following brief commentary reflects:

> Hong Kong society and its population have always been in a hybrid state greatly affected by immigration into and out of the territory. Historically, the 'visiting' and transient mentality of the 'dwellers' domicile in Hong Kong, as it was almost a norm before the Second World War, was documented also officially in such dossiers as the Butters Report on Labour and Labour Conditions in Hong Kong (Ng, 1996a: 39).

Ng Sek Hong and Carolyn Poon, University of Hong Kong

The watershed year was 1949, when the Communists won decisively over the Nationalists in the traumatic civil war and liberated the nation by introducing a doctrinal socialist government which was inhospitable towards private business. The massive escape of Chinese capital, alongside the industrial know-how and technical labour it brought to Hong Kong as an asylum, was the prelude to the first wave of industrialization. The territory's *entrepot*-based commercial economy was hence restructured into an industrial one, as an offshore base for foreign capital of relatively cheap labour producing manufactured or semi-manufactured products for export to Europe and America. Hong Kong's first experience of economic restructuring has been described in such terms:

> The civil war ended with the establishment of a Communist regime in China in 1949. Under the pressure of these political events, a huge inflow of labour, capital and entrepreneurial skill from China to Hong Kong occurred during the period 1948–51. Those taking refuge in Hong Kong included young and energetic people who were intelligent and willing to work hard, people with much money capital, and skilled entrepreneurs who were mostly Shanghainese industrialists engaged in the textile industry. This huge inflow of human and capital resources from China formed the basis of subsequent industrialisation (Chen, 1995: 2).

As Hong Kong advanced industrially, its traditional mix of commercial and mercantile activities began to recede. Such a de-commercialization process was to a large extent accelerated by the trade embargo levied upon China by the US and UN in the aftermath of the Korean War. This almost halted the previous voluminous flow of goods between the Mainland and the rest of the world which were processed through Hong Kong's *entrepot*. In spite of attrition in these *entrepot* activities, the territory's new industries were able to benefit substantially and strategically by inheriting a well enshrined trading infrastructure. This included, notably, an efficient and stable banking system, an effective network of domestic and international telephone services, a stable and competent civil service bureaucracy, as well as a web of established retail outlets and public transport support, plus a low taxation regime. Such an infrastructural endowment gave its new manufacturing base, which was labour-intensive and featured 'low-tech' assembly-line processing activities, a salient competitive advantage over other neighbouring NIEs (such as Singapore, Taiwan and South Korea) which were also on the eve of their respective industrial take-off dramas (Ng and Lethbridge, 1995a: 213).

Although Hong Kong had consolidated a significant base of light industries during its process of de-commercialization, heavy industrial and engineering activities had been conspicuous by their absence. Such a bias has affected the composition of the labour force and the employment practices and HRM adopted in enterprises. In the 1960s, Hong Kong was basically a low-cost production centre: the labour force was predominantly semi-skilled and unskilled, with workers hired in manufacturing industries often on a casual or semi-casual basis engaged on piece-work arrangements. It was a case of Hong Kong's restructuring into an industrial base due to defaults in historical events and crises, especially hostilities like the (Mainland) Liberation, Korean and Vietnam Wars and associated upheavals, rather than by design of the state planners (Ng, 1996b: 296–97). By contrast, in other Asian Pacific economies, the imperative of state planning and intervention has been far more noticeable, as in South Korea, Taiwan and Singapore (Maeda and Ng, 1996: 167–72; and respective pieces in this volume).

In such a context, what has evolved in Hong Kong is a labour market where there has been a steady improvement in employees' real wages and living standards. This was basically sustained by its industrial growth and advances in export markets, and upgraded productivity resulting from advances in both technology and educational levels of the workforce. Moreover, labour shortages stemming from a growing demand in the economy and a consolidating population (as the birth rate declines) have, in turn, raised the general wage level. A relatively free labour market also helps to distinguish Hong Kong from other state-led cases of Asian NIE's industrialization, such as South Korea and Taiwan, where coercive state control of organized labour before political democratization in the late 1980s contained pay advances so strenuously that it laid the seeds for the explosion of vociferous industrial strife (Maeda and Ng, 1996: 183–92; Park and Lee, 1995: 38–9). Transformation of the Hong Kong economy into a base of secondary manufacturing activities and subsequently into the higher realm of post-industrial (tertiary service) industries, produced by the beginning of the 1980s an affluent level in people's living standards by Asian standards (Labour Department, 1995: 29, para. 2.12.).

THE CYCLICAL SYNDROME OF ECONOMIC DEVELOPMENT

Recent wage improvements have also been caused, however, by a steady reversal process in the territory's economic restructuring. The transformational process this time has been the drain of industrial activities, coupled with the recovery of *entrepot* trade as well as the growth of financial, business, and other tertiary commercial services. However, Hong Kong restructured itself spontaneously, almost by the reign of the marketplace alone, and made possible by the 'China factor'. As argued earlier, the economic and labour history of Hong Kong is actually a drama representing an outgrowth of external and contextual changes in the politico-economic arenas of the Mainland, East Asia and the global paradigm impinging upon the commercial status and viability of the territory. It began when Hong Kong's initial prewar role as an *entrepot* was emasculated by the civil upheavals of the Mainland, the military confrontation besetting the Taiwan Straits, the hostilities of the Korean War and the UN trade embargo against China. It was a dualistic engine of the 'invisible hand' combining both the market imperative and geo-political history in the region, which explains Hong Kong's legendary transformation into a leading NIE in East Asia around the 1960s through the 1980s (Chen, 1995: 2–13).

Again, in the mid-1990s the territory is basically responding, in spite of its purported flexibility and prudent adherence to the law of the 'invisible hand', to the exogenous pressure of competitive business and trade in the global and regional economies, as well as the shifting parameters of its own political future (due to the transfer of sovereign power to China). In such a context, and against the background of such a traumatic history of labour and capital migration from the Mainland, it can be argued that such restructuring is not novelistically new, but merely a re-visit to its previous experiences. Moreover, such restructuring can hardly be de-associated from the territory's political economy, which is about to enter a realm of post-industrialism and become an autonomous self-governing entity, as a Special Administrative Region of China. It is a paradox of sanctioned contradictions, permitted by virtue of an international (Sino–British) treaty and a China-ordained Basic Law to conserve its capitalist status quo, within the rhetorical framework of 'one country–two systems' which China devised as the formula of its re-unification (Miners, 1991; Ng and Lethbridge, 1995a: xi–xii).

Thus, the 'China factor' has once again become a crucial source, or even the key determinant, causing the territory's de-industrialization. Preambled by the 'Four Modernizations', China began its long march of modernizing its 'command economy' by a creeping process of prudent adjustments to introduce decentralized marketplace activities and attract foreign capital investment. Since the beginning of the 1980s, China (especially along its coastal areas) has witnessed vigorous state sponsored economic reforms to institute a nationwide system of 'market socialism' with 'Chinese characteristics'. The process has provided Hong Kong with expanded markets, capital and low-cost hinterland to relocate labour-intensive light manufacturing. These contextual shifts happened at a time of labour shortages and wage–price spirals that pushed Hong Kong into a high-cost production base (Chen, 1995: 5–22). As the bastion of 'free-wheeling' capitalism, Hong Kong has been able to expand and advance its business, financial trading and hospitality industries at the tertiary level, on a regional (Asia Pacific) and global scale, by hiving off the lower value-adding manufacturing activities in textiles, garment-making, electronics, plastics and watch assembly across the border. These industrial activities, financed and branded by Hong Kong capital, have succeeded and prospered by engaging a native labour force of more than three million workers in its hinterland. Moreover, the re-activation of China's external trade relations with the West and other industrial nations via the Organisation of Economic Co-operation and Development (OECD) and General Agreement on Trade and Tariff (GATT), now the World Trade Organisation (WTO), has stimulated an unprecedented volume of Sino trading activities worldwide.

Such a commercial nexus has in turn enabled the territory to re-cycle itself again back into an *entrepot*, as the gateway to China.

However, it must be said that, in today's post-industrial context of advanced information and telecommunication services, Hong Kong's advantages due to geo-political proximity may no longer suffice when competing with neighbouring NIEs like Singapore, Macau, or even Shanghai. As increasingly recognized by the administration, and succinctly acknowledged by the Governor in his annual policy addresses, it is imperative that Hong Kong is able to excel in the quality of service industries and support which it provides to local and foreign business – whether in the China sector or in the Asia Pacific region. The key to Hong Kong's advances in its service domain rests strategically, the argument follows, with its human infrastructural back-up and its continuous improvements and upgrading (Patten, 1995: 14–16, para. 35–8). By implication, it is considered imperative that commensurate labour market reforms are introduced in its human infrastructure in order to sustain its excellence as a service centre.

Compounding the theme of restructuring in Hong Kong's economy and business is the commercialization of the corporate stock and share markets, which raises in turn the 'trendy' issue of corporate governance and performance in order to attract investors in the capital fund market. The economy's transformation entails, *inter alia*, its hastened and pace-setting development into Asia's largest financial market for stock and share transactions (almost second to Tokyo, presently on parity with Singapore). As this capital and share market becomes internationalized, the resulting pressure of globalized competition in the capital fund market has also induced companies listed on the public stock exchange to improve corporate performance in order to attract potential investors. This has posed, in turn, a strong incentive upon their managements to seek leverage in such cost-saving devices as 'downsizing', 'de-layering' or 'de-bureaucratization'. The apparent rationale is to improve the performance image (commonly measured in terms of yield or return to share investment) of listed public companies in annual reports disclosed to shareholders. That human resource issues are increasingly recognized worldwide as a pertinent aspect of improving corporate governance in processes of business restructuring is noted by Verma *et al.* (1995a: 26) in presenting such an agenda:

> The central issue is how industrial relations and human resource policies and practices fit into the pattern of corporate governance found in the enterprise? To what extent, and how, are employee interests articulated in the strategy formation and governance processes of the enterprise? What roles, if any, are played by unions, works councils, codetermination, human resource managers, or other processes or institutions in corporate governance?

Labour overheads are popularly seen as the culprits for burdening business bureaucracies – whether they are the highly sophisticated and professionally managed Western-style technocracies (which once won admiration as 'model' corporations like IBM, Philips, General Motors, Ford or General Electric, British Telecom, etc.) or large-scale and once 'socialist' structured state-owned enterprises (SOEs) in China, which are anxious to scale down their over-manned organizations in order to remain viable when converted into autonomous business units under the reforms. It has, hence, become a world-wide fashionable prescription for corporations to streamline their size by employee cutbacks and retrenchment into leaner and smaller units. However, supportive empirical evidence has remained elusive, clouded and inconclusive, as in Western Europe (Hyman and Ferner, 1994: 8–13). Even in Asia, as argued by Verma *et al.* (1995b: 337), the problems facing countries in the process of restructuring 'are quite different', so that 'the constraints under which they seek solutions vary a great deal'. Anyway, the anxiety of many company boards in Hong Kong is to position their enterprises pro-actively to face an impending unknown of a (economically) competitive and (politically) uncertain future, as well as to erect a performance-oriented image in the capital fund market of stock and share transactions. This psychology has reportedly caused a growing number of corporate bureaucracies to view downsizing as the 'standard' recipe of, and key to, innovative management and business competition.

EMPIRICAL CLUES

However, data obtained by the authors are useful to help elucidate the Hong Kong 'drama' of economic restructuring and how it has affected industry and individual enterprises in coping with the shifting terrain of the marketplace. The findings from a series of case studies illustrate the labour implications of these processes. For ease of exposition, data are organized into three clusters. The first uses two corporate case studies of business restructuring activities in process at the time of writing. The second reviews the business and manpower profile of the retail trade sector with reference to department and chain fashion/convenience stores. The third comprises a group of three enterprises also belonging to the service industry,[1] focused upon the patterns of business restructuring and adjustments and examined not only the implied human resource and labour markets changes emanating from these shifts, but also the roles of culture and institutions (Ng *et al.*, 1995: 81–9).

Cluster 1: Corporate Employers Adjusting Business Strategies and Human Resource Approaches

There is now an apparent syndrome, as commonly advanced by management in the corporations we investigated and others in Hong Kong, that business and manpower restructuring is almost imperative in order to compete effectively. This is especially because the territory's transfer of sovereign authority and the turn of millennium (suggesting a new paradigm of a postmodern economy and industrial order) are both imminent. Our two corporate case studies in the first cluster are seemingly trapped in such a syndrome, as narrated below.

The first and almost classic illustration of such corporate-wide adjustments in business and human resource strategies is Cathay Pacific, the Hong Kong based airline. This carrier has built up its international reputation as one of the world's few highly competitive and profitable airlines – despite being relatively small (by international standards) and managed entirely as a private business unit owned by a leading commercial 'noble house' (one of the British old-style trading *hongs*). However, its competitive edge began to face slow yet steady decline (in profit margins) from its zenith in the mid and late 1980s. The airline embarked upon a proactive but ambitious renewal programme of organizational development (OD). Given its high optimism about the prospect of a fast-growing airline industry, such an OD prescription was expansionist and globalized. The exercise, however, inadvertently (and drastically) altered the conservative and paternalistic managerial culture of the corporation. Moreover, the initial endeavours of the airline's 'change agenda' were so impersonal and bureaucratic that it provoked in late 1992 and January 1993 a wave of disputes with its house union organizing the predominantly young, female cabin crew staff (Ng and Lethbridge, 1995b: 82–3).

For the company, the air stewardess strike was traumatic and costly. It lasted 17 days, almost unprecedented in Hong Kong's postwar labour history, and was organized, surprisingly, by a basically non-recalcitrant union of its cabin attendants. In addition to direct losses, it demoralized heavily a defeated, apprehensive and suspicious cabin workforce. These were combined spontaneously in a multicultural mix but demonstrated ill organized militancy in the strike. However, the gestation, incidence and aftermath of this stoppage seemed to be calculated by top management as a 'necessary' price to be paid, as 'shock therapy' to traditional organizational culture. Management's victory served to levy upon the 'tamed' workforce a new mandate and eventually, by furthering the OD 'dosage', to secure renewed 'consent' to restructuring. The hardline approach was also intended to act as a signal to middle-layers of the organization's previously 'lukewarm' management, alerting the entire bureaucracy to the imperative agenda of change.

However, the real test actually arrived a few years after the collapse of the strike. These new constraints are essentially geo-political, associated with China in the settings of both the reversion of the territory's sovereign rights and the prospects of 'Sinolization' and 'East Asianization', in addition to 'Japanization', as the likely motors of the world's economic growth and prosperity. Adding to these are the competitive uncertainties specific to the global airline industry moving towards de-regulation and privatization of nationalized flag-carriers, and challenges from the new Second Airport due to open in 1998. The latter is expected to heavily erode Cathay Pacific's present privileged single carrier status (by virtue of its

British linkage), and its air-cargo handling and engineering service subsidiaries are also due to lose their quasi-official franchises as sole agencies.

The airline has interpreted such a shifting business milieu as a paradoxical source of both inhospitality and new opportunities. It has accordingly re-aligned its pre-1993 strategy of business restructuring to concentrate upon a narrower focus of excelling in Asia rather than worldwide, in spite of its continued global flight service. First, it has secured the participation of Mainland China capital in corporate management and ownership tiers, thereby converting its governing board of directors into a Sino–British joint 'administration'. The purpose is both to procure political insurance and to pre-empt entry of China backed competitors into the sector. Second, for political security it has re-located some key operational activities to lower cost areas like Guangzhou in Southern China, such as its accounting department and part of its ticketing clerical support, or even Sydney, to which the core of its Management Information System has been re-sited. Third, it has sourced from its various outport bases in Asia potential cabin crew, making the airline's image more multicultural as well as saving on labour costs such as pay and benefits, notably overseas housing allowances.

Thus, a theme of 'Asianization' has become central, as visible in the airline's communication to its staff and passengers about restructuring. The 'Asian image' is now ingrained in the carrier's logo. However, the principal concern remains the clouded prospect as to whether it can excel as a leading Asian carrier now that the bulk of its customers are Asians (making up about two-thirds of its passenger volume). While its reform agenda is primarily to save costs, the company has made explicit that it would not consciously downsize but instead upgrade and enhance its human resource conserve and advance its purported 'core competency' – the provision of quality 'customer service' flavoured with a modern Asian style.

Notwithstanding such a vision, the airline's human resource agenda is laden with a variety of thorny issues. While human resources are identified as the key lever for advancing the standard of customer service, implementing its new cost-saving plans impinges heavily upon its staff. Moreover, there prevails the lingering misgiving that 'problematic' staff relations persisted in the aftermath of the 1993 strike and that 'the wounds need to be healed' before morale and commitment can be restored, especially since the crew's attitudes are key to achieving quality customer service.

The globalized nature of competition in the air travel-cum-hospitality industry has implied the almost inevitable control device of 'benchmarking' in measuring staff and corporate performance. In this context, it is likely that performance appraisal will be enhanced as a 'core' instrument, especially in the 'key result areas'. Seemingly, there is a growing convergence of this airline with other corporations in having fashioned, almost worldwide, a human resource ideology of 'postmodern' managerialism. Four personnel sub-functions are commonly emphasized as the popular prescription for building their competency and competitive niche. These are, first, recruitment that exalts selection by inculcating the notion that the intake needs to be highly selective and controlled by measured assessment. Second, performance appraisal, with moves towards workplace appraisal, evaluation and assessment, is now applied to all parties and to every stage and aspect of employment, including recruitment and intake, performance, training, promotion, transfer, etc. The third personnel function involves training, education and socialization. This is to be consistent with the strategy of investing in human assets as capital that pays off in yielding 'value-added' contributions. However, ideologically, such activity can also 'programme' staff values, assumptions and actions: by indoctrinating the workforce in order that it can be assimilated into the sanctioned corporate culture, with consent elicited to the change process (see also Hochschild, 1988). Fourth, human resource planning is to provide the strategic linkage to top-level corporate planning as well as giving a coherent framework for integrating those above key personnel activities (Storey, 1991: 8–9; Ng, 1995: 6–7).

The rationalization of human resource policy and practices of this company by such a strategy is imminent, and in some aspects already in progress. The prescription is remarkably Westernized in its assumptions, in spite of the business theme of Asianization which such restructuring activities are purported to address. Its convergence with a Western-style approach to 'de-bureaucratization' is, in addition, evidenced by another personnel feature – the imminent introduction of a variety of flexibility arrangements and contractual 'package' deals. These are designed to stimulate incentive and performance as well as to reduce labour costs. The contradiction is in the emasculation of a stable internal labour market, which its celebrated corporate culture used to enshrine. In terms of what was represented to us by its management, the internal labour market has been made less structured and more competitive, fluid and amenable to intra-organizational mobility, transfer and open bidding for promotion and advancement opportunities. Yet, the invisible bond of the 'psychological contract' in binding the parties' mutual commitment has become transient instead of 'life-long' in horizon.

This has led a new policy of hiring in an increasing number of jobs (including some core managerial positions) via fixed-term contracts – a practice reminiscent of contract labour now adopted in China to alleviate cost burdens on over-staffed SOEs (Warner, 1996: 196–7). A dualistic advantage of such a flexibility measure is claimed by management because the financial obligations implied by fixed contracts are readily ascertainable and hence controllable, while the parties' delimited period of commitment indirectly induces them to excel in serving each others' expectations in order to justify and maximize a 'fair deal' at work. Parallel to this, 'flexi-hire' arrangements are also expected to help source and procure better 'quality' human resources in the professional/managerial skill markets.

What is to be instituted next on the human resource agenda is the changeover to a 'flexi' remuneration package to allow staff scope for individual choices in opting between both cash disbursement and payment in kind (such as housing, medical or money equivalents in lieu and immediate and deferred payment with a 'saving' factor of investing in the company's superannuation scheme as well as a 'security' factor in retirement). Such a flexible configuration is justified, in addition, because of its role in contributing to cost consolidation and overhead savings (of organizing and providing in-house, medical and other employee welfare benefit fixtures).

Obviously, it appears premature to attempt to assess in totality the significance and implications of such a relatively generic approach by this air carrier to engineer and steer a holistic, ambitious process of restructuring its corporate structure (in its capital 'make-up' in ownership), business and work organization, as well as its hardware and human infrastructure. The outcome and relative success of these restructuring strategies are influenced by a number of key imperatives. These are largely of a politico-economic nature, which are themselves in the process of gestation. The company appears to have chosen to initiate a pragmatic approach in search for corporate consolidation and de-centralized reforms so as to equip itself with its basic competency to compete better. The nexus of its advances is possibly located in the Asian domain and articulated in business qualities like 'passenger/customer services', where it has always claimed a niche as its corporate tradition.

Inasmuch as the downsizing corporate mentality is common worldwide, the Cathay Pacific perspective of business rationalization can hardly be seen in isolation as a parochial or specific culture-bound issue. Yet, there is the moral pledge made by its management that it is not to take on wholesale the downsizing formula *per se*, although, quite unavoidably, its human resource agenda is designed to be one of austerity and economizing on fixed labour overheads. As noted already, what is likely to be unfolded on the human resource agenda is the adoption of an increasing variety of flexible arrangements like flexi-pay packages, 'open' bidding for senior openings, contract hiring, part-time employment, localization of recruitment (in place of overseas assignment of office staff and cabin crew), and outsourcing. Thus, there will be a steady run-down of its elitist enclave of an expatriate (essentially British) core of house managerial staff, recruited from Britain and groomed for corporate leadership by a system almost equivalent to the cadet or administrative officers in the civil service.

The second case of corporate re-adjustment is one of the territory's two franchised power companies, China Light and Power (CLP). It serves the more industrialized Kowloon Peninsula and the New Territories, while its smaller counterpart operates on the urbanized Hong Kong Island (which is patronized largely by office and residential customers). The Kowloon-based power plant achieved its 'peak' in the early and mid-1980s – at a time when industry was at its zenith in its export-oriented production activities, aided by the euphoria of the opening up of China and its reforms. Widespread optimism was nurtured by its business success, because of industry's high propensity to consume energy commensurate with its prosperity in the mid-1980s; sustained industrial affluence of the local population and a potentially huge and enlarging volume of cross-border trade and commercial activities with the Mainland; and the availability of a major market in Southern China importing electricity to feed light industries. Such optimism was evident in the ambitious corporate planning of this power plant in the mid and late 1980s. Such an expansionist strategy was epitomized by its joint venture with China's Ministry of Energy in building the first nuclear generation plant on the Guangdong coastline adjacent to Hong Kong.

However, such expansion soon became problematic, triggered off again, ironically, by the China factor. This was, in the first place, the unanticipated *en masse* migration of manufacturing activities to the Mainland in search of cheaper labour and land. Hong Kong's industrial workforce halved in size to just about 600,000 over a five-year span to the mid-1990s. This reduction was especially problematic for CLP which had a hitherto bias in catering for manufacturing. There was also the inception of nuclear power in the early 1990s, the sale of which has been guaranteed and accorded priority over that of the company's local conventional plants. Thus, due to the territory's shifting politico-economic milieu for business activities, CLP's corporate agenda is now confronted with drastic decline in domestic industrial consumption of energy. This is compounded by the possible loss of its privileged position as a power monopoly sheltered by an officially sanctioned franchise. Hong Kong is systematically deregulating the area, opening it up to new entrants so as to enhance its competitiveness, efficiency and 'value-for-money' to consumers/users. The company's response is to diversify its outlets, both geographically to penetrate Southern China and neighbouring NIEs, as well as vertically to promote a more varied and sophisticated mix of product lines to cater to domestic industrial and household consumption.

A niche which the power station enjoys as an established 'player' in the industry is a highly structured and competent infrastructure of power generation, transmission and distribution network in terms of both hardware 'back-up' as well as its managerial and control system. What emerges as a clear theme of its business restructuring vision is to conserve and improve such a key competitive advantage, accompanied by a vigorous corporate-wide endeavour to achieve excellence in its customer service. However, for a long established, conservative, bureaucratic and engineering-biased utility monopoly, the changeover involved in its re-positioning to become a federal-like conglomerate of decentralized and autonomous business units (which exalts, instead, the primacy of customer service) is clearly 'revolutionary' to both the organization itself and its staff. For this purpose, a re-vamped approach to its HRM strategy and policy is imperative.

It appears that such a corporate orientation towards strategic renewal is to a certain degree comparable to that identifiable in the airline case – inasmuch as the corporate vision in either places a seemingly paradoxical emphasis upon two aspects. First, its Asianization as a regionally-oriented business unit, which necessarily entails a cross-border or cosmopolitan horizon of strategic expansion steered by the Hong Kong headquarters. Second, an austerity action plan to save on cost and labour overheads to enhance competitiveness in productivity, quality performance and customer service. The 'consolidation' nexus is probably imperative on CLP's change agenda – in the aftermath of its over-expansion a decade ago, and beset by a 'glut' and a less hospitable industrial setting emanating from opening up energy production.

A three-tier blueprint of CLP's vision to restructure and re-image itself as a regional business corporation in Asia has been outlined by its chairman. It suggests a prescription of corporate entrepreneurial initiatives, pledging commitment to three domains. First, to retain Hong Kong for its 'core' operations. Second, to advance growth in China: focusing upon China – the most prospective market as a hinterland to the core business (it created a representation office in Beijing in 1995 and entered into a number of joint venture arrangements with its Mainland counterparts, including the construction and operation of the nation's first nuclear plant). Third, to develop transnational activities and collaboration in Asia: by participating in power development projects and investing in the supportive infrastructure in areas like India, Taiwan, Thailand and Indonesia, given its niche in engineering and technology (China Light and Power Company, 1995a: 14–15).

What has emanated from these contextual shifts is a corporate agenda which has to cope with not only change and reform, but also the complexity of managing such changes strategically and pro-actively in order to accommodate all these. As a sequel to the recommendations of a comprehensive consultancy review, the company has now adopted a dualistic restructuring mission, termed a 'Strategic Plan' for the long-term, and accompanied by an operational 'Change Plan' for steering structural reforms and business/human resource adjustments. This is aimed at improving its core strengths and using these to meet the differing aspirations of its customers, employees and shareholders – the principal parties commonly cited in the stakeholder theory of corporate governance and decision-making (ibid: 16; Tricker, 1984: 153–4, 157–60).

The corporate pledge to ascertain, appraise and advance the company's core competence and strength brings into focus a sensitive issue of measuring performance, both of the enterprise and staff. It apparently subscribes to the practice of benchmarking, anchored in the critical HRM activity of performance appraisal, aimed at 'improving utilisation of assets and resources, streamlining procedures and setting and achieving performance targets benchmarked to world best practice' (China Light and Power, 1995b: 2, 7). An inventory of such 'threshold' benchmarks is in the process of being developed, with references drawn against selected model establishments across industry, as well as in a transnational context. This will constitute a corporate-wide scheme of department-specific checklists and criteria to appraise the enterprise and its workforce.

In spite of these procedural reforms in establishing measured norms of business and work performance in key areas of excellence, uncertainty clouding its future is rooted in the fluidity of having to transform itself from a public utility with a heavy engineering tradition into a modernized energy supplier excelling in the user market by advancing quality of customer service. Consistent with the macro shift of Hong Kong into a postindustrial economy, CLP is adjusting its image to become a service enterprise which places a premium on customer friendliness. It aspires to excel more than as a power generation plant *per se*, for which customer satisfaction used to be trivial or even irrelevant, especially when covered by a government sanctioned public franchise. Apparently, the power plant is anxious to change from its bureaucratic 'cage' as a civil service-like hierarchy, into a 'leaner' organization made up of a coalition of semi-autonomous business units. In turn, its renewal needs radical changes in its HRM policies and activities. Such an enhanced and re-structured approach to its HRM agenda involves actions and adjustments.

The first 'recipe' involves a corporate-wide re-engineering of organizational culture, now oriented towards a total quality management (TQM) philosophy and approach to business and work. Its HRM activities, which have been re-organized to devolve control from the headquarters to the constituent business units now made semi-autonomous in HRM decision-making, are aimed to cultivate a staff awareness of and ideological commitment to, serving their customers. The search for excellence in service becomes the litmus test for the corporation in assessing and determining its competitive strengths, its core competencies.

Second, top management has pledged its commitment to the 'humanization' of the corporation's culture as a service enterprise. A caring, personal and hospitable approach to users is now promoted, with the establishment of a network of customer service centres. What is patently new and important is this theme of hospitable interface with 'end users', the domestic and business customers. Its core activity is no longer limited just to delivering energy from its power plants. It also includes cultivating and soliciting good human relations with customers by practising the ethos of 'user friendliness'. This is indicated by a checklist on its performance pledges to customers, reproduced in Table 1.

The HRM activities involved are both direct and indirect. They begin with a subtle task of building and re-building a new spirit of staff commitment to achieving service excellence. What follows next on the agenda is a mixed-bag of personnel selection, training, skill upgrading and performance appraisal activities designed to yield and sustain an integrated system of corporate competency by grooming an human infrastructure of commensurate quality and proficiency.

The development of a body of its key 'corporate competencies' is hence

TABLE 1
CHINA LIGHT AND POWER PERFORMANCE PLEDGES

Performance Pledges	Achievement (%) 1995	Target (%) 1996
1. Reliability of electricity supply to exceed target	99.98	99.99
2. New connection and supply of electricity within 24 hours after satisfactory installation inspection	99.60	>99.60
3. Arrive at site of loss within one hour of receipt of notification	95.07	>95.07
4. Keep queuing time at cash collection points to within five minutes	97.74	>97.74
5. Answer customer phone calls within four rings:		
• China Light's 10 Supply Districts	98.00	>98.00
• Customer Telephone Services Emergency	75.53	95.00
• Customer Telephone Services Enquiry	55.70	95.00
6. Notify customers 3 working days in advance of planned outrage	new target	95.00
7. Reconnect supply within one day after payment of outstanding charges is received	new target	95.00
8. Keep queuing time for customer service enquiries to within 20 minutes	new target	95.00

Source: China Light and Power (1996: 14).

the third theme of the programme of restructuring its human resources to sustain and advance such pledges in harmony with its re-adjustment strategy. The programme, designated as the 'Competency Development Suggestions' (CDS), enables its managerial staff to coach and instruct their subordinates, by combining both Management By Objective and TQM approaches, to advance their awareness, appreciation and performance in an identified mix of company-specific competencies, defined as 'the preferred behaviours (which) the company wants to promote throughout the organisation' (China Light and Power, 1995b:3). These corporate competencies are classified into three tiers of competencies clusters, ranging from 'value orientation', through 'human relations' skills, to the technocratic capabilities needed in job performance. Basically, they correspond to the qualities of: (1) Cultural Competencies: customer orientation, business mindedness, continuous improvement, concern for safety and the environment and teamwork and co-operation; (2) Taking People With You: team leadership, communication for impact, and developing self and others; (3) Planning For Results: performance driven, critical thinking, expertise and organizational commitment. These three layers of core competencies are applied and tailored to fashion staff performance and assessment in various grades in the hierarchy, including the status strata of the governance and management boards at the apex; the leadership echelon of senior managerial staff; the middle layer of managerial and professional staff; the lower middle layer of professional and technical staff; and the supporting staff.

The design of these core competencies, now central to the fashioning of its HRM activities, is indicative of the new theme of quality customer service. It is a strategy of de-bureaucratization and de-centralization aimed at yielding a renewed, flexible and organic business/commercial entity. In support, a parallel corporate concern is to re-build and consolidate a solidaristic spirit of workforce commitment in aligning the individual's personal interest with the company's needs, priorities and goals.

To contribute to the consistent, coherent and focused enhancement of the above identified core competencies strategic to corporate reform and advances, CLP has reinforced its provisions and facilities in its training and skill development activities. The new qualities sought are creativity, sociability, lateral thinking abilities and quality awareness, and so on. A range of new courses have been developed and existing ones have been reinforced at the Training Centre, which historically enjoyed an esteemed reputation in Hong Kong by virtue of its comparative rigour and professional resources. A cursory review of the broadened and renewed inventory of training courses suggests they are likely to yield a more adaptive, flexible, multi-skilled and innovative workforce, with a higher consciousness about customer service, quality, and excellence, in an 'organistic' service bureaucracy.

Of course, the obvious ramifications of redefining and refining the qualities of the workforce are drastic for HRM and the recruitment, selection and retention of staff. New criteria for ascertaining candidates' suitability have been introduced. Compounding the new HRM agenda is the urgent need to consolidate the establishment and workforce size. This is because of the above noted shifts. A painful process of downsizing, affecting in particular the craft tradeworkers, technicians and engineering staff, is almost impossible to avert. However, downsizing could unwittingly weaken staff commitment to the new organizational culture which CLP has painstakingly devised and cultivated.

Cluster 2: Business Restructuring in the Retail Service Sector

A second cluster of data is based upon a small-scale investigation of the retail industry, conducted in the summer of 1996.[2] The Hong Kong Department Stores and Commercial Staff General Union has a membership of about 20,000, out of 700,000 salaried employees in this highly diversified and fragmented trade. However, such modest strength has to be appreciated against a historical background of the mainstream retail trade anchored in the large department stores. These workplaces typically offered more favourable conditions for workers to combine and the union to organize.

Anyway, because of the distinctively core position of the department stores in the retail shop trade, their employees used to constitute the 'labour aristocracy' located in a relatively advantaged position *vis-à-vis* a heterogeneous fringe of low-paid and long-hour salesworkers typically hired by a vast number of small shops, boutiques and grocery stores. It also helps explain a small nucleus of organized labour.

However, it was apparent that neither the membership of the union of department stores staff nor their employers were able to sustain any longer such a 'lead' position in the sector by the end of the 1960s. With significant advances in income and affluence, there have been conspicuous shifts in lifestyle towards a more consumption-oriented one. The rise of a consumer society – concerned first with the availability of mass consumer goods and later with quality, brand differentiation and choice of products – has induced this once casually structured retail sector, predominated by petty capital (save the mainstream department stores), to re-configurate. The sector has now become increasingly diversified and pluralistic in outlet arrangements, varying in style from the department stores, through the supermarkets, grocery and stationary stores, street-corner stalls and peddlers to the trendy variety of boutiques, shopping arcade stores, chain convenience stores and fashion stores, specialist gift shops and network direct marketing.

As the sector grows in competitiveness and diversity, continuing viability requires the dualistic concern for productivity and performance, which have taken on increasingly qualitative dimensions – that is, a quest for excellence in customer service and satisfaction. While the core capability of 'salespersonship', backed by the 'classic' incentive of sales bonus or commission, have remained 'custom and practice', HRM policies and norms have become more technocratic in design as the importance of modernizing human resource utilization and management gains growing recognition as the key to business success.

Our sample of five case studies (including a local department store, owned by a Chinese business family, a Japanese department store, a group of Mainland China product department stores, a chain convenience store and a chain garment fashion store), as well as our interviews with the union's leadership and officials of the Hong Kong Retail Management Association, have illustrated an important number of shifting HRM and other practices. These have, paradoxically, made both more central and marginal the contribution of human resources in business performance. This is, noticeably, in hiring part-timers instead of permanent staff to save on labour overheads and facilitate flexibilities in work arrangements and business activities.

Transformational shifts within the large department stores mirrored advances in Hong Kong's society and economy which affected affluence, lifestyle, consumption and shopping behaviour. As a sequel to more sophisticated shoppers' tastes, as well as their higher aspirations for a better variety of choices, and a flair about fashion and status goods, the department stores have shifted in pattern to become less dominated by local Chinese family businesses and led by Japanese stores instead. The latter began to penetrate at the beginning of the 1980s because of their niche in areas of fashion and style, variety and choice, accessibility and hospitality to customers. Earlier, the standard locally-owned department stores distinguished themselves as luxury good stores catering to the upper class and later to the white-collar 'central class'. They grew in popularity in the 1960s, patronized often as family stores at weekends and holidays. Their heyday also coincided with the rise of another important stream of department stores specializing in the sale of Mainland China products. Labelled as Hong Kong's national merchandise department stores, they were centrally co-ordinated and supervised by a SOE belonging to China's Ministry of External Trade.

These China product emporium stores operated like a cartel in selling inexpensive necessity and consumer goods to the grass-roots labouring masses. Often their extensive network of outlets (inasmuch as most of these established several large branches catering to various districts in different locations) also served as the *de facto* collecting points for working-class shoppers to purchase in bulk low-cost merchandise to be taken back to their Mainland relatives. This cluster of stores reached its zenith in the mid-1970s when cross-border movement began being liberalized. Anyway, these Chinese stores, despite their proliferation and locational dispersion, were conspicuous for their high level of inter-store standardization in product mix, physical layout, sales strategy and HRM practices.

Concomitantly, the influx of Japanese department stores since the early 1980s led to substitution of local stores as sectoral 'pattern-setters'. These stores epitomize lead practices not only in product merchandising, but also in customer service, sales promotion, inventory control, corporate image and consumer's culture enhancement, as well as HRM – employment norms, human resource utilization and work organization. Particularly noticeable has been their success in re-inventing a sub-letting system of consignment, enabling sale areas to be leased by agreement to franchisees which are brand differentiated (especially on items like garments, cosmetics, jewellery and gift accessories). They have also served as benchmarks in employment benefits and arrangements which are emulated by others in the trade. However, they have selectively transplanted celebrated home practices like tenured hiring and seniority advancement. In the Sogo Japanese Store, '...staff, especially those in the lower level, are having lots of promotion chances. ... these multi-step graded staff scale are actually rooted in the Japanese concept of lifetime employment. ...to cultivate Sogo's staff belongingness and allegiance' (Ng and Poon, 1997).

What has become, however, a paradox is the piloting of shift patterns by some Japanese stores to marginalize some of their workforce, in the wake of the economy's recession which started to afflict the consumer service trades, particularly the retail business, in the mid-1990s. These shifts involve basically changes to such flexi-hiring practices as part-time employment, which have been popularized in the West (and now even in

Japan as well) as instruments of business restructuring. Although instrumental in enabling less competitive stores to reduce operational costs and labour overheads, these flexible employment practices have caused significant apprehension among a basically docile workforce.[3]

Anyway, Sogo has succeeded in maintaining intact its lead position as the most successful retailer. It has pledged to conserve its HRM policy of full-time and permanent employment and limiting its size of part-time hiring to less than five per cent of its workforce. Nevertheless, there have been consistent signs suggesting the retreat of the mainstream department store business in the increasingly pluralistic and competitive domain of retail sales. Coinciding with the slow-down of the economy, there has been a recent succession of business failures causing the closure of several Japanese branch stores and of a number of Chinese emporium shops (which are probably the most feeble competitors in the trade), and heavy losses by those few local Hong Kong stores still in operation.

The apparent marginalization of the department store mainstream and its retreat from a central position in the retail trade have to be seen in context. Basically, its restructuring is attributed to Hong Kong's advances in economy, technology, productivity, income level and hence, consumption and life-style. Heralded by a global mass culture of materialism and consumerism which defer to fashion, status goods and conspicuous consumption (Handy, 1995: 360–3), nostalgic qualities like 'austerity' and 'product durability' are increasingly outdated and displaced by consumer yearning for convenience, accessibility, style, variety and 'past-time' leisure as the key basis of their choice and behaviour in patronising the retail service. Apparently, the consumers' quest and the industry's consciousness for quality has seemingly taken on a re-adjusted connotation – now quality is judged in terms of service, and not just the product and its durability.

Perhaps the most distinctive feature of the industry's advances into the realm of 'modernity' is the rise of the decentralized chain stores (first, in supermarket, and later in convenience provisions, garment fashion, gift and other specialist retails) and the housing of upmarket boutique shops in shopping arcades. We were able to study, *inter alia*, one of the leading chain garment fashion stores as well as a convenience store operating as a mini-supermarket chain. These two chain stores are purportedly practising 'scientific management' by hiring 'technocratic' professional managers (Galbraith, 1972: 75–80), backed by corporate capital or modernized big family business. Their penetrative marketing strategies led to a geographically dispersed network of retail outlets which seemingly addresses ecological constraints of urban over-crowding and suburbanization. These branches are usually small shops, yet located in chosen sites readily accessible to customers who are offered a variety of reasonable choices of merchandise at inexpensive prices. However, as a fashion shop, the clothing chain store we investigated needs to compete not only by the quality of its customer service but also by way of brand/product differentiation. Conversely, the chain convenience store holds it niche in its locational accessibility and a broad spectrum of convenience items, imaging itself as a hybrid of a small department store, supermarket and stationary store.

However, the rise of the chain store system of multiple outlets offers an important alternative to the multi-storey department stores as a new mainstream division in the organization of retail business in Hong Kong. Such retail arrangements are reminiscent of the old-style, trendy small shops or stalls as family businesses based on petty capital. Yet, unlike the latter, these small street corner shops are owned by corporate capital and managed by salaried professionals as a structured network of branch outlets monitored centrally by a nerve-centre of control (Handy, 1995: 364–7). The headquarters acts like the old-timer *compradores* in past systems of wholesale distribution, being responsible for such strategic decisions as design, choice and adjustment of product lines. Not only are marketing activities such as promotion, discount sales and advertisement highly standardized among outlets under the head office's prerogative, but the hiring of sales staff in the branches is also governed by corporate-wide HRM policies, in some cases, centrally administered by the headquarters. The HRM implications of such a decentralization-cum-standardization pattern are several-fold. First, there is the paradox of bureaucratization and de-layering as the wholesale, distribution and retail activities are integrated at the centre of a fringe of its nominally autonomous small retail units. Second, there is the distinction between the 'core' staff at the headquarters of the chain and the 'peripheral' personnel hired in the retail branches as sales staff. Third, there is the impersonalization and rationalization of the workplace relations of the shop assistants, who are now more the salaried staff of corporate chain business than employees of small shopkeepers and owners. In a sense, they are also the beneficiaries of corporate development in the business organization of the small shops/stalls, given the long hours, low pay and sweat shop conditions that used to prevail in traditional retail shops.

Our case studies on these chain stores suggest that sales workers in these are converging in their employment conditions with their counterparts in the mainstream department stores. Of course, the sales workforce is itself highly stratified within the retail industry, whose 'labour aristocracy' is probably located within such upstream fashion boutiques as those housed in the 'aristocratic' parts of the city or among the leading Japanese department stores, such as Sogo. At the other end of the spectrum, employment in the traditional small shops, like the street-corner grocery stores or those specializing in miscellaneous merchandise items (including the sale of jewellery and accessories), has a long history as being marginal *vis-a-vis* other types of white-collar employment outside retail services.

Outside the mainstream of full-time sales staff hired in the large department stores, a classic study of the sales assistants in the early 1970s illustrated an industry-wide doldrum of low pay, marginal status, poor job security and long hours in this class of retail workers, trapped in 'work life impoverishment'(Chaney, 1971: 262–70), and marginally located in the white-collar labour market possibly due to the predominance of untrained and poorly educated woman workers. There has been consistent modernization of these retail stores because of technological, managerial and human resource advances, made possible by the entry of corporate capital into grocery retailing (namely, the rise of the supermarkets) and later into chain store marketing of fashion wear, gifts and other specialist items. Nevertheless, current official statistics illustrate that pay and earnings in wholesale and retail trades continue to occupy the lower or lower-middle layers in the wage/salary hierarchy stratified by industry. Pay packages are probably better than those in the manufacturing and restaurant and catering groups, but still below others like community social and personal services; transport, storage and communication; and finance and business services. (Hong Kong Government Secretariat, 1995: 123; 1996: 138). In spite of rationalizing shifts towards a more corporate form of human resource investment and application in the transforming retail industry, these statistics seem to suggest hardly any significant improvements in the conditions of the retail sales workforce.

Cluster 3: Business Restructuring and Advances – Cultural and Institutional Constraints

In the third cluster, three service establishments, including a commercial trading house (one of the *hongs*), a tourist agency and a local Chinese bank – all confronting changes implied by corporate renewal or business advances or consolidations – were studied. Their HRM activities were the core instruments supporting re-adjustment strategies, which were proactive in one organization, *laissez-faire* in another and conservative in the third. An important discovery was an increasing and common managerial concern to advance competitiveness and upgrade the quality of services as the key 'mission' of HRM, in spite of a culture-bound ambivalence about the relatively elastic notion of measuring and benchmarking service output and performance.

These studies lead us to highlight the importance of the inter-related issues of the receptivity of both the workforce and its management to change, the elasticity of workplace relations in responding to reorganization in work methods and transformation in business activities, as well as the reputed flexibility of Hong Kong's institutions and its marketplace business ideology and work values (Ng et al., 1995: 58–62, 75–9, 88–9; Ng and Lethbridge, 1995a: 212–3). However, we observe that culture-specific factors such as a 'trust' nexus in the Chinese heritage and the adaptability of Hong Kong's business are also conducive to these enterprises' restructuring and their versatility in accommodating the old and new, and the conserved and innovative, in aspects like technological hardware, business and HRM, as well as work values and strategies in human resource utilization. Hong Kong industry, now increasingly oriented towards high-value activities and tertiary services, has adopted fashionable business practices to move towards organizational consolidation, downsizing and de-layering, etc. In parallel, however, Hong Kong has also thrived because of its resilience in maintaining its celebrated institutions of Confucian instructed norms: reciprocity, mutual trust and commitment between the employer and employed, the manager and the managed at the workplace. As illustrated by the case of the local Chinese bank, many family businesses are hence trapped in similar dilemmas which now constrain downsizing activities in SOEs in China (Warner, 1996: 202–5, 207–8). In essence, this dilemma betrays a potential drift in weakening an 'Oriental style' of invoking trust as the 'invisible contract' for binding employee commitment. This erosion is due to the insecurity and transient nature which employment relations are now being re-interpreted under the pervasive imperative of business restructuring and rationalization.

DISCUSSION:
LABOUR MARKET CONVERGENCE OR DIVERGENCE?

In summary, the Hong Kong drama of economic restructuring is basically a hybrid of both its de-industrialization and re-commercialization, touched off by the China factor but also pushed by a market imperative of advancing into high value-added activities because of escalating land and labour costs in the last two decades of fast growth. The search for business flexibilities and improved human resource performance is characteristic of restructuring strategies and practices in the West, which has led authors in both industrial relations as well as HRM to postulate the rise of a 'new managerialism'. (Hyman and Ferner, 1994: 4; Storey, 1991: 8–9) In Western Europe, the prevalent and pervasive pattern across nations has been:

> a series of transformations in production: an increased differentiation and segmentation of product markets; exploitation of microprocessor-based technological innovation to achieve rapid change in product lines; more decentralised production, often based in ... a more differentiated labour force, some key groups possessing new technical skills, but many others marginalised from the central productive process (Hyman and Ferner, 1994: 9–10).

There has been a process of segmentation and 'flexibilization' which Hyman and Ferner attribute to the brunt of globalized competition (posed by the NIEs), blended by a paradox of market liberalism, and 'anarchic vagaries of international finance, and the far more calculative interventions of giant transnational firms' (ibid.: 10–11). A core concern is apparently for cost control and competency advance in order to strengthen corporate competitiveness (Storey, 1995: 11–6; 25–9).

Such a trend has also affected the Asian NIEs, as instructed by the convergence thesis and its prescription for development strategies in such classic works as *Industrialism and Industrial Man*, which canvasses the notion that industrial societies are converging towards a range of institutional arrangements and alternatives: 'pluralism of the state, the enterprise or association ... a "two-way partial convergence" between market capitalism and state socialism with the possible addition of some syndicalist elements' (Kerr *et al.*, 1973: 297–8). In Asian business and managerial practices, as well as their impacts on economic growth and labour markets, there has been a cyclical process. This has involved emulating the 'mainstream' industrial practices of the West, followed by a departure from this course in pursuit of a culture-specific niche of Asianized or Easternized traditions, and shifting back again to borrow from – or benchmark against – the best practices of business restructuring and resource arrangements espoused by European and American corporations. Given an almost universal quest by business for flexibility as it becomes 'a key source of competitive advantage within firms across all the advanced industrialized nations' (Verma *et al.*, 1995a: 8), the question of whether an element of cultural distinctiveness is identifiable in, and between, these Asian NIEs can be posed. As Verma *et al.* (1995b: 336) succinctly remark: 'The success of many high growth economies in Asia has led to the question of whether there is an 'Asian' model of economic growth? We pose the same question in human resource terms: are there specific HR/IR responses that characterise rapid economic growth?'

Our three clusters of empirical findings on the Hong Kong experience of its industrial advances and business adjustments and restructuring suggest an interesting hybrid. This is composed of both converging patterns analogous to the West, Japan and other Asian societies, as well as divergent practices which are probably distinctive to Hong Kong.

The first cluster presented corporate reforms in two benchmarking bureaucracies, which are reminiscent of the Western approaches to HRM, which prompts and justifies a corporate prescription for satisfying 'the need both to reduce costs and to meet customer service needs', to 'adopt flexible contracts more strategically' (Rothwell, 1995: 192–3). Similarly, in our cluster two study of the retail trade, the consistent in-road achieved by part-time hiring suggests a peril of de-skilling in the labour process and an 'alienable' reconfiguration and emasculation of the traditional full-time, eight-hour day, five-day week or 48-week year in the 'mainstream' department store sector.[4]

However, when reviewing our third cluster, a culture 'divide' differentiating an Asian approach from mainstream Western practices – inspired by the nexus of a Confucian heritage – appears to be ascertainable. Such a property helps explain some of the comparabilities in HRM practices among Japan, Taiwan, South Korea, Singapore, Mainland China and Hong Kong. Our case studies suggest, *inter alia*, that the sustained stability of employment in the trading house, tourist agency and the local Chinese bank have been instrumental in backing and advancing business restructuring. Even in our first case, management articulated a clear preference not to downsize but to retain its existing workforce as a tacit trade-off to secure consent and commitment. These are to facilitate greater numerical (for example, in terms of rationalizing cabin crew deployment in the airline) and functional (as evidenced by CLP's rigour in re-imaging its staff to become a consumer caring workforce) flexibilities introduced to enhance their excellence in quality and competitiveness in a de-regulated market.

Interestingly, in Mainland China, although reforms aimed to remove the 'iron rice bowl' mentality which used to stifle work incentives, the introduction of the labour contract system and staff-cuts in SOEs are still constrained by its apprehension about the excessive amount of unemployment created, as well as the alienness implied to the notion of job security enshrined in the nation's Confucian heritage (see Warner in this volume). In Japan, where the Confucian ethics also prevails, Benson and Debroux (in this volume) have also noted as well the continued resilience of lifetime employment practices in spite of business and work practice adjustments in coping with its recent recession. Similarly, in South Korea Park and Lee (1995) have observed that lay-offs have been limited for business restructuring. Instead, work flexibility has been practized largely by way of adopting labour subcontracting inside plants. Typically, these putting-out jobs are farmed out to the in-service employees under a practice called the 'small president system', which is 'a kind of piece rate system' (ibid.: 47–8).

However, convergence among Asian patterns does not altogether preclude diversities. In this connection, Hong Kong seemingly differs from other Asian economies inasmuch as business restructuring appears to bring about a sharper concern in enterprises for controlling performance, as attested by our case studies in all three clusters. Severe business competition has pushed these enterprises towards excelling in quality service as Hong Kong advances into a service-oriented, postindustrial economy. As a result, the twin issue of productivity and work performance claims increasingly high priority at the enterprise level – as reminiscent of the advanced Western economies (see, Storey, 1995: 8, 11; Illes and Salaman, 1995: 222–3; Kochan and Dyer, 1995: 339–42; Brewster, 1995: 312–9). Part of the corporate answer to this performance agenda, being practiced now with growing rigour, is HRM based – to institute a sensitive, fair, acceptable and practicable system of staff performance appraisal and to ensure its adequate linkages with pay and promotion. The strategic role of appraisal as a core instrument in eliciting quality performance, work commitment and incentive is a visible theme of business rationalization in services to enhance its niche of core competencies.

Anyway, several features are worth noting in this context of advances in performance and appraisal control. First, direct payment by results (like individual bonuses and commission) has become less common for stimulating improved performance. We have noted that a corporate concern for 'bettering' customer service in the chain fashion stores has led to the popularized design of an appraisal-based system of variable annual salary adjustment, supplemented by a collective bonus for the sales force in the retail outlets. Similarly, in the large department stores, the individual commission system, previously popular 'custom and practice' in the petty retail shops, is being steadily phased out as divisive and prone to breeding inter-group rivalry among shopworkers. Second, an increasing reliance now placed upon the linking function afforded by performance appraisal also reflects upon the diversity and non-standardized nature characteristic of service activities. Performance appraisal provides an integrative measuring rod for assessing the relative quality of services offered to customers, especially if these provisions are now spatially dispersed, as in the case of a network of multiple sales and trading outlets, rather than being concentrated at a single workplace. The variability and plurality of such services make it essential for a common conversion tool, as in the form of centrally designed performance appraisal, to be applied across all offices/departments/sections within the enterprise for ascertaining individual achievements. A system of performance appraisal linked fairly to merit pay increments and career advances has given these enterprises an integrated mechanism to recognize and regulate staff efforts, contributions and performance on an organization-wide basis. Third, in spite of the advent of flexibility in permitting a broader spectrum of options in selecting alternative packages of remuneration for individual employees, there prevails a widespread managerial assumption that simplicity in design helps fashion arrangements which have worked well in soliciting effective, dedicated efforts from employees. Conversely, a highly sophisticated, complex structure of pay and incentives is abhorred by both employers and employees because its sensitivity is blunted unwittingly by its cumbersome nature.

There is, however, a pervasive apprehension precipitated by performance appraisal among employees that it can be used by management as a control instrument to identify and weed out the 'inferior' performers. This is reflected in the case of CLP, where the union articulated its qualms several years ago when appraisal was introduced among the blue-collar ranks (Townley, 1991: 99–100; 103–6). To the extent it betrays a nexus of corporate control, performance appraisal is an apparatus of packaging a new managerialism: a drift towards the model of 'individualised HRM – high priority to HRM with no industrial relations' (Guest, 1995: 124). These tendencies are reminding us of the neo-Marxist radical critique, such as those espoused by Braverman (1974) in the 1970s, that the management of workplace control is intensifying instead of being liberalized in later (or post)-capitalist societies of the industrialized West (Poulantzas, 1975; Carchedi, 1983; Giddens, 1982; Mackenzie, 1982; Mandel, 1983). The question is: is Hong Kong converging with these societies because of the enhanced agenda to advance performance in the currency of business restructuring today?

CONCLUSION

Benchmarking for business success has become a popular theme of corporate advances and restructuring in Hong Kong. It has led to adoption in many service enterprises of Western inspired HRM practices, having been popularized for advantages of flexibilities and securing competitive niches in aspects such as quality excellence. To that extent, Hong Kong businesses seem to be converging with, or at least emulating, their counterparts in Europe and America, especially where fashionable labels such as consensus, flexibility and commitment actually conceal, as argued by Storey (1995: 8), a disguised concern for 'greater managerial control' of costs and quality of products and services – and hence of performance. However, the convergence parallel appears only partial rather than complete, as some of Hong Kong's practices also betray the normative influences of Asian traditions, notably rooted in its Confucian heritage.

However, Hong Kong itself is also distinctive for its hybrid practices which suggest its celebrated property of so-called 'institutional permissiveness', which gives it a global reputation as the bastion of free market capitalism. This character is considered as a source of industrial strength and flexibility: in spite of its comparative industrial advancement in physical and fiscal infrastructure, many of its institutional arrangements remain in a relative state of 'immaturity' and openness, notably in light of 'the feebleness of collective bargaining and the absence of a minimum wage floor and statutory human rights safeguards' (Ng and Lethbridge, 1995a: 213). Ironically, this is 'both an advantage which assists Hong Kong as the world's focus of the marketplace nexus, as well as a liability contributing to the territory's dispute as an immature trading partner in the domain of international economics and trade relations' (ibid.). Yet, a pervasive belief prevails among businesses that such a permissive system has served them well in avoiding normative and institutional rigidities in structural adjustments to cope with the exigencies of rapid market shifts. Indeed, many of the firms we investigated claim to owe much of their human resource and business flexibilities to this uncrystallized and hybrid character of Hong Kong which is, by its nature, hard to emulate for other new or rejuvenated Asian economies. This is largely because its economic restructuring process 'would not have crystallised in its present form if not for the modernisation and economic reforms' going on inside China (Ng, 1996a: 297). The Hong Kong drama of business advances and transformation is a hiatus stemming more from defaults in history than designed by state policy. China is itself now in the process of rapid modernization. It recognizes Hong Kong's distinctiveness by devising a prudent accommodative formula of 'one country, two systems'. Now China's Special Economic Zone however, 'the Hong Kong legend' appears to raise 'serious doubts as to whether it can offer much as an instructive model, notably in terms of postwar development among the NIEs' (ibid.).

NOTES

1. The sponsoring body for this cluster was the Asian Productivity Organisation (APO), based in Tokyo. APO was interested in advancing a new and holistic perspective of productivity for three broad reasons. First, the rise of services as the mainstream of industry now conceived to be a value-adding exercise. Second, the shift towards a quality nexus in perceiving, interpreting and appraising productivity, previously measured mechanically in big manufacturing plants. Third, a growing academic appreciation that productivity, once put in the organic context of a system or process treatment, has to be reconciled with 'cultural relativism'. In practice, this means that it needs to be managed with elasticity, so as to assimilate better human aspects like incentives, performance and work values, in harmony with the organization's own institutional arrangements and its constraints, both inside and outside the workplace (Ng *et al.* 1995: 48–50).

2. This was sponsored by the principal trade union organizing the sales and associated staff in the retail and department store trade. This study aimed to profile business transformation as well as its human resource implications since the immediate postwar years, in the context of Hong Kong's industrialization and advancing affluence.

3. Indeed, as hinted to us by the Department Store and Commercial Staff Union, it could have been its membership's qualms about the adverse impact of the these austerity measures which instigated its appointment of our study on the industry.

4. Thus, we were asked by the apprehensive union organizing the sales staff to investigate the potential scope for temporary, part-time working hours, or other flexible working models currently practised by local authorities and business corporations in the UK where working hours are, as in Hong Kong, relatively unregulated by statutory provisions (Rothwell, 1995: 193; Ng, 1982: 277–9). However, the UK is under pressure via the European Union's agenda of legislative enactments to regulate work hours and protect part-time employment. An example is the 48-hour working week directive, which seeks to create greater harmony among member states.

REFERENCES

Braverman, Harry (1974) *Labor and Monopoly Capital: The Degradation of Work in the Twentieth Century.* New York: Monthly Review Press.

Brewster, Chris (1995) 'HRM: The European Dimension', in John Storey (ed.) *Human Resources Management: A Critical Text.* London: Routledge, pp.309–31.

Carchedi, Guglielmo (1983) 'The Global Function of Capital', in Richard Hyman and Robert Price (eds) *The New Working Class? White-Collar Workers and Their Organisations.* London: Macmillan.

Chaney, David (1971) 'Job Satisfaction and Unionization: The Case of Shopworkers', in Keith Hopkins (ed.) *Hong Kong: The Industrial Colony.* Hong Kong: Oxford University Press, pp.261–70.

Chen, Edward K.Y. (1995) 'The Economic Setting' in Ng Sek Hong and David G. Lethbridge (eds) *The Business Environment in Hong Kong*, Third edition. Hong Kong: Oxford University Press, pp.1–43.

China Light and Power Company, Limited, Hong Kong (1995a) *Annual Report.* Hong Kong: China Light and Power.

China Light and Power Company Limited, Hong Kong (1995b) *The CLP Competency Guide.* Revised edition. Hong Kong: China Light and Power.

China Light and Power Limited, Hong Kong. (1996) *Delivering Absolute Customer Satisfaction.* Hong Kong: China Light and Power.

Galbraith, John Kenneth (1972) *The New Industrial State.* Second edition. Harmondsworth: Penguin.

Giddens, Anthony (1982) 'Power, The Dialect of Control and Class Structuration' in Anthony Giddens and Gavin Mackenzie (eds) *Social Class and the Division of Labour.* Cambridge: Cambridge University Press.

Government Secretariat, Hong Kong Government (1995, 1996) *Third Quarter Economic Reports.* Hong Kong: Government Printer.

Guest, David E. (1995) 'Human Resource Management, Trade Unions and Industrial Relations', in John Storey (ed.) *Human Resource Management: A Critical Text.* London: Routledge, pp.110–41.

Handy, Charles (1993) *Understanding Organisations*. Fourth edition. Harmondsworth: Penguin.

Hochschild, Arlie Russell (1983) *The Managed Heart: Commercialisation of Human Feeling*. Berkeley, CA: University of California Press.

Hyman, Richard and Anthony Ferner (1994) 'Introduction: Economic Restructuring, Market Liberalism and the Future of National Industrial Relations System' in Richard Hyman and Anthony Ferner (eds) *New Frontiers in European Industrial Relations*. Oxford: Blackwell, pp.1–14.

Iles, Paul and Graeme Salaman (1995) 'Recruitment, Selection and Assessment', in John Storey (ed.) *Human Resources Management: A Critical Text*. London: Routledge, pp.203–33.

Kerr, Clark, John T. Dunlop, Frederick Harbison, and Charles A. Myers (1973), *Industrialisation and Industrial Man*. 2nd edition with a postscript. London: Harmondsworth.

Kochan, Tom and Lee Dyer (1995) 'HRM: An America View' in John Storey (ed.) *Human Resources Management: A Critical Text*. London: Routledge, pp.332–51.

Labour Department, Hong Kong Government (1995) *Report of Commissioner for Labour 1994*. Hong Kong: Government Printer.

Levin, David A. and Ng Sek-Hong, 'From an Industrial to a Post-industrial Economy: Challenges for Human Resource Management in Hong Kong' in Anil Verma, Thomas A. Kochan and Russell D. Lansbury (eds) *Employment Relations in the Growing Asian Economies*. London: Routledge, pp.119–57.

Mackenzie, Gavin (1982) 'Class Boundaries and the Labour Process' in Anthony Giddens and Gavin Mackenzie (eds) *Social Class and the Division of Labour*. Cambridge: Cambridge University Press.

Maeda Masahiro and Ng Sek Hong, with Jon-chao Hong and Jenn-yeu Lin (1996) 'The Role of the State and Labour's Response to Industrial Development: An Asian "Drama" of Three New Industrial Economies' in Ian Nish, Gordon Redding and Ng Sek Hong (eds) *Work and Society: Labour and Human Resources in East Asia*. Hong Kong: Hong Kong University Press, pp.167–97.

Mandel, Ernest (1983) 'Scientific Intellectual Labour' in Richard Hyman and Robert Price (eds) *The New Working Class? White-collar Workers and their Organisations*. London: Macmillan.

Miners, Norman (1991) *The Government and Politics of Hong Kong*. Fifth edition. Hong Kong: Oxford University Press.

Ng Sek Hong and David G. Lethbridge (eds) (1995a) *The Business Environment in Hong Kong*. Third edition. Hong Kong: Oxford University Press.

Ng Sek Hong and David G. Lethbridge (1995b) 'Labour and Employment' in Ng Sek Hong and David G. Lethbridge (eds) *The Business Environment in Hong Kong*. Third edition. Hong Kong: Oxford University Press, pp.64–88.

Ng Sek Hong (1995) 'Human Resources Management: An Introductory Note', *Working Paper*, School of Business, University of Hong Kong.

Ng Sek Hong (1996a) 'Immigration, Emigration, Migrant Labour and Employment in Hong Kong' in Institute of Development Economies (ed.) *Hong Kong 1997: Society in Transition, IDE Spot Survey*. Tokyo: Institute of Developing Economies, pp.39–44.

Ng Sek Hong (1996b) 'The Development of Labour Relations in Hong Kong and Some Implications for the Future' in Ian Nish, Gordon Redding and Ng Sek Hong (eds) *Work and Society: Labour and Human Resources in East Asia*. Hong Kong: Hong Kong University Press, pp.289–300.

Ng Sek Hong and Carolyn Poon (1997) *A Report on the Retail Industry and Its Restructuring: The Case of Hong Kong*. Hong Kong: University of Hong Kong, cyclostyled.

Ng Sek Hong, Sally Stewart and Fun Ting Chan (1995) 'Socio-Cultural Impact on Productivity: The Case of Hong Kong' in Kwang-kuo Hwang (ed.) *Easternization: Socio-Cultural Impact on Productivity*. Tokyo: Asian Productivity Organization, pp.47–96.

Park, Young-bum and Michael Byungnam Lee (1995) 'Economic Development, Globalisation, and Practices in Industrial Relations and Human Resource Management in Korea' in Anil Verma; Thomas A. Kochan and Russell D. Lansbury (eds) *Employment Relations in the Growing Asian Economies*. London: Routledge, pp.27–61.

Patten, Chris (1995) *Hong Kong: Our Work Together* (Address by the Governor, the Right Honourable Christopher Patten at the Opening of the 1995/96 Session of the Legislative Council). Hong Kong: Government Printer.

Poulantzas, Nicos (1975) *Classes in Contemporary Capitalism*. London: Verso.

Rothwell, Sheila (1995) 'Human Resource Planning' in John Storey (ed.) *Human Resource Management: A Critical Text*. London: Routledge, pp.167–202.

Storey, John (1991) 'Introduction: From Personnel Management to Human Resource Management' in John Storey (ed.) *New Perspectives on Human Resource Management*. London: Routledge, pp.1–18.

Storey, John (1995) 'Human Resource Management : Still Marching On, or Marching Out?' in John Storey (ed.) *Human Resource Management: A Critical Text*. London: Routledge, pp.3–32.

Townley, Barbara (1991) 'Selection and Appraisal: Reconstituting "Social Relations"?' in John Storey (ed.) *Human Resource Management: A Critical Text*. London: Routledge, pp.92–108.

Tricker, Bob (1983) 'Perspectives on Corporate Governance: Intellectual Influences in the Exercise of Corporate Governance' in Michael J. Earl (ed.) *Perspective on Management: A Multidisciplinary Analysis*. Oxford: Oxford University Press, pp.143–69.

Verma, Anil, Thomas A. Kochan and Russell D. Lansbury 91995a) 'Employment Relations in an Era of Global Markets: A Conceptual Framework Chapter' in Anil Verma, Thomas A. Kochan and Russell D. Lansbury (eds) *Employment Relations in the Growing Asian Economies*. London: Routledge, pp.1–26.

Verma, Anil, Thomas A. Kochan and Russell D. Lansbury (1995b) 'Lessons from the Asian Experience' in Anil Verma, Thomas A. Kochan and Russell D. Lansbury (eds) *Employment Relations in the Growing Asian Economies*. London: Routledge, pp.336–57.

Warner, Malcolm (1996) 'Economic Reforms, Industrial Relations and Human Resources in the People's Republic of China', *Industrial Relations Journal*, Vol.27, No.3, pp.195–210.

HRM in Japanese Enterprises: Trends and Challenges

JOHN BENSON and PHILIPPE DEBROUX

Accompanying the success of Japanese manufacturing has been the belief that the superior performance has been due to the nature and configuration of human resource management (HRM) practices that exist within the large Japanese firm (Whitehill, 1991). These firms, however, constitute only a small proportion of firms in a given industry and are distinguishable by their size, complexity and markets. Nevertheless, these firms, with an emphasis on market share, sophisticated production systems and stable relationships between all stakeholders, have been a major factor in the international competitiveness of Japanese manufactured products.

In these firms, HRM practices have been characterized by a strong internal labour market, consultative decision making and enterprise unionism. Such practices, individually and collectively, encourage the incorporation of employees into the culture of the enterprise. The result is a strong employee identification with the firm and a high commitment to innovative production practices that enhance firm performance. In return the enterprise, albeit informally, provides job security and higher rewards. According to Moore (1987: 143) these practices are a 'highly rational and effective means for inducing worker identification with the enterprise and for creating a highly skilled and pliable core of employees adaptable to rapid technological and organizational change'.

In an attempt to emulate Japanese success, Western firms focused on the HRM practices found in these large manufacturing firms. This interest was promulgated by a number of commentators who focused on the behaviour of Japanese firms abroad. Terms like 'Japanization' became part of the vocabulary on Japanese management practices and academics rushed to study the practices of the so-called Japanese transplants. This was despite the dearth of studies as to what were the actual practices in Japan and how these practices were evolving. In short, the standard model of Japanese management practices was an ideal that was limited and was situated in the practices of large firms in the 1970s.

These issues form the focus of this contribution. We contend that the rise in the Western concept of HRM parallels the international success of Japanese manufacturing enterprises and, to a large degree, is based on Japanese management practices. This proposition is discussed in Section Two. In particular, the failure of research to establish the widespread use of

John Benson and Philippe Debroux, Hiroshima City University

the HRM model in the 1980s suggests it was part of a wider ideological agenda to improve the competitiveness of Western firms. The Japanese model was the most appropriate choice, though with an emphasis on union-free workplaces. The article then discusses the trends in Japanese management, locating such developments in their economic and social context, and concludes by considering the implications of these trends, both for Japanese industry and for the adoption of the HRM model in Western firms.

HRM: A JAPANESE PHENOMENON?

The dramatic rise in Japanese exports during the 1960s and 1970s and the success of many large Japanese manufacturing firms in establishing offshore facilities in the 1980s led to debates concerning the organization of work and models of labour–management relations (Elgar and Smith, 1994: 1–2). The success of Japanese firms, with their emphasis on people as the key resource, became a model for Western managers (Dulebohn *et al.*, 1995: 30; Goss, 1994: 4). Industrial relations was seen as too conflictual and the cause of many of the underlying problems of Western firms. Without unions, management would be able to compete with the Japanese by adopting new practices: practices that emphasized commitment rather than control (Walton, 1985). This idea appealed to Western management, not only for advocating union-free workplaces but also because the responsibility for the poor performance of their firms could be deflected from themselves and placed on unions.

The global success of Japanese firms led Western management to restructure and develop 'leaner and fitter' organizations. In addition, declining union power in the 1980s in many Western countries led to a reassertion of managerial rights. In the UK and the US this was with the assistance of conservative governments, although this was not a necessary pre-condition, as the Australian case demonstrates. These conditions led to the emergence of the HRM model (Goss, 1994: 5). What is not clear is what is meant by the term HRM. Some argue that HRM is 'old wine in new bottles' (Fowler, 1987; Legge, 1989), while others distinguish between 'hard' and 'soft' versions of HRM (Storey, 1989; Legge, 1995). Despite these differences there does appear to be some agreement that HRM is about achieving improved organizational performance through a flexible, committed and integrated labour force (Guest, 1987).

Storey (1995: 6–10) operationalized the HRM approach by suggesting it consists of four dimensions: beliefs, strategic qualities, critical managerial roles, and key levers. Using these dimensions Storey develops a checklist of 25 items to measure the extent of HRM practices in British firms. Case studies of 15 large British firms conducted in the period 1986–88 revealed that the majority of firms had introduced many of the individual aspects of HRM. Nevertheless, 'most cases failed to offer much in the way of an integrated approach to employee management, and still less was there evidence of strategic integration with the corporate plan' (ibid.: 14). For many firms HRM thus consisted of discrete elements rather than an integrated package. This may explain why research has failed to show a positive correlation between HRM and firm performance (Brewster and Hegewisch, 1994: 2).

On the other hand, many large Japanese firms would rate highly on each of the four dimensions and would appear to have integrated their labour strategies with their corporate plans. This is demonstrated later when case study evidence is presented on the current use of these HRM practices in four Japanese firms. This suggests that in practice HRM approximates a stylized model of Japanese labour–management relations, though with a greater emphasis on individual effort and reward. This does not deny HRM's usefulness to Western firms, but it does suggest that the *configuration* of HRM practices is important and that the firms' context may cause a modification of these practices. The research by Storey (1992) indicates that these issues have not been considered by Western firms.

It appears, therefore, that HRM lacks strategy, at least in the way it is being implemented in Western firms (Storey, 1992; Beaumont, 1993). For these firms HRM involves the piecemeal adoption of Japanese-type management practices. For these practices to be effective requires a high commitment from employees. Individual and performance related reward systems, despite the lack of evidence, are seen as the major avenue to this increased commitment. Given the extent of restructuring and redundancies that has characterized Western firms in recent years it is difficult to see how this commitment can be achieved. Moreover, the structure of trade unions in Western countries has led HRM to deviate from Japanese management by advocating a unitarist position. The absence of enterprise unions from this model may mean a less than optimal outcome for both management and labour (Weinstein, 1994). As union-free workplaces will not occur rapidly, HRM has attempted to marginalize union activity. As Storey (1995: 14) found, a dual system has been created. Unions maintain involvement in traditional areas, such as collective bargaining, but are being isolated from the new HRM initiatives. The extent of this duality will, however, depend on the responses of trade unions (Martinez-Lucio and Weston, 1992).

While this stylized version of Japanese management is being introduced in Western firms under the title of HRM, Japanese firms are examining new approaches to the management of their human resources. The competitiveness of international trade, especially since the entry of a number of newly industrialized Asian economies, the increased value of the Yen, and the deregulation of the Japanese economy have placed pressure on Japanese firms to restructure and reorganize their labour practices. Recruitment methods and wage systems are two practices that have come under intense media speculation and comment. How have Japanese firms responded to these pressures? Are Japanese firms moving towards a new model of HRM? Before considering these questions in detail it is necessary to examine the changing context of the Japanese firm.

ECONOMIC AND SOCIAL CONTEXT

The postwar Japanese economy experienced high and sustained growth in real gross domestic production (GDP) until 1992. While real economic growth of around ten per cent ceased after 1970, Japan still experienced growth of more than five per cent for the next 20 years. This period was not a period of constant growth but one characterized by declining real GDP growth and a series of economic cycles. The years 1992 to 1995 found the Japanese economy in a severe downturn. Growth in GDP in 1991 was over four per cent; in 1992 real GDP growth reached only one per cent. During 1993 there was a 0.2 per cent decline in economic growth, while for 1994 and 1995 growth in real GDP remained under one per cent.

Economic growth in 1996 was about three per cent mainly due to a production surge in export-oriented industries induced by the weaker Yen. This has caused a growth in corporate earnings, especially in the manufacturing sector (*The Nikkei Weekly*, 18 October 1996: 1). A relatively slow growth trend remains, however, the most likely scenario for the long-term. Investment in capital equipment has slowed down, and returns on investment have fallen. The size of the labour force is expected to fall in the future and the returns on education have fallen significantly (*The Nikkei Weekly*, 25 November 1996: 2). Productivity levels are about two-thirds of those in the US, although in recent years they have been growing at about the same rate (Ostrom, 1996: 3).

The rapid expansion of the economy in the mid-to-late 1980s created a labour shortage. This situation has now changed due to the low growth of the early 1990s and the fall in exports caused by the long-term increase in the Yen. The manufacturing sector's share of GDP and employment has fallen over the past five years. This has been especially noticeable among small and medium-sized enterprises (SMEs). Japan had 874,000 manufacturing SMEs in 1989. By 1994 this figure was 817,000; a fall of 6.5 per cent in five years. The number of workers employed by such companies dropped proportionally from 10.4 million in 1991 to 9.74 million in 1994; a decline of 6.3 per cent (*The Nikkei Weekly*, 13 June 1995: 9).

Large firms have not been immune from these developments, with 60 per cent of such firms reporting a fall in regular employment (Recruit, 1996: 47). These developments have impacted on the unemployment rate which in 1996 stood at 3.3 per cent, up from 2.1 per cent in 1991 (*Labour Issues Quarterly*, 1996: 9). Firms have recently re-commenced hiring, mainly of young male graduates. Nevertheless, recruitment has not returned to its pre-1991 level and so the unemployment of young people, especially women, remains relatively high at about six per cent (MOL, 1996a: 6). Many of the new jobs are in small companies in the service sector and this trend is expected to continue (ibid.).

It is estimated that over a million jobs, about nine per cent of the current manufacturing workforce, are likely to disappear over the next five years due to the restructuring of firms and their relocation abroad (MITI, 1996:

19). However, Japanese firms remain reluctant multinationals, with overseas production accounting for substantially less than Western multinationals (Ostrom, 1996: 9). This attitude, coupled with this likely supply of quality labour, means that it is not clear that firms will expand their overseas production if they can export competitively again. Indeed, the recent fall in the value of the Yen has seen firms like Matsushita, Hitachi, Toyota and Honda, announce the relocation of some production activities back to Japan (*The Nikkei Weekly*, 4 November 1996: 1, 23).

These economic factors, coupled with a changing demographic profile and social attitudes, will affect work and employment in Japan in a variety of ways. First, younger employers are less confident of their long-term employment and promotion prospects. As a consequence, the level of commitment of young employees is lower than that of the previous generation (Takezawa, 1995: 136–9). Second, a growing segment of the labour force believes that traditional management practices are unfair to good performers and to employee privacy. These attitudes are part of a wider change in Japanese society where many young Japanese are increasingly adopting more individualistic attitudes and a dislike for the 'groupism' of Japanese society (Miyanaga, 1991: 27). Third, long-term employment and the seniority wage system requires that young workers outnumber older workers. Such a demographic profile no longer exists. The decline in the birthrate, now the lowest in the developed world, will only further accentuate this problem. In addition, the aging population will increasingly make the system unsustainable under its current form because of rising wage and welfare costs (Tsuchida, 1996: 2). Fourth, a governance structure embedded in economic, political and social relations and subsuming capital interests, has insulated companies from the short-term demands of shareholders. In times of recession, Japanese firms have cut dividends before reducing labour costs. This practice may no longer be sustainable. Individual and institutional investors are beginning to demand higher dividends due to the fall in the capital value of shares and the higher interest rates on offer overseas (Debroux, 1996: 249). Fifth, deregulation is now advocated by many industrial associations (Nikkeiren, 1995: 5) and by the government (MITI, 1996: 3). In the manufacturing industry, for example, it will become more difficult to persuade employers to bargain with unions to avoid large scale redundancies. In a period of increased competition, some firms may adopt a tougher union policy so as gain a competitive advantage. Fear of losing competitiveness might force others to adopt the same policy. Finally, the Japanese Government has so far met the threat of rising unemployment with the use of subsidies to employers to maintain their labour force and retrain excess workers (*Tokyo Business*, 1994: 15). Special programmes also continue to protect SMEs and some regional areas against the forces of economic change. It is likely that, as in the other developed countries, technological changes and market liberalization will lead to structural unemployment and a widening gap in earnings (OECD, 1993).

TRENDS IN JAPANESE MANAGEMENT PRACTICES

The economic and social changes outlined above have exerted pressure on the Japanese system of HRM and have resulted in changes to managerial practices and strategies. This section will document the extent of these changes using survey and case study evidence.

Employment security

Reduction of overtime, reassignment and transfer of workers were widely used in the most recent recession. Cutting costs through these methods was preferred as the retrenchment of regular workers involves large pay-outs and so is not financially practical in the short-term. In the automobile industry, worker exchanges between companies has increased (*The Nikkei Weekly*, 6 November 1995: 13). Interestingly, the labour market participation rate for males in 1993 reached its highest level for those aged 55–59 years (94 per cent), and its highest point since 1982 for the 60–64 year age group (MOL, 1995: 347). Employment tenure has increased for both blue and white-collar workers (MOL, 1992: 18). Average tenure of workers covered by the Ministry of Labour survey rose from 12.5 years to 12.8 years in the period 1990 to 1994 (MOL, 1995: 351).

A significant decline occurred in the period 1990–94 in the number of temporary workers employed in the manufacturing sector. This finding suggests that these workers acted as a buffer for regular employees. This decline was partially offset by an increase in service-oriented jobs where companies are shifting towards the use of non-permanent employees for clerical and sales occupations (*The Nikkei Shimbun*, 6 November 1995: 13). Overall, few workers were retrenched or forced to take early retirement. The small increase in redundancies can be almost entirely explained by cyclical factors. There appears no clear trend to replace core employees with temporary and contract workers. Outsourcing has been mainly directed at clerical female workers and ancillary functions. The proportion of the workforce regularly employed remained around 80 per cent in 1992 (MOL, 1995: 351). There is, thus, little evidence of a departure from the long-term employment guarantee or the development of a stronger core-periphery labour market.

There remains strong support for lifetime employment among workers. A recent survey indicated that two-thirds of employees in large companies think that the system of long-term job guarantees should be maintained (Recruit, 1995: 19). Even among employees in their thirties, 56 per cent supported that view, although they also expressed a stronger willingness to change jobs. This finding reflects the perception among many younger employees of the increasing difficulties in gaining management positions (*The Nikkei Shimbun*, 9 November 1995: 12). As a consequence, younger employees are now placing more importance on developing their expertise than to getting a higher position in the hierarchy.

Yet, it would be wrong to conclude from these figures that the system of

employment will not change. The importance of lifetime employment as a
managerial strategy is declining. One survey of 6,000 companies found that
more than half did not include lifetime employment as a key element in their
HRM. This was 11 per cent more than the result of the same survey three
years earlier (MOL, 1996b: 52). An Economic Planning Agency (EPA,
1996:12) survey supported this finding. Some 44 per cent of the firms
intend to make changes to their lifetime employment policy in the next three
years compared to the 13 per cent who made changes in the past three years.
Part of the problem for most firms is the large number of excess white-collar
employees. In the past the problem could be overlooked as firms were able
to achieve efficiency gains by applying pressure on suppliers to reduce costs
and improve efficiency. The limitations of this approach are now being
realized.

Compensation

For the majority of firms, basic wages are based on group affiliation and
non-task related criteria rather than on qualifications and ability (Recruit,
1995: 3). There is, however, an emerging consensus on the need to revamp
the system of automatic annual wage rises and allowances. In particular,
there is a strong trend to reduce allowances or link them to job activities
(*The Nikkei Shimbun*, 12 November 1995: 12). An increasing number of
Japanese companies are adopting annual pay systems in an attempt to do
away with automatic salary increases. In a recent survey, 32 per cent of
respondents replied that they intend to annualize wages (Recruit, 1995: 28).
In most cases where annualized pay has been introduced it has not
suppressed bonus payments or transport, family, and housing allowances.

In addition, companies are beginning to link wages and bonuses more
directly to individual performance. In many of these schemes employees
will have part of their wage and employment conditions based on their
performance in the preceding year. A 1992 survey found that performance-
related pay systems were used by only about 15 per cent of Japan's largest
companies (MOL, 1992: 65). By 1995 this figure had more than doubled to
32 per cent (MOL, 1996a: 252). This trend is likely to continue. An EPA
(1996:18) survey found that 60 per cent of managers felt that the weight
given to individual performance in the determination of wages and
promotion in the next three years will rise to about 70 per cent. This is an
increase from 50 per cent over the previous three years. The objective of
most companies is to maintain the long-term job guarantee for core
employees, but nevertheless to combine it with a performance-related pay
system (Recruit, 1995: 3).

Change in compensation arrangements will not occur rapidly. The
notion that compensation must be related to age and family composition has
roots going back to the immediate pre-war period (*The Nikkei Business*, 16
September 1996: 21,27). During these 60 years there was a growing
departure from the notion of linking wages to the job itself and thus to
market mechanisms. In addition, labour and its associated costs are

interpreted differently in Japanese corporate accounting practices. In Japanese firms, labour and capital are treated equally as factors of production. In most Western firms labour is a variable cost – a cost that can be readily adjusted. This difference means that Japanese firms have less compensation options available in responding to economic changes.

Overall, wages and bonuses increased in real terms during the period 1991–95, but at an increasingly lower rate each year. Wage agreements for 1996 halted this trend, with wage increases equalling the 1995 figure of 2.7 per cent (*The Nikkei Weekly*, 30 December 1996; 6 January 1997: 4). A widening gap between the wage levels of large and SMEs occurred as large companies sought and gained cuts in subcontract prices. These lower wage increases have been accompanied by a wider variation of bonus and a progressive demise of some allowances (*The Nikkei Shimbun*, 7 November 1996: 3).

Recruitment

Recruitment from schools and universities remains the major source of new labour for Japanese firms. Some firms have diversified their recruitment of new graduates by employing not only in April, the traditional period, but also later in the year (*Japan Labour Bulletin*, 1996: 3). The employment of workers later in the year mainly involves young graduates from overseas universities or specialists (*The Nikkei Shimbun*, 9 November 1996: 10). Although all year recruitment is only practiced by about ten per cent of major firms it is likely to increase in importance, particularly for larger firms (*The Japan Times*, 2 December 1996: 15). One of the reasons for this change is that Japanese firms require a greater diversity of employees to be competitive internationally. Moreover, it may begin to break down the pervasive feeling among firms that recruits hired in a particular year are all equal (ibid.).

Some firms are placing less emphasis on educational credentials in the hiring process. These include Orix (*The Nikkei Weekly*, 22 May 1995: 8), Sumitomo Bank, supermarket chains such as Daiei, Ito-Yokado and Nichii, and Mitsubishi Electric (Koyo Shinko Kyokai, 1994: 91, 163, 247). In a recent survey some 74 per cent of companies said they do not place significant emphasis on the prestige of the universities of new graduates; a 15 per cent rise since 1984 (Recruit, 1994: 21). Nevertheless, graduates of good universities have a better chance of gaining lifetime employment in large firms. Thus, university entrance examinations remain the critical determinant of future job opportunities.

In the case of natural science graduates, recruitment through professors in a limited number of specific universities is still the norm at the post-graduate level. The informal contract that some firms have with certain universities is as crucial as their entrance examination in providing employees with the required characteristics. In these cases the firms' selection costs and risks are substantially decreased and so there is little pressure for change to the recruitment process. While reliance on new graduates is still high, there is a growing interest in mid-career recruitment, although at this stage firms are only taking limited steps to recruit more mid-career employees (JIL, 1995b: 68). In addition, the use of headhunting agencies is becoming more common for top managers and specialized technicians.

So far, the system of recruitment has served Japanese firms well. This explains their reluctance to implement major changes. Some pressure for change is coming from the supply side, inasmuch as a growing number of employees do not want to commit themselves to one company for their entire working life. In addition, companies are seeking more workers who do not expect lifetime employment and tenure. Some changes may also occur if reforms developed by the Ministry of Education (MOE) for schools and universities to train young specialists succeed (MOL, 1994: 145).

Training

A generalist background is normally required for those in a lifetime employment position, while specific attributes are required for contract, part-time and temporary jobs. For lifetime employees, internal and firm-specific training will remain the norm (Nikkeiren, 1995: 62). At the same time, the high placement rate for students graduating from technical schools, and the relatively lower placement rate for graduates from general schools, indicates that companies are looking for people with more specialist skills (*The Nikkei Shimbun*, 4 July 1996: 10). Thus, the recent policy of the MOE for an integrated learning approach, and the offering of lifelong learning opportunities at universities, will help to meet the new market demand. Japanese firms are just beginning to consider the opportunities offered by the universities for the supply of trained graduates. Similarly universities are only now considering the need for closer contact with the business world.

Promotion

Promotion in most firms is based on a mix of seniority and ability (Morishima, 1995: 623). In an increasing number of cases managerial promotion is being linked to internal examinations based on strict merit criteria (Sangyo Rodo Chosa, 1994: 3). In the case of Nippon Express this is linked to a system of merit points without any consideration of educational credentials (Koyo Shinko Kyokai, 1994: 221). Honda, for some time, has been bypassing its internal hierarchy to promote talented people (*The Nikkei Business*, 13 October 1994: 23). Orix, a major leasing firm, has decided to open career-track management positions, hitherto set aside for the graduates of top universities, to graduates of two-year vocational schools and junior colleges. One factor influencing the company's decision was their success in recruiting mid-career employees. These employees now account for 20 per cent of Orix staff in their thirties and about 50 per cent of those in their forties (*The Nikkei Weekly*, 22 May 1995: 8).

Some companies now have a system of status downgrading for under-performing executives. At Fujisawa Pharmaceuticals, for example, a system of merit and demerit points can lead to differences from three to eight years in the hierarchy (Sangyo Rodo Chosa, 1994: 216). Some companies are also simplifying their hierarchy through the removal of titles (*The Nikkei Business*, 16 September 1996: 27). Most companies still pursue a policy of giving what is effectively a 'dummy' title for those older employees who have not made the grade. Despite the reduced availability of titles due to delayering, this practice will continue, at least in the short-term. There is, however, growing opposition by younger employees to 'dummy' titles that do not lead to higher managerial positions and serve only to save face. In response, some companies are removing formal titles up to the level of middle management and replacing them by titles such as 'group leader'. Those titles are not assigned on a permanent basis but according to the *ad hoc* responsibility given for a specific project.

Title removal or flexibility supports a more objective use of job classifications. In many firms, positions linked to a particular classification are openly contested by all eligible employees. The overall trend appears to be towards a more quantitative classification of jobs, more transparency in job evaluation and a higher degree of fairness. It seems that connections and personality will be less important in the future (ibid.: 29). This has led, as in the case of Sekiyu Department Stores, to a number of older employees having their pay reduced substantially after the introduction of the new scheme (*The Nikkei Business*, 16 September 1996: 24).

As in the UK and the US much of the delayering has been targeted at the large number of middle managers employed in Japanese firms. This has led to unionization emerging among middle managers who have doubts about the commitment of the company and perceive their job to be threatened by restructuring moves (Sataka and Shibara, 1995). The Trade Union Law does not recognize managerial unions as negotiating bodies, as these workers are supposed to represent the interests of their employer. Nevertheless, more recently these unions have demanded recognition (Tokuzumi *et al.*, 1994: 2) and a recent court decision indicates that the courts are ready to accommodate the request (*The Japan Times*, 10 July 1996: 8).

The Role of the Personnel Department

Mitsubishi Corporation, in perhaps the most radical reform to date, outsourced all the administrative functions of the Personnel Department to a newly established subsidiary (*The Shakai Keizai Seisansei Shimbun*, 1996: 5). The new company is to deliver personnel services as required by Mitsubishi Corporation, but it will also be allowed, in future, to sell its expertise outside. Another innovative practice has been implemented at Nippon Hewlett-Packard. If an employee is declared redundant by their department they are required to join a programme conducted by the Personnel Department called 'Second Career Assist'. If the employee is unable to find another position in the company within a given time they must resign (*The Nikkei Business*, 16 September 1996: 26).

In most cases, changes to the role of the Personnel Department have been more gradual. The overall trend is towards a more advisory role to line management (ibid.: 22). Examples of this trend include Hankyu Railways and Sekiyu Department Stores (ibid.: 23–4). In both cases the Personnel Department is now more of an internal job agency. Their major task is to find employment in other sections of the firm for employees who have lost their job in their own department. Line managers are increasingly involved in the appraisal process and increasingly, although to a lesser extent, the selection of employees for promotion and the recruitment process. In these cases the Personnel Department and other line managers in the same department usually become involved.

To improve line managers' skills, Mitsubishi Electric places all key line managers in the Personnel Department for a short period (Yashiro, 1992: 52). Many white-collar workers in large companies are opposed to line managers having more responsibility for the re-assignment of employees (Inoki, 1993: 129). This reflects a concern about the arbitrary nature of the process given the lack of well-defined procedures. The influence of the Personnel Department within the firm is persuasive as it collects and files information, both formal and informal, on all employees (JIL, 1995b: 54). Moreover, to avoid inconsistent policies arising many of these companies are devising systems to ensure some company-wide consistency. These systems will be controlled by the Personnel Department (ibid.: 43) and so much of the flexibility generated by giving line managers more authority will be lost.

Equal Employment Opportunities

Recent surveys show that many women who stopped working after marriage believe that it would be possible to work in a full-time job if the right environment existed (ibid.: 116). Moreover, many women are no longer satisfied to simply support the work of their male colleagues. Nevertheless, barriers continue to exist and limit the job opportunities for female workers. Ten years after its introduction, the Equal Employment Opportunity Act remains largely without effect because of the absence of penalties and the lack of enforcement of the Act's employer obligations (*The Asahi Shimbun*, 1996: 14).

Some companies have implemented career paths for those women who want to pursue a management career. In most cases, this has resulted in longer hours of work involving more complex tasks but with little financial reward and long-term managerial opportunity (ibid.). The flexibility of working hours for female workers advocated in the Act will only assist a small number of women unless supporting structures like child-care are made available. A significant step in providing more employment for women could come from the liberalizing of the temporary job service industry. This would extend the right of private agencies to deal with clerical workers who, in the main, are women. However, while this would help counteract the growing level of female unemployment, it would do little to provide women with regular full-time positions.

Trade Unions

The decline in unionization in Japan has paralleled that of a number of Western countries. By 1993 union density had fallen to 24 per cent (JIL, 1995a: 48). Part of this decline has been due to sectorial shifts, with an increasing number of workers being employed in the service industry. These sectors are poorly organized and many of the workers are employed as peripheral workers (Tsuru, 1995: 14). Freeman and Rebick (1995: 603) argued that the fall in unionization can be primarily attributed to the falling rate of new organization. They found that the probability of being a union member in a new firm was significantly less than for established firms.

Other reasons, however, exist. Tsuru (1995: 15) found that the size of union–non-union wage differential in Japan is virtually non-existent for both men and women. Thus, he argued that Japanese employers have little incentive to resist unions, although profitability has been found to be significantly lower in union firms (Benson, 1994: 10–11). On this basis, Tsuru (1995: 15–16) suggested that the decline in unionization is partly due to the low expectation employees have of unions. The minimal effect of unions on wages could be compensated by other activities related to sources of dissatisfaction. Union membership was not related, however, to higher job satisfaction and lower turnover. The effect of 'voice', he argued, is not highly valued by individual workers. This is despite the success of unions in gaining legislation to cover child-care leave (1991) and part-time employment (1993), as well as income tax cuts in 1994. Unions, it appears, get little credit for their positive achievements for workers (*The Nikkei Weekly*, 5 October 1996: 7).

CASE STUDIES IN HRM PRACTICES

The previous section outlined the major HRM changes taking place in Japanese firms. While the process of change could be best characterized as an incremental approach it is clear that some of the changes have the potential to seriously challenge the present configuration of Japanese management practices. How have these changes impacted on the configuration of HRM in the Japanese firm, and do Japanese firms represent the exemplar of the HRM approach? To explore this issue further four case studies were conducted in Japanese companies in 1995.[1] Three of the companies were located in Tokyo and one in the Osaka area. While not representative, these firms covered the following:
• Electronics (Company A – 80,000 employees),
• Instrumentation (Company B – 7,800 employees),
• Cosmetics (Company C – 21,000 employees) and
• Distribution (Company D – 8,700 employees).

Using a modified version of the 25 item checklist (Storey, 1992: 10) each of the four companies were classified on ten dimensions (as in Warner and others in this volume). The classification of each company is given in Table 1.

From these cases, three key features stand out. First, there exists a high

TABLE 1
PERSONNEL/IR VERSUS HRM IN THE JAPANESE FIRMS

| Dimension | Firms | | | |
	A	B	C	D
Rules	x	%	x	%
Behaviour	✓	✓	✓	✓
Managerial Role	✓	✓	✓	✓
Key Managers	✓	✓	✓	✓
Personnel Selection	✓	✓	✓	✓
Payments	%	%	%	%
Work Conditions	✓	✓	✓	✓
Labour–Management	x	x	x	x
Job design	✓	✓	✓	✓
In-house Training	✓	✓	✓	✓

Key:
✓ practice present
% practice present to some degree
x practice not present

Source: Adapted from Storey (1992).

degree of consistency between all companies. On seven of the ten dimensions the HRM approach was evident and is what is generally referred to as the Japanese management style. These were: the importance placed on values and mission statements, a managerial role of nurturing, the key role of the line manager, personnel selection focusing on integrated key tasks, harmonized work conditions, job design based on teamwork, and continuous in-house training. These practices were not new, having been introduced in all companies many years earlier, although in the late 1980s all companies had redefined their mission and corporate values and began to give more responsibility to line managers. These dimensions are mutually supporting and the absence of one will make the effect of the others less significant.

The second feature of these results is that on two of the three remaining dimensions most of the firms had undertaken some change towards the HRM approach and were basically in the same stage of development. Payment systems were being developed that reduced the number of grades and emphasized performance. In addition, clear rules were slowly giving way to more employee flexibility in two of the companies (B, D). We would expect this will also become the case in the other two firms. Finally, labour–management relations were still characterized by collective bargaining agreements and are likely to be so in the future. Indeed, Japanese managers made the point that it is difficult to achieve harmony, teamwork and continuous learning if a collective approach is not adopted.

The current economic and social context has caused each company to assess their HRM practices. The companies intend to maintain a long-term commitment to their core employees. Some changes in working conditions will take place and are mainly focusing on introducing a larger performance element in the pay system. Job classifications are likely to be modified and this will be applied, in the first instance, to sales and other functions where teamwork is not so important. In all the companies, a flattening of the hierarchy is noticeable. Three of the firms (A, B, C) intend to delayer and remove about half of the positions and titles. The overall objective is to improve communication and to provide more opportunity for younger employees to take initiatives.

In the distribution company (D), mid-career hiring is increasing. For these employees, contracts are negotiated individually with renewal clauses depending on their performance. This represents a departure from collective bargaining, although the collective bargaining agreement still forms the basis of the contract. In the other three companies, mid-career hiring remains the exception. All the companies also recognized the need for transparent reward and appraisal systems to satisfy younger workers. Managers still have a clear nurturing role, but this has not precluded the development, via Management by Objectives, of a more comprehensive monitoring role. For administrative activities, three of the firms (A, B, C) have contracted a US consulting company to devise a comprehensive system of control and monitoring.

The four companies had created an express career track for promising young employees. Managers were, however, concerned that this scheme may create large disparities among people belonging to the same cohort. In all the companies, line managers appeared to have gained more autonomy in the award of titles, and in three companies (A, B, C) these managers had the authority to promote employees. It was pointed out that these decisions involved others, including staff of the Personnel Department. The scarcity of promotional opportunities in all the firms meant that decisions to promote are made only after substantial input from relevant parties. Given the role of the Personnel Department in this process it remains the key decision maker.

DISCUSSION

Japanese firms are examining new approaches to the management of their human resources. The reform of HRM practices is, however, proceeding slowly with an emphasis on promotion, recruitment and performance-related compensation. Lifetime employment practices have remained intact and regular employees were protected from the recent economic downturn by the traditional adjustment measures. These included reduced overtime and bonus payments, reassignment and dispatching of workers, reduced recruitment of new graduates, dismissal of part-time and temporary workers, extended vacations, temporary factory closure, and the voluntary retirement of workers.

Management's strategy during the recession was to support the internal labour market so as to keep down contingency costs and maintain worker morale. Thus, for most firms the internal labour market rules are still in place for most aspects of wages, job design and classification, the deployment of labour and employment security. Although some changes were considered radical by Japanese standards, they were introduced slowly and usually after extensive discussions and, finally, agreement with the unions. For instance, the reforms at Nippon Hewlett-Packard took place over a ten-year period and were only introduced with the collaboration of the union. Even in those companies which have pursued change, care was taken to maintain the social cohesion and to respect the implicit mutual contract. For example, at Honda, while managers' wages are annualized, they still receive housing and family allowances (*The Nikkei Business*, 13 October 1994: 27). Similarly, at Asahi Beer although wage increases associated with promotion are based solely on merit, basic regular salary increases are guaranteed (*The Nikkei Business*, 2 November 1994: 19). In most cases the payment and size of bonuses were not affected (JIL, 1995: 121). Some firms did, however, incorporate business performance into their 1996 bonus offers (Egami, 1996: 8).

The changes documented in the preceding sections illustrate that no employment system can, or does, remain static. Many of the changes can be related directly to the changed economic and social context, although as Benson (1996a: 29) has noted, similar economic situations in the past left the employment system intact. Equally, it should be recognized that all systems undergo change as contexts vary, new ideas emerge and world markets shift. What appears critical for Japanese firms is whether the changes reinforce other components of the HRM approach.

The Japanese HRM approach in large firms is based on the development of a highly skilled, flexible and committed workforce that can rapidly respond to changes in technology and markets (Sano, 1995). Employees recruited from schools and universities enter the company as general employees. Employment security and seniority-based promotion enhances long-term commitment and promotes acceptance of managerial control (Whitley, 1992: 39). These factors encourage firms to invest in on-going and firm-specific training (Cole, 1992). The wage system and the enterprise structure of unions provide further support for these HRM objectives. In short, the configuration of HRM practices in Japanese firms is both internally consistent and mutually supporting (Beaumont, 1993: 28).

A critical element in Japanese HRM is the recruitment of new employees. The recruitment process is taken seriously by firms and involves extensive socialization and indoctrination programmes (Clark, 1979: 156–64). While there has been a shift towards more mid-term and year-round recruitment, the major source of new recruits remains graduates from secondary schools and universities (Murdo, 1995: 10). In addition, the impact of recruitment changes will remain minimal if, as has been the practice to date, these involve specialist positions or temporary and part-time jobs. While seniority remains an important part of the promotion strategy, firms are clearly moving to performance based promotion. In the long-term this will lead to a more transparent evaluation system and a higher degree of equity.

Changes in compensation also have the ability to effect the basic configuration of HRM in Japanese firms. Annualized pay schemes and the linking of pay to performance has been introduced in some firms, although there is little evidence to suggest that this has improved worker motivation. It should also be noted that while traditionally seniority played an important part in the compensation package, other factors, such as skills and work performance, were also important. These pay attributes reinforce other employee and human resource policies. As Morishima (1995: 624) argued, a 'skill-grade pay system provides a strong incentive for Japanese employees to learn and improve their skill'. The changes implemented to date have placed only a small percentage of an employee's pay at risk and, given that the other components of the salary package have remained intact, it is unlikely that these changes will greatly effect worker morale or commitment.

Japanese firms usually have only one union, which is specific to that firm. These enterprise unions have tended to adopt management's objectives, but this does not mean they are not, at least to some degree, independent (Benson, 1996b). As unionization is declining in Japan does this mean the possibility of union-free workplaces as advocated by some advocates of HRM? For large firms, particularly in manufacturing, this remains unlikely. For smaller firms, and those firms in the hospitality, retail and service sectors, this may occur. In this case it is likely that other forms of collective determination of workplace rules will be developed. This process is well underway where joint management–labour consultative bodies have been established. Interestingly, 80 per cent of unionized firms and 40 per cent of non-unionized firms have already established such bodies (Nakajima, 1995: 12). Whether this system will develop the duality evidenced in British workplaces (Storey, 1995: 14) remains to be seen, although Japanese unions appear to remain closely involved in both collective bargaining and discussions over changes to recruitment, compensation and restructuring.

Considering the historical and institutional background of Japanese corporate governance, Japanese managers are unlikely to respond to international competitiveness by discarding their management strengths. Instead, they will selectively borrow aspects of Western HRM that are compatible with the Japanese management system. Moreover, it is likely that internal factors will, in the next few years, act as a major impetus for change in Japanese firms. In particular, the low dividends normally paid to shareholders is unlikely to be sustained given the low capital growth in recent years. This will entail accommodating shareholders in a more 'Western way' with respect to capital return, transparency and managerial accountability. These reforms have the potential to effect HRM in Japanese firms. An increased emphasis on capital return will require a substantial effort to maintain the prevelant internal labour market system. In the pursuit of profit, firms may in the short-term be prepared to cut costs by reducing both the quantity and price of labour.

The strategy of Japanese management, at least to now, has been to undertake change slowly and to maintain the basic configuration of Japanese employment practices. As such, it would be premature to conclude that the Japanese are moving towards a new model of HRM. A shift to a new HRM paradigm would mean an understanding and acceptance of the values of individualism, increased flexibility in recruitment, training and compensation, and a rejection of consensual decision making. Given the economic, social and institutional context of the Japanese firm it is unlikely that such reforms will take place or would improve performance.

CONCLUSION

The approach to HRM reform in Japanese enterprises can be characterized by three distinctive features. First, notwithstanding the pressure to restructure and reorganize their labour practices, Japanese firms have not lost sight of their prime objective of the development of a flexible and committed workforce. While some firms have implemented major innovations most firms have reacted cautiously. Japanese managers have tended to examine what aspects of HRM can be discarded, what aspects can be modified and what needs to be retained. For the Japanese firm HRM is the basis for their competitive advantage and so any innovations must be considered within the overall strategy of the firm.

Second, Japanese managers recognize the configuration of HRM practices must remain internally consistent. Consequently, change in the Japanese firm will usually be introduced on a small scale or in one section. This allows management to monitor and measure the effect before introducing the reform throughout the firm. Many of the innovations referred to earlier had been introduced into the white-collar or managerial levels only. Thus, by the time they are introduced to production areas, there has already developed a general consensus on their value and the issues to be resolved.

Finally, most changes that have taken place in Japanese firms were not short-term reactive strategies to counter the effects of the economic downturn. Japanese firms are aware that they are dependent on a productive, committed workforce and that their recovery does not just depend on improved product markets. This explains, to a large degree, why the lifetime employment system is intact and why the internal labour market has been retained for core workers, albeit in smaller numbers, in large firms. While Japanese firms are prepared to experiment with new HRM practices they appear to be aware that adoption of Western HRM practices must be located within their social, economic and institutional environment.

These findings have implications for the adoption of the HRM model in Western firms. The argument advanced here is that the Western concept of HRM approximates a stylized version of Japanese labour–management relations, though with a greater emphasis on individual effort and reward. This hybrid system of collective and individual management practices may mean that the Western model of HRM is not internally consistent and lacks a coherent strategic focus. For HRM to become more strategic will require Western firms to modify Japanese practices to take into account their different social and institutional environment. Moreover, the configuration of practices will need to form a consistent and integrated approach to the management of human resources.

Yet, such an agenda may prove difficult for Western firms to adopt. Western firms have less autonomy to act independently of shareholders than do their Japanese counterparts. This places the financial function in a dominant role and leads to a strategy based on short-term capital gains. Management has little loyalty to employees and perceives their role is to serve the interests of outside capital. In this model, employees are expendable. The purpose of HRM is to a produce a committed and low cost workforce: objectives that are mutually exclusive. The emphasis on profits means that managements will adopt a short-term focus. New ideas, particularly ones that promise cost savings, are likely to fall on fertile ground. In this environment new HRM practices will be adopted irrespective of the social, economic or institutional context of the firm.

In addition, the adoption of HRM practices on an individual basis will mean that the configuration of HRM practices in Western firms will not be mutually supporting or consistent. This appears to be the case to date. The British research indicates that few firms had developed an integrated set of practices and most had tended to introduced policies that reduced costs and marginalized unions (Storey, 1992; Duberley and Walley, 1995). While this may be a useful short-term solution it will do little for the long-run competitive advantage of the firm. As Beaumont (1993: 30) claimed, HRM practices in most firms do not constitute a coherent management strategy. The Japanese model with a more individualistic focus is one possible strategy. Yet, within this framework there are inconsistencies that lead to an unstable configuration of practices. Until Western managers can make a choice between ideology and strategy the situation is unlikely to change.

NOTES

1. The interviews were conducted in April and May 1995 by one of the authors. In each company four managers were interviewed: the Personnel Manager, the Training and Development Manager, and two managers from other areas of the firm's activities. The interviews were supplemented by company documents and reports.

REFERENCES

Asahi Shimbun (The), August 23, 1996.

Beaumont, Phillip (1993) *Human Resource Management: Key Concepts and Skills*. London: Sage.

Beaumont, Phillip (1995) *The Future of Employee Relations*. London: Sage.

Benson, John (1994) 'The Economic Effects of Unionism on Japanese Manufacturing Enterprises', *British Journal of Industrial Relations*, Vol.32, No.1, pp.1–21.

Benson, John (1996a) 'Change and Continuity: Contemporary Employment Practices in Japan', *International Employment Relations Review*, Vol.2, No.1, pp.21–31.

Benson, John (1996b) 'A Typology of Japanese Enterprise Unions', *British Journal of Industrial Relations*, Vol.34, No.3, pp.371–86.

Brewster, Chris and Ariane Hegewisch (1994) 'Human Resource Management in Europe: Issues and Opportunities' in Chris Brewster and Ariane Hegewisch (eds) *Policy and Practice in European Human Resource Management*. London: Routledge, pp.1–21.

Clark, Rodney (1979) *The Japanese Company*. Tokyo: Tuttle.

Cole, Robert (1992) 'Issues in Skill Formation in Japanese Approaches to Automation' in Paul Adler (ed.) *Technology and the Future of Work*. New York: Oxford University Press, pp.187–209.

Debroux, Philippe (1996) 'Japanese Mergers and Acquisitions: Overcoming Obstacles to Improved Systemic Efficiency', *Atlantic Economic Journal*, Vol.24, No.3, pp.244–56.

Duberley, Joanne and Paul Walley (1995) 'Assessing the Adoption of HRM by Small and Medium-sized Manufacturing Organizations', *International Journal of Human Resource Management*, Vol.6, No.4, pp.891–909.

Dulebohn, James, Gerald Ferris and James Stodd (1995) 'The History and Evolution of Human Resource Management' in Gerald Ferris, Sherman Rosen and Darold Barnum (eds) *Handbook of Human Resource Management*. Cambridge, MA.: Blackwell, pp.18–41.

Egami, Sumio (1996) 'Spring Wage Struggle System at Turning Point', *Labour Issues Quarterly*, Summer.

Elgar, Tony and Chris Smith (1994) 'Introduction' in Tony Elgar and Chris Smith (eds) *Global Japanization: The Transnational Transformation of the Labour Process*. London: Routledge, pp.1–24.

EPA (1996) *White Paper on the Economy*. Tokyo: Economic Planning Agency.

Fowler, Arthur (1987) 'When Chief Executives Discovers HRM', *Personnel Management*, Vol.19, No.1, p.3.

Freeman, Richard and Marcus Rebick (1989) 'Crumbling Pillar? Declining Union Density in Japan', *Journal of the Japanese and International Economies*, Vol.3, No.4. pp.578–605.

Goss, David (1994) *Principles of Human Resource Management*. London: Routledge.

Guest, David (1987) 'Human Resource Management and Industrial Relations', *Journal of Management Studies*, Vol.24, No.5, pp.503–21.

Inoki, Takao (1993) *Atarashii Sangyo Shakai no Joken: Kyoso-Kyocho-Sangyo Minshushugi (Conditions for a New Industrial Society: Competition-Cooperation-Industrial Democracy)*. Tokyo: Iwanami Shoten.

Japan Labour Bulletin, 1 December 1996.

Japan Times (The), various editions.

JIL (1995a) *Japanese Working Life Profile, 1994–95*. Tokyo: Japan Institute for Labour.

JIL (1995b) *Human Resource Management of White-Collar Workers*. Tokyo: Japan Institute of Labour, November, No.68.

Koyo Shinko Kyokai (1994) *Case Studies on Policies to Systemize and Stabilize Employees' Careers*. Tokyo: Keie Shoin.

Labour Issues Quarterly (1996), Autumn.

Legge, Karen (1989) 'Human Resource Management: A Critical Analysis' in John Storey (ed.) *New Perspectives on Human Resource Management*. London: Routledge, pp.19–40.

Legge, Karen (1995) 'HRM: Rhetoric, Reality and Hidden Agendas' in John Storey (ed.) *Human Resource Management: A Critical Text.* London: Routledge, pp.33–59.

Martinez-Lucio, Miguel and Sid Weston (1992) 'Human Resource Management and Trade Union Responses: Bringing the Politics of the Workplace Back into the Debate' in Paul Blyton and Peter Turnbull (eds) *Reassessing Human Resource Management.* London: Sage, pp.215–32.

MITI (1996) *White Paper on Trade.* Tokyo: Ministry of International Trade and Industry.

MOL (1992) *White Paper on Labour.* Tokyo: Ministry of Labour.

MOL (1994) *White Paper on Labour.* Tokyo: Ministry of Labour.

MOL (1995) *White Paper on Labour.* Tokyo: Ministry of Labour.

MOL (1996a) *White Paper on Labour.* Tokyo: Ministry of Labour.

MOL (1996b) *Survey on Employment Practices.* Tokyo: Ministry of Labour.

Moore, Joe (1987) 'Japanese Industrial Relations', *Labour and Industry*, Vol.1, No.1, pp.140–55.

Morishima, Motohiro (1995) 'Embedding HRM in a Social Context', *British Journal of Industrial Relations*, Vol.33, No.4, pp.617–40.

Miyanaga, Kuniko (1991) *The Creative Edge.* New Brunswick: Transaction Publishers.

Murdo, Fred (1995) *Is There Still a Fit Between the Japanese Education System and Labour Market Needs?* Washington, DC: Japan Economic Institute.

Nakajima, Shigeya (1995) 'Labor–Management Consultation System in Japan', *Labour Issues Quarterly*, No.27, Spring, pp.2–4.

Nikkei Business (The), various editions.

Nikkei Shimbun (The), various editions.

Nikkei Weekly (The), various editions.

Nikkeiren (1995) *A New Era for Japanese Style Management.* Tokyo: Nikkeiren.

OECD (1993) 'Earnings Inequality: Changes in the 1980s' in *Employment Outlook.* Paris: Organization for Economic Cooperation and Development.

Ostrom, Douglas (1996) *Japan's Long-Term Economic Prospects: Growth, Trade and Foreign Investment.* Washington, DC: Japan Economic Institute.

Recruit (1994) *Survey on Employment Practices.* Tokyo: Recruit Co.

Recruit (1995) *Survey on Employment Practices.* Tokyo: Recruit Co.

Recruit (1996) *Employment Report.* Tokyo: Recruit Co.

Sangyo Rodo Chosa (1994) *Case Studies of Employment Practices.* Keiei Shoin: Tokyo.

Sano, Yoko (1995) *Human Resource Management in Japan.* Tokyo: Keio University Press.

Sataka, Makoto and Kyotsugu Shibara (1995) *Kanrishoku Union Sengen (Declaration of Executives Union).* Tokyo: Shakaishisosha.

Shakai Keizai Seisansei Shimbun (The), November 20, 1996.

Storey, John (1989) 'Introduction: From Personnel Management to Human Resource Management' in John Storey (ed.) *New Perspectives on Human Resource Management.* London: Routledge, pp.1–39.

Storey, John (1992) *Developments in the Management of Human Resources.* Oxford: Blackwell.

Storey, John (1995) 'Human Resource Management: Still Marching On, or Marching Out' in John Storey (ed.) *Human Resource Management: A Critical Text.* London: Routledge, pp.3–32.

Takezawa, Shin-ichi (1995) *Japan Work Ways.* Tokyo: Japan Institute of Labour.

Tokuzumi, Kenji, Yukio Inoue and Tatsuo Ozuka (1994) *Kanrishoku Kumiai (Managers' Unions).* Tokyo: Chuo Keizaisha.

Tokyo Business, April 1994.

Tsuchida, Takeshi (1996) 'Welfare Provision as They Stand Today', *Labour Issues Quarterly*, Autumn.

Tsuru, Tsuuyoshi (1995) 'Determinants of the Union Decline in Japan', *Labour Issues Quarterly*, Winter.

Walton, Richard (1985) 'From Control to Commitment in the Workplace', *Harvard Business Review*, Vol.6, No.3, pp.60–66.

Weinstein, D. (1994) 'United We Stand: Firms and Enterprise Unions in Japan', *Journal of the Japanese and International Economies*, Vol.8, pp.53–71.

Whitehill, Arthur (1991) *Japanese Management: Tradition and Transition.* London: Routledge.

Whitley, Richard (1992) *Business Systems in East Asia.* London: Sage.

Yashiro, Atsushi (1992) *Daikigyo ni Okeru Honsha Jinjibu no Soshiki to Kino (Organization and Function of the Central Personnel Department of Large Companies).* Tokyo: Nippon Rodo Kenkyu Kiko Kiyo Dai 4 Go.

Beyond Seniority-Based Systems: A Paradigm Shift in Korean HRM?

JOHNGSEOK BAE

The economy of South Korea (hereafter Korea) is at a turning point. Many large firms are now making efforts to move from imitation towards innovation, from labour-intensity to capital-intensity, and from focusing on quantity to quality. Large companies have also been driven to become real global players. After realizing that Korean goods are too expensive to compete against goods from the Third World, and are of too low quality to compete against goods from more developed countries, Korean firms began to invest aggressively for innovation and self-renewal. Significant attention has been given to human resource management (HRM) recently as Korean executives realize that competitive advantages can come from human resources.

Along with other newly industrializing countries (NICs), Korea has been the focus of many writers. Although many studies have dealt with rapid economic growth and management in general, HRM systems in Korea are relatively little known. In this piece we will attempt to fill this gap by delineating HRM in Korea in the context of macro environments and organizational contingencies, recent trends in HRM, and an international and comparative framework.

First, we will start with a discussion of the political, economic, and cultural environments of business organizations, management in general, and their effects on the formation of Korean HRM systems. Second, both traditional aspects of Korean HRM, and current trends, the so-called 'New HRM (NHRM) Systems', are dealt with. Finally, a summary of the field data collected by the author is discussed in an international and comparative framework. Four country groups (Korea, USA, Europe, and Japan) are included in the analysis. Along with the literature review, the data from interviews, case studies, and a questionnaire survey are used to analyze both Korean local firms and foreign subsidiaries of multinational enterprises (MNEs).

BACKGROUND OF HRM SYSTEMS

While Western European countries were experiencing dramatic changes such as the Reformation, the Renaissance, the Industrial Revolution, and the French Revolution, *Choson* (an old name for Korea which existed from

Johngseok Bae, Hanyang University, Seoul

1393 to 1910) was known by the beautiful nickname of 'the country of the morning calm'. However, after the Japanese colonial period (1910–45) and a transitional period, Korea was full of noise due to hammering, digging, constructing, and so forth. This was the first step in the industrialization of the country.

From the American military government period (1945–48) through the Korean War (1950–53) up to the first military coup (1961), Korea was one of the world's poorest countries, characterized by an agricultural economy. Then, General Park Chung Hee, who was the ringleader of the military coup and became president, launched the first five-year economic development plan (1962–66), which marked the beginning of the move towards an industrial economy. From the first plan to the seventh five-year economic and social development plan (1992–96), the economic development plans have settled down as nationwide movements. In this section we focus on the macro environments of the HRM system.

Economic Development

Over the past three decades, Korea has achieved rapid economic growth (see Table 1 for macro-economic and labour statistics). *Per capita* Gross National Product (GNP) leapfrogged from a mere US $87 in 1962 to US $10,076 in 1995. While in 1962 the proportion of agriculture, manufacturing, and services in the economy was, respectively, 37, 16.4, and 46.6 per cent, by 1995 it had changed to 7, 27.2, and 65.8 per cent, respectively.

When we look into the economically active population (EAP), both male and female EAPs have increased. The labour force participation rate has steadily increased for females from 28.6 per cent in 1962 to 48.3 per cent in 1995, while the male participation rate has remained more or less stable. Average weekly working hours decreased steadily until 1990, as shown in the last row of Table 1. With the recovery of the economy in 1993, both regular and overtime work increased to some extent. One reason is that companies tried to increase the numerical flexibility of internal labour markets through overtime work instead of recruiting new workers when they encountered high labour costs and environmental uncertainty (Korea Ministry of Labour, 1995).

After World War II Korea lacked physical capital and human skills, but had abundant unskilled labour. For effective development it chose a strategy that used the scarce resources economically and the abundant resources lavishly (Papanek, 1988). Korea, therefore, focused on labour-intensive manufacturing industry in its first stage (as Taiwan did in the early stage of its economic development). Furthermore, export-oriented industrialization was one way to overcome small and saturated domestic markets. Amsden (1989) took the Korean economy as a model of 'late industrialization'. As a good 'learner', Korean firms developed their industrial technology through the implementation of imported technology, assimilation of product diversification, and improvement of enhancing competitiveness (Kim,

TABLE 1
SELECTED MACRO-ECONOMIC AND LABOUR STATISTICS IN KOREA

Variables \ Year	1962**	1965	1970	1975	1980	1985	1990	1995
GNP Per Capita: US $*	87	105	243	573	1,592	2,242	5,883	10,076
Economic Growth Rate (GNP)	2.2	5.8	7.6	7.1	−3.7	7.0	9.6	9.0
Exports: US $ million (Growth Rate)	55 (34.15)	175 (47.06)	835 (34.24)	5,081 (13.92)	17,505 (16.27)	30,283 (3.55)	65,016 (4.23)	125,058 (30.25)
Inflation Rate (%)	6.7	13.6	16.1	25.3	28.7	2.5	9.3	4.7
Male EAP*** (Participation rate)****	5,386 (79.8)	6,001 (76.0)	6,752 (75.6)	7,822 (77.4)	9,019 (76.4)	9,617 (72.3)	11,030 (74.0)	12,433 (76.5)
EAP (Participation rate)****	2,156 (28.6)	3,198 (37.3)	3,624 (39.1)	4,371 (40.4)	5,412 (42.8)	5,975 (41.9)	7,509 (47.0)	8,363 (48.3)
Unemployment Rate (Non-farm households)	8.4	7.4	4.5	4.1	5.2	4.0	2.4	2.2
Hours of Work Per Week (Manufacturing)	57	57	52.5	50.5	53.1	53.8	49.8	47.8

*   Nominal dollars in each year.
**   Male and Female EAPs figures are from 1960.
***   Economically active population (thousands)
****   '[Fe]Male EAP' 'all [fe]male population of 15 years and over'

Sources: Year Book of Labour Statistics (ILO, Various Years); International Financial Statistics (IMF, various years); Monthly Statistics of Korea (National Statistical Office, Korea, various issues).

1980). Now Korean firms are shifting their efforts from imitation to innovation.

During the 1960s and 1970s, the abundant supply of young, low-wage workers contributed to the rapid expansion of the economy. National competitive advantage came from the lower cost of labour and products, and firms focused on quantity rather than quality. The world economic environment was generally good for the Korean economy. However, both the internal and external environments of the national economy have dramatically changed since the mid-1980s. *World Development* (1988) published a special issue entitled *Korea: Transition to Maturity*, in which articles explained Korea's period of transition. Korea was seen to be on the brink of the final stage of development and undergoing a rapid structural change of industry into an OECD-type mature economy (Leipziger, 1988).

We can draw implications for HRM from Korean economic development. Korea as a late starter achieved rapid economic development in just a few decades. This shortening of the development period did not allow Korean firms enough time for the formation of an indigenous HRM system. In many cases Korean firms merely adopted the Japanese or

American HRM model without giving much consideration of the Korean situation.

The Role of Government

The role of the government in the process of economic development in Korea has been well noted (Amsden, 1989; Wilkinson, 1994). As Kihl (1987) pointed out, the East Asian development model is more based on 'neo-mercantilism' (that is, state-led economic development). For uninterrupted economic growth, governments protected important industries from external competition through import controls and restricted labour disputes through legislation. While the government encountered complex and uncertain environments, strategic industries could keep producing goods with efficiency. The state in late industrializing countries 'can stimulate or stagnate the economy; it is a necessary, if not a sufficient, cause for development' (Lie, 1991: 502). With reciprocal relations between the state and the firm, 'the state [could] exact certain performance standards from firms' in direct exchange for subsidies (Amsden, 1989: 146). In short, the government fostered those things that could help the growth of economy and checked those things that might hamper economic development.

Yet, the economic success of Korea has come not under Western-style democratic government, but under authoritarian ones. Further, this success was actualized not by the principle of the 'invisible hand' of the free market[1] but by the 'visible hand' of a strong and authoritarian system. This authoritarianism has often worked well to drive growth, since it can carry out a policy, without interruption, by taking austere measures. This is more understandable when we consider the inefficiency of market forces for driving economic development in NICs (Sharma, 1985).

Governments as 'the prime agent of industrialization' and 'industrializing elites' have a profound impact on the evolution of industrial relations patterns in NICs (Kerr et al., 1960; Sharma, 1985). In the early stages of development governments catered less favourably for workers in many cases (Deyo, 1989). The roles of the Korean government in industrial relations and HRM can be nicely summarized as following four stages: market-driven repression (1963–71); authoritarian corporatist repression (from 1972 to mid-1987); immature pluralism (mid-1987 to mid-1989); and transition towards maturity (from mid-1989) (Park, 1993). As Wilkinson (1994: 95) pointed out, 'the most obvious change by the state in 1987 was a shift from an unambiguous role of controlling labour on behalf of capital to one of "hands off in industrial relations".' However, the general strike triggered by the revision of labour laws on 26 December 1996 represented another type of authoritarianism by the government, which initiated the change for the enhancement of national competitiveness (Bae et al., 1997).

Social and Cultural Factors

To understand the general context of HRM and management, we need some understanding of the role of Confucianism. Although it is impossible to introduce all the Confucianist beliefs here, we can capture some sense from a code of ethics consisting of five moral disciplines in human relations. They are: filial piety; the subservience of women to men; the precedence of the elder over the younger; mutual trust among friends; and absolute loyalty of subjects to sovereigns. Basically, human relations are based on predetermined, unequal relationships. Confucian beliefs also emphasize the importance of self-discipline, education, and one's family and clan. These Confucian teachings are socially desirable, and all people are strongly expected to follow this moral code. Strong social norms do not allow anyone to defy these precepts. Similarly, as in Taiwan, the employer–employee relationship is seen as an extension of familism. This type of employment relationship may be influenced by Confucian beliefs which are influential in Taiwanese society.

As national culture generally affects HRM practices (Lawler and Bae, 1996), Confucian culture has impacted on both workers' behaviours and HRM practices (Moore and Ishak, 1989). HRM systems in Korean companies are characterized by strict seniority, though this has been challenged recently. A strong work ethic can also be ascribed to the Confucian tradition (Koch *et al.*, 1995). Another prevailing consequence of the Confucian tradition is its emphasis on education, which has contributed greatly to enhancing the general quality of the workforce. For example, Korea's adult literacy rate was 96 per cent in 1994 (US Department of Labour, 1995).

Recently, some scholars have pointed out that the Confucian tradition had been affected by Western culture and had formed the 'new Confucian ethics', a blending of East and West, of old and new, or of collectivism and individualism (Koch *et al.*, 1995; Lee, 1993). Therefore, it can be argued that Korean people still stick to traditional values, and at the same time they also place high value on individualism and personal achievement.

Management in General

Before World War II the Japanese 'military style' heavily influenced Korean society as a whole. Those who were trained in the Japanese military got involved in political affairs after the military coup of 1961, and many of these people in turn came into the business world. The blending of the military tradition, the bureaucratic government style, Confucian culture, and a close connection between government and management together brought about an 'authoritarian management style'. Other aspects of Korean management display a 'paternalistic management style'. Lee and Yoo (1987: 75) summarized the distinguishing characteristics of Korean management as:

> clan management; top-down decision making; flexible lifetime employment; high mobility of workers; Confucian work ethic; paternalistic leadership; loyalty; compensation based on seniority and merit rating; bureaucratic conflict resolution; highly bureaucratic and

yet less degree of formality and a standardized system; close government–business relationship within the company.

All these characteristics are closely related to the aforementioned macro environmental factors. The relationships of these factors are presented in Figure 1.

FIGURE 1
ENVIRONMENTAL AND ORGANIZATIONAL FACTORS
AND HRM SYSTEMS

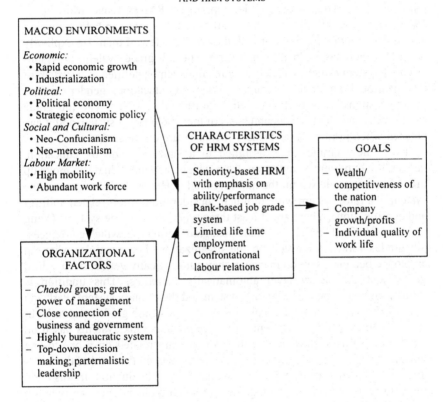

To sum up, the most important goal in Korea during the last several decades was 'economic well-being'. There was little objection to this national goal among the Korean people. Under this unquestioned goal other factors subordinately worked together and affected the formation of Korean HRM systems. Now we will turn to some specific HRM practices.

TRADITIONAL HRM PRACTICES

Before moving on to an explanation of Korean HRM systems, we need to make a distinction between 'traditional' HRM systems and recent trends, as the latter can look like more fundamental changes. What we call traditional HRM systems are related to seniority-based systems, which were dominant until mid-1980s. Current changes seem to be a paradigm-shifting movement which started in the late 1980s. First, traditional HRM practices are discussed,[2] followed by more recent trends in the next section.

Work Systems

In this section we want to explain some aspects of work systems within Korean HRM. Two interesting features of work systems are broadly defined jobs and job grade systems. Like Japanese HRM systems (Morishima, 1995), Korean systems have broadly defined jobs and flexible job assignments. Although there are job descriptions, few of them are explicitly related to their tasks. In its broad sense, the job grade system, a person-oriented system rather than task-oriented one, can be defined as a system of organizational employee hierarchy based on education, gender, tenure, ability, responsibility of tasks, and so forth (Ahn, 1996). The job grade system provides the fundamental basis of the whole HRM system and it can be used when promotion and salary increases are considered.

Every new employee is assigned to a starting grade by education, gender, job experience, and so on, from which each individual can move up to the highest grade within the mobility ladder. However, in most cases the system is a rank system without much consideration of job-related abilities and qualifications. There are at least three types of job grade systems (Yang and Ahn, 1992). The first one is the post grade system, in which employees' job grades follow their rank in the organization. For example, when an employee becomes section manager, they automatically get, let us say, third grade, and the salary level automatically increases. This tradition is influenced by the Japanese factory system and the military system (Park and Lee, 1995). This system is a typical Korean type of job grade system. Until the late 1980s job grade systems were regarded as rank systems based on seniority. In this system, rank and job grade are related on a one-to-one matching basis. Second, job grade is literally based on the level of the task's difficulty, which is determined by job analysis and evaluation. In this case, job values and job grades go together. This is a typical American-type job grade. Finally, a third type of job grade system is based on employees' skill and knowledge development, which is commonly found in Japanese firms (Morishima, 1995).

There exists a dual job grade system in Korean firms: one for production employees and another for managerial and administrative employees (see Table 2). Their hierarchical structures are different from each other. Usually, managerial and administrative jobs have about eight grades, yet production jobs have about three or four grades. Therefore, production employees have fewer opportunities for promotion, lower pay, and worse work conditions (Park and Lee, 1995). Even managerial and administrative employees can be terminated in their forties and fifties. Those who do not expect to be promoted usually leave for other jobs before they are made redundant.

TABLE 2
CORRESPONDING RELATIONSHIP OF JOB GRADE
AND RANK (L COMPANY)

Job Grade	Managerial and Administrative Jobs		Production Jobs	
	Matching Rank	Minimum Years for Promotion	Matching Rank	Minimum Years for Promotion
First Grade (A)	General Manager			
First Grade (B)	Deputy General Manager	4 years		
Second Grade (A)	Section Chief (A)	4 years	Foreman	
Second Grade (B)	Section Chief (B)	2 years		
Third Grade	Deputy Section Chief	3 years	Group Leader	7 years
Fourth Grade	Senior Administrative	1 year	Team Leader	7 years
	Junior Administrative	2 years		
Fifth Grade (Male)	Employee	4 years	Team Member	10 years
Fifth Grade (Female)				

* *Source:* Adapted from Lee and Kim (1991:249).

Korean HRM systems look similar to Japanese ones, except that they have very limited (or 'flexible' from a management perspective) lifetime employment practices.

Human Resource Flow

(1) Inflow: recruitment and selection. Recruitment in small companies and firms in rural areas usually relies more on personal connections, especially for production employees (Koch *et al.*, 1995). However, large companies have more formal recruitment processes and hire a cohort of new school graduates each year. Graduates from the leading universities often have better treatment. Each *chaebol* recruits the total number of new employees necessary for its subsidiary companies. The process includes written exams and interviews (for both job-related ability and personality). Firms usually use both objective and subjective employment tests. Employment exams typically include English proficiency, general knowledge, and sometimes knowledge of their major fields.

Historically, new graduates are preferred to experienced ones, and generalists, rather than specialists, were preferred until late 1980s (ibid.; Von Glinow and Chung, 1989). In this aspect, Korean and Japanese firms are alike, in contrast to American firms, which prefer specialists with experience. Also, similar to Japanese firms (Morishima, 1995) is the fact that both Korean employers and employees use the cohort as a reference group for the evaluation of employee progress and position in the organization. However, one different aspect is first assignment practices. While Japanese firms typically assign new employees to jobs in the field, Korean firms are more likely to assign excellent college graduates to jobs at corporate headquarters in such areas as strategic planning, finance, and accounting (Koch *et al.*, 1995).

New recruits are assigned to a specific job grade according to their educational background, gender, and so forth. For example, as shown in Table 2, female high school graduates are assigned to the lower fifth job grade, and their male counterparts to the upper fifth job grade, while college graduates to the fourth job grade. These initial job grade assignments represent the starting points from which they progress up the job ladder.

Most foreign subsidiaries have different recruitment and staffing practices from those of Korean firms. While most Korean firms recruit employees from new graduates for more generalist employment positions, foreign subsidiaries recruit new employees when they need people for specific positions. There are at least two factors that explain this variety. One is national difference, and the other is size difference. The size of firms of foreign subsidiaries is relatively small, thus they sometimes do not need formal large scale recruitment activities. Rather, they conduct recruitment and selection on the basis of vacancies throughout the year.

(2) Throughflow. After several years of service, most employees can predict the possibility of their career success in the organization. When promotion is considered, seniority and educational attainment are important factors, traditionally and still today (Park and Lee, 1995). However, at higher levels of management, actual performance is a more important factor than seniority in promotion (Koch *et al.*, 1995). Additionally, family connection is a critical factor for higher level management in family-owned *chaebols* (Von Glinow and Chung, 1989).

(3) Outflow: termination and retirement. The previous Korean Labour Standard Act did not allow the termination of employees without just cause. However, this clause brought totally different responses from employers and employees, who had polar opposite views on this. While the human resource managers interviewed commented that it was really difficult to terminate employees, in contrast employees said that their jobs were really insecure. However, the newly amended law includes a clause of 'discharge upon business crisis', which allows employers to lay off their employees for the reasons of financial deterioration, structural adjustment, technical

innovation, and change of business for the enhancement of productivity. By such revisions of labour law, it is expected that firms will become more flexible. Compared to their Japanese counterparts, Korean companies do not widely practice permanent employment, whatever its actual extent in Japan, which is debated (Kang, 1989; Koch *et al.*, 1995; Lie, 1990; and Benson and Debroux in this volume). Japanese companies take the responsibility for poor performance in the sense that firms try to find ways to improve employees' performance or assign them to different positions (Kang, 1989). However, in many Korean firms individual employees and managers bear the responsibility for poor performance.

Retirement is mandatory in Korean companies, with some variation in age limits. Typically, a lump sum retirement payment is paid, usually amounting to one month's salary for each year of service. Large Japanese firms enhance the flexibility of staffing practices through '[the] practice of transferring employees out of the parent firm to its subsidiaries and related companies' (Morishima, 1995: 136). This practice partly allows for employment level adjustment and redundancy control with regard to older employees. However, this is rarely used in Korea (Koch *et al.*, 1995).

Training and Development

When new recruits come into companies, the first thing they do is attend group-level socialization camps. From the very beginning of the employee's company life, firms pursue an indoctrination process designed to inculcate its corporate culture and business philosophy. Another purpose of such camps is to develop 'all-purpose' general skills to enhance team-spirit, 'can-do spirit', adaptability to new environments, problem-solving abilities, and so forth. In addition to this, most *chaebols* have their own training and development centres. For example, LG Inwhawon (LG Group's Research and Training Institute) provides such support services as general and special management skill training, internationalization training, consulting services, multi-media materials support, and other cultural services.

Many large companies also have several programmes for business–university partnership activities, as many US firms do (Ferris *et al.*, 1995). In addition, overseas training programmes also provide opportunities of training and 're-education'. Many companies provide some opportunities to their employees who have certain qualifications (such as language proficiency and high ranking in performance evaluation) to study in universities of foreign countries. In Samsung, the 'region expert' programme has operated for several years. Samsung sends its brightest junior employees to other countries for a year, without any obligation, except to obtain language and cultural acquaintances: this is seen as a 'Goof off' mission. According to *the Wall Street Journal* (1992), the programme costs about $80,000 a year per person.

For job-related skills and knowledge, job rotation is a popular programme. Yet, it is less systematic than Japanese counterparts, and the practice of job rotation and multi-skills training varies among industries

(Park and Lee, 1995). Production employees are usually involved in on-the-job training for the enhancement of job-related skills. However, although retraining is needed due to automation and technological changes, an adequate amount of retraining is not provided by the majority of firms (ibid.). A survey conducted by the author of 138 Korean local and foreign firms in 1996 showed that, on average, about 59 per cent of employees in each firm participated in training programmes, and that the average hours of training a year per employee was about 32 hours.

Performance Appraisal and Reward Systems

In most cases the purpose of performance appraisal is an administrative one, with only a minimal developmental purpose in Korean firms. About 50 per cent of the firms surveyed in 1994 used performance appraisal to make a rank order for promotion candidates (Ahn, 1996). Relative appraisal systems, assigning certain predetermined percentage to each grade, rather than absolute ones have been used. Appraisal systems have also focused much on person-related attributes such as 'proper' attitudes and loyalty. In most firms (81.4 per cent), only top-down appraisal is used, and there is usually no feedback to employees (ibid.).

After 1987, Korean wages rapidly increased. Between 1986 and 1995 nominal and real wages rose at an annual rate of 14.25 per cent and 7.93 per cent, respectively, in the whole of industry, and 15.42 per cent and 9.07 per cent, respectively, in manufacturing. These high increases are due to trade union expansion and high economic performance (Park and Lee, 1995). Three basic components in wages are basic salary, allowances, and bonuses. Basic salary is the largest portion and provides a central skeleton for remuneration. The starting level of basic salary is determined by educational background and experience and annual salary increases occur according to seniority. In their earlier career stages, employees are usually paid less than their contributions, while salary exceeds contributions later in their careers. This answers a question posed by human capital theorists: 'Why do firms use seniority as the basis of pay although seniority is not related to productivity?' (Kaufman, 1994). It seems employees can develop a 'property right' in their jobs as they stay longer in the organization (Mitchell, 1982). This explanation is probably not the reason that Korean firms employed seniority-based pay systems, but systems could be interpreted in this way *ex post facto*.

Although Korean pay systems are based on seniority, they are different from Japanese ones. Survey results from 1994 showed that the proportions of basic salary, various allowances, and monthly average bonus are 52.6 per cent, 20.5 per cent, and 26.9 per cent respectively (Yang *et al.*, 1994). In Japan, base pay accounts for about 60 per cent, and skill-grade pay about 40 per cent, of total take-home pay on average (Morishima, 1995). While Japanese firms reflect much of their employees' skills and knowledge in pay levels, in contrast Korean firms minimize the proportion. When Korean firms use both seniority and skills, management use them very strategically to meet both employee needs and company goals (Bae and Form, 1986). In addition, while large Japanese firms institutionalized training programmes rather systematically, so as to enhance skills and knowledge as tenure increases, Korean firms operate less systematically. As a result, seniority-based pay systems bring different results in the two countries. Compared to Japanese cases, the relationship of seniority and productivity would be smaller in Korea. Allowances, another part of salary, include allowances for overtime, service-area, family, transportation, and so on. One feature of the reward systems in Korea is the complexity of wage structure, principally due to these various types of allowances. The amount of bonus is fixed annually (for example, 400 per cent or 600 per cent of a month's gross salary). As a result, bonus systems cannot function as a motivator.

In sum, the characteristics of the traditional HRM system in Korea can be seen in Figure 1. These include: seniority-based systems, rank-based job grade systems, limited lifetime employment, and confrontational employment relationships.

NHRM SYSTEMS

The HRM function is probably the least rationalized management function in Korean companies. However, it was not problematic until mid-1980s, partly because of a favourable economic environment and labour supply (Kim, 1994). Now new environments are pushing companies to change HRM systems fundamentally. When we say a 'new' HRM system, it generally means that the Korean HRM system is experiencing a paradigm shift from a seniority-based system to an ability-based one. Some companies use the term 'new' system when they introduce any new technique, while others employ it when they change the HRM system more fundamentally (Ahn, 1996).

Three major themes, which guide the directions of NHRM systems, are as follows: ability/performance, rationalization, and fairness. The traditional seniority-based HRM system has been challenged, moving towards an ability- and performance-based system. The irrational factors in the traditional system have been pointed out as requiring redress. These factors are discussed in the next section. Finally, as employees' desire for both distributive justice and procedural justice grows (see Greenberg, 1990), traditional HRM systems have been challenged.

Background: The Cause of Current Trends

Both external and internal factors have affected recent NHRM trends. External factors include international competition, declining economic growth, labour force shifts, and changing industrial structure and technology. First, recently the world economy has dramatically changed and can be characterized by 'unlimited competition', and the economy of one country cannot be separated from others. However, internationalization or globalization is often taken for granted, yet this is a debated area in itself (see Hirst and Thompson, 1996). Nevertheless, this kind of environmental change has motivated management to reconsider HRM systems. Second, the decline of economic growth in Korea. Korea enjoyed rapid economic growth for about three decades. However, it is becoming difficult to keep up the pace. The HRM system which had a good fit when the economy was growing, may not fit so well now. Third, there are labour force changes. For instance, not only is there a high education level, but also an aging workforce, more female participation, and a shift in workers' mentality. These changes are not aligned with a seniority-based HRM system. Finally, as industrial structure and technology change, the positive relationship between the length of service and skill level is no longer linked. Rather, younger workers with better knowledge and skills in information technology perform better in some industries. In addition, the number of these kinds of industries has increased. Thus, traditional seniority-based HRM systems do not perform as well.

There are also some internal factors that have encouraged NHRM systems. First, management recognized that seniority-based HRM systems are weaker motivators under these environmental changes. For example, as mentioned earlier, traditional HRM practices, such as a seniority-based pay system, fixed-amount bonuses, and dual rank systems between white and blue collar workers, do not provide much motivation. Second, management realized that traditional systems are inadequate for human resource development. In traditional HRM systems, there is little effort to identify highly talented employees for special training and fast promotion from the early stage of their careers. Highly talented people usually remain as seemingly 'normal' people with little vision. Management wants to choose the right people for the right place as early as possible. In sum, traditional HRM systems have limitations in developing workers' skills, knowledge, and abilities on the one hand, and in motivating those workers to exert all their competencies on the other.

NHRM Practices
To overcome those problems many Korean companies, especially large ones, have introduced various NHRM practices in some or all of the HRM functions. How these practices are commonly introduced will be described by starting with the job grade system. Two problems related to the job grade system are the post-centred characteristic and dual approaches. To resolve these problems many firms made single job grade systems for both managerial/administrative employees and production employees. In addition, traditional post-centred job grade systems have been changed to skill-grade systems following the Japanese model. In addition, the number of grades is increasing. For example, in the case of Samsung, the job grades have increased to 11 steps, each divided into three groups: Junior, Senior, and Manager. They include five Junior grades (J1 to J5), three Senior grades (S1 to S3), and three Manager grades (M1 to M3). Another popular practice is the team system, to integrate departments and divisions both horizontally

and vertically so that firms can achieve tasks efficiently and quickly (Lim, 1995).

In recruitment and selection, many companies use internship programmes and 'blind' interviews. Promotion by selection, disregarding incremental promotion following job ladders, has also been adopted in some companies. In the past, employees would spend certain periods of time in the same job grade in order to be considered for promotion. Under NHRM systems, most firms disregard such time serving, rather they consider skills, knowledge, and abilities for upgrading in the skill grade systems. In the compensation area, skill-grade pay, individual or group-performance bonuses, monthly salary, rather than hourly wages, for production employees, and annual salary practices have all been introduced. The most prominent feature of the change is the emphasis on ability and performance *vis-a-vis* seniority.

To enhance fairness and objectivity, many firms have begun to use multi-rater performance evaluation and absolute appraisal, as opposed to traditional relative evaluation, practices. Furthermore, the purpose of performance appraisal is moving towards a more developmental role. To achieve this goal, firms have begun to give feedback to employees.

In 1995 a survey was conducted by the Korea Employers' Federation to find out the extent of the introduction of these new practices (Ahn, 1996). A total of 283 firms out of about 3,000 firms of over 50 employees were included in the final report. The sample consists of both manufacturing (71 per cent) and non-manufacturing (29 per cent) firms. The results are shown in Table 3.

On average, about 20 per cent introduced NHRM practices, ranging from 2.5 per cent for 'subordinate/peer performance evaluation' to 43.3 per cent for 'single rate basic pay'. In addition, about nine per cent were considering introducing NHRM practices. This implies that more firms will introduce NHRM practices in the future. To sum up, the comparison of traditional and current HRM practices is presented in Table 4. The upper part shows some general differences, and the lower part shows HRM practices.

Finally, to evaluate NHRM practices we employed the concept of 'fit' in three different aspects: internal, external, and social fit. Internal fit means the coordination or congruence among the various HRM practices (Schuler and Jackson, 1987; Wright and McMahan, 1992; Wright and Snell, 1991). Many Korean firms adopted some individual NHRM practices that seemed attractive to their firms without full consideration of other practices in the existing systems (Ahn, 1996). This may be partly due to the inherent contradictions of the concept of HRM (see Legge, 1989). Furthermore, the internal consistency of the 'soft' version of HRM, which puts the stress on the term 'human' (Storey, 1992), aims at generating quality, commitment and flexibility at the same time. Take the case of commitment, the basic assumption of pursuing commitment is that it can generate desirable outcomes for both individual and organization (Beer *et al.*, 1985). However,

TABLE 3
THE EXTENT OF THE INTRODUCTION OF NHRM PRACTICES

HRM Areas	NHRM Practices	Introduced (%)	Not Introduced (%)	Under Consideration (%)	Total Cases (N)
Recruitment and Selection	Internship	18.2	73.6	8.2	280
	First Fellowship Next Recruitment System	10.8	85.9	3.2	277
	Blind Interview	9.8	85.5	4.7	275
	Recruiting Specialists	30.2	57.9	11.9	271
	Promotion by Selection	33.8	56.5	9.7	278
	Equal Promotion Opportunity to Female	36.2	57.2	6.6	271
	Career Development Plan	18.8	65.3	15.9	277
Work Systems	Skill Grade Systems	7.9	92.1	0.0	278
	Separation of Post and Job Grade	40.9	57.0	2.2	279
	Single Job Grade System	23.5	71.3	5.1	272
Reward Systems	Skill-grade Pay	25.1	57.0	17.9	279
	Single Rate Basic Pay	43.3	51.3	5.4	277
	Individual Performance Bonus	14.7	72.8	12.9	277
	Group Performance Bonus	28.3	58.0	13.8	276
	Annual Salary	7.2	74.2	18.6	279
	Monthly Salary for Production Employees	27.9	69.3	2.9	280
Performance Evaluation (PE)	Multiple-Rater PE:				
	1) Subordinate Evaluation	2.5	92.1	5.4	278
	2) Peer Evaluation	2.5	90.1	7.4	278
	3) Self Evaluation	25.8	65.9	8.2	279
	MBO (Management by Objectives)	21.5	67.2	11.3	274
	Absolute Appraisal System	25.3	65.3	9.4	277
	Appraisal Feedback	11.4	78.6	10.0	281
	Behaviourally Anchored Ratings	10.9	81.2	8.0	276
Retirement	Honorary Retirement System	17.3	73.7	10.0	278
	Retirement Within Job-Grade Systems	10.0	84.9	5.0	279

Source: Adapted from various tables in Ahn (1996).

'[t]he possibility of multiple and perhaps competing commitments [to organization, career, job, union, work group, and family] creates a more complex set of issues' (Guest, 1987: 513). In sum, the introduction of NHRM policy in Korea seems to be *ad hoc* and piecemeal, which prevents firms from generating expected outcomes. In addition, 'internal fit' does not seem to be achieved easily due to some inherent conflicts.

A second concern is external fit, which means the linkage and congruence between HRM practices and organizational goals or business strategy (Lengnick-Hall and Lengnick-Hall, 1988; Tichy *et al.*, 1982;

TABLE 4
COMPARISON OF TRADITIONAL HRM AND NHRM SYSTEMS

Dimensions	Traditional HRM	NHRM*
Economic Development	• Rapid growth stage • Favourable export markets	• Stable growth stage • Global competition
Wage and Labour Supply	• Relatively low wages • Abundant labour supply	• Relatively high wages • Labour shortage
Competitive Advantages	• Low cost • Mass production	• Innovation/quality/speed • Customization
Some Characteristics in HRM	• Tradition focused • Undifferentiated equality • Job stability	• Breaking tradition • Differentiated equity • Flexibility
Important Factors in HRM	• Age, educational background, and seniority	• (Potential) Ability and performance
Human Resource Flow	• Recruitment of new graduates • Preferred generalists • Socialization and indoctrination	• Internship programmes • Blind interview • Recruiting specialists • More steps in the rank system • Promotion by selection
Reward System	• Seniority-based payment • Monthly salary • Complexity of pay structure • Traditional boss-subordinate form of appraisal (less rigorous)	• Ability- and performance-based payment (with keeping seniority system) • Skill-grade pay • Annual salary • Monthly salary for production employees • Multiple-rater performance measurement • Appraisal feedback
Work Organization	• Department or section basis • Broadly defined jobs and flexible job assignments • Job grade systems	• Team basis • Skill grade system • Separation of rank and position • Single job grade systems for all employees

* The HRM practices mentioned in this column have been introduced in Korean companies. This does not mean that every company uses those programmes. Rather, it means that these techniques, which have really been unfamiliar to most Korean companies, have been introduced or have been considered to be introduced by many companies at the same period for the first time.

Wright and McMahan, 1992). Of course, this argument is highly dependent upon the definition of HRM. Legge (1989: 29) argued that integrating HRM policy to business strategy contradicts pursuing the normative 'soft' version of HRM because while the former argues 'a contingent design of HRM policy', the latter argues 'an absolute approach to the design of employment policy'. The external factors that brought NHRM to Korea require the 'hard' version of HRM which emphasizes 'the idea of "resources", that is something to be used dispassionately and in a formally rational manner'

(Storey, 1992: 26). Therefore, the underlying assumption of NHRM policy in Korea is that the integration of HRM policy with business strategy is desirable. However, many firms introduce NHRM practices opportunistically rather than strategically simply because other firms adopt them without evaluating their own goals, strategies, or capabilities. Perhaps this is an example of poor 'benchmarking'. Some internal factors that created NHRM require the 'soft' side of HRM as well. How can Korean firms reconcile this contradiction? As labour costs have increased, firms now may need to gain competitive advantage based on quality, variety, and/or speed. This change of business strategy would resolve the contradiction to some extent, though 'a higher degree of homogeneity in business strategy among organizations' is suggested (Legge, 1989: 34).

Finally, social fit is another barrier to the adoption of NHRM practices. While many employees want NHRM practices, these practices are not congruent with Confucian seniority-based culture, which is deeply rooted in the sentiments of many Korean people. This is perhaps the opposite phenomenon that occurred when 'lean production' systems, which demand some characteristics of collectivism, were introduced in individualistic societies. Taira (1996: 152) pointed this trouble out:

> Organisation-specific behaviour of individuals is in part driven or constrained by broader ethical and cultural life forces. Lean production demands certain organisation-specific behaviour. Unless such behaviour is congruent with the culture and society at large, individuals will be torn between the demands of organisational commitment and those of effective citizenship in the larger community.

While Taira's argument is rather macro by distinguishing culture in the organization from that of whole society, some UK researchers focused on the shift of emphasis from collectivism to individualism within organizations (Legge, 1989; Sisson, 1994). Just as the UK's use of HRM has a potential conflict between emphasizing the virtues of individualism and pursuing collectivist characteristics such as team work and functional flexibility (Legge, 1989), Korean NHRM encounters similar conflicts that need to be resolved. Many Korean companies are finding it a challenge to pursue more individualistic and performance-oriented HRM policies and, at the same time, more collectivist features, because Korean society is rooted in seniority and collectivism. Keeping a balance between 'individualism' and 'collectivism', with a minimum of adverse effects is a critical task to be achieved in many Korean firms. In sum, a major concern is that there is a wide gap between the 'rhetoric' of NHRM and the 'reality' of new practices.

COMPARATIVE AND INTERNATIONAL ASPECTS

An Argument

As a late starter, the Korean HRM system needed to follow those of its forerunners. The two most influential countries were the US and Japan. For this reason, many Korean scholars have raised such questions as: 'is the Korean HRM system similar to the Japanese system or the American system?' Considering cultural similarity and physical proximity, the Korean HRM system may be similar to the Japanese system, but this is not the case, as explained above (Kang, 1989; Lie, 1990). However, it did not follow the American model either.

Bird and Beechler's (1994) and Schuler's (1989) studies used three types of HRM strategy: accumulation, utilization, and facilitation. An accumulation strategy is much like the typical Japanese HRM system, characterized by building up human resources in the organization for long periods of time to satisfy the needs of companies. A utilization strategy, pursuing short-term efficiency, matches human resources to specific task requirements with little training and development. Finally, a facilitation strategy is a mixed one. It emphasizes new skills and knowledge which are usually acquired by self-motivated personnel (Schuler and Jackson, 1987).

When we roughly match, at the expense of oversimplification, these strategies to the HRM systems of the US, Japan, and Korea, the following typology appears: accumulation can be paired with the Japanese system, utilization with the American system, and facilitation with the Korean system. Korean HRM systems are characterized by a mix of Japanese and American systems. Most Korean companies recruit new employees immediately after they graduate from school, as do Japanese companies. However, lifetime employment and internal labour markets take place in only a limited way compared to Japanese counterparts (Koch *et al.*, 1995; Lee and Yoo, 1987; Lie, 1990). Although the Korean HRM system is based on a seniority system, it is also different from the Japanese one. While Japanese firms make efforts to improve employees' skills and knowledge through their career paths in systematic ways, this is less likely to occur in Korean firms.

However, recent trends in HRM systems in these three countries show some convergence. Japan has already made some changes by mixing jobs and skills, resulting in skill grade systems. Firms in the US also experienced some transformation (Appelbaum and Batt, 1994; Kochan *et al.*, 1986). Pfeffer (1994) suggested 16 of the most effective practices for managing people: employment security, selectivity in recruiting, high wages, incentive pay, employee ownership, information sharing, participation and empowerment, teams and job redesign, training and skill development, cross-utilization and cross-training, symbolic egalitarianism, wage compression, promotion from within, long-term perspective, measurement of the practices, and overarching philosophy. Many US firms are undertaking major changes in work organization. Although these changes

vary among companies, a common thread is that 'firms gain a strategic
advantage from training front-line workers and utilizing their full
participation and that of their representatives at various levels of the
organization' (Appelbaum and Batt, 1994: 24). While these practices still
emphasize fairness and performance, as before, the most dramatic change is
perhaps in moving towards the internalization of workers, which was
traditionally part of the Japanese HRM system. On the other hand, the
Korean HRM system is moving towards a more ability-oriented system.
Furthermore, Korean firms have also begun to adopt Japanese skill grade
systems. It seems that these changes reflect that the HRM systems of the
three countries are at least partly converging.

Case Studies with Ten Dimensions

In most US organizations, the term HRM in place of personnel management
has been recently used to indicate 'the awareness of the critical importance
of the human element' and 'the extent to which the success of an
organization must be balanced with the ability of the individuals in it to
develop to their full potential' (Ferris *et al.*, 1995: 2). Although there are
several ways of conceptualizing HRM, the dominant approach has been to
define HRM by delineating its essential features which stand in contrast to
the more familiar characteristics of personnel management (Storey, 1992).
Following Storey's 27 points that identify differences between personnel
management and HRM, in Table 5 we use the ten dimensions focused on by
Warner and others in this volume. We use ticks, percentage marks and
crosses, following Duberley and Walley (1995), based on a survey and
interviews with HRM managers.

    Five companies were selected for the case studies: a large Korean firm
in electronics and communications with over 3,000 employees; a small
Korean firm in electronics with over 350 employees; a US firm in chemicals
with over 400 employees; a Japanese firm in electronics with over 450
employees; and a European firm in pharmaceuticals with over 400
employees. All these firms have trade unions except the US firm. The
results of the classification of the five firms are provided in Table 5.
Although each firm is not necessarily representative of its group, the results
from the case study are generally consistent with those of the survey data
collected by the author.

    From these results, several comparisons can be derived. First, there are
considerable differences between large and small Korean firms. While the
large firm scored positively on the HRM-type approach in eight dimensions,
the small firm is characterized by limited training, seniority-based pay
system, and collective bargaining contracts. The dimensions that have been
marked with 'ticks' for the small firm are perhaps due to the tradition of
Korean HRM practices rather than trends of transformation towards an
HRM-style approach. Second, the US firm showed a very similar pattern to
that of the large Korean firm. Both firms experienced some NHRM
development. Third, the European firm is somewhere between the large and

TABLE 5
PERSONNEL VERSUS HRM IN THE KOREAN SAMPLE

Dimensions	Korean Large Firm	Korean Small Firm	American Firm	Japanese Firm	European Firm
Rules	✓	%	✓	%	%
Behaviour Referent	✓	%	✓	%	✓
Managerial Task	✓	✓	✓	✓	✓
Key Managers	✓	%	✓	✓	✓
Selection	✓	%	✓	✓	✓
Pay System	%	x	%	x	%
Work Conditions	✓	✓	✓	✓	✓
Labor–Management	%	x	%	x	%
Job Design	✓	✓	%	✓	%
Training	✓	x	✓	x	%

Key:

✓ practice present

% practice present to some degree

x practice not present

Source: Adapted from Storey (1992).

small Korean firms. The HRM manager said that thus far many European firms in Korea allowed Korean HRM managers to take responsibility for all HRM-related activities. Since most foreign firms are small, there were few systematic approaches towards human resources.

Finally, the Japanese firm is similar to the large Korean firm in five dimensions: managerial task, key managers, selection, work conditions, and job design. However, unlike its parent company and the large Korean firm, the Japanese subsidiary has little in-house training. Similar to the small Korean firm, the Japanese firm has seniority-based pay and collective bargaining contracts. According to the survey data, Japanese subsidiaries have much higher scores for 'job security' practice than subsidiaries from other countries, partly due to strong unions and, according to HRM managers in Japanese firms, possible anti-foreign sentiments of Korean employees towards Japanese managers. Therefore, the Japanese firm adjusted its workforce level by controlling the recruitment of new employees. While the US firm and the European firm have Korean HRM managers, the Japanese firm has a HRM manager from Japan.

Results from the Field Data

To look into the issues empirically, data were also collected with a questionnaire survey and interviews during the summer of 1996. This is from 40 Korean-owned firms and 98 foreign firms operating in Korea (41 subsidiaries and joint ventures [JVs] of American firms, 42 European firms, and 15 Japanese firms). Among the 98 foreign firms, 64 (65.3 per cent) are wholly-owned foreign companies, while 34 (34.7 per cent) are JVs. The sample represents many industries, covering 20 different two-digit Standard Industrial Code categories. In the case of company size, while 85 per cent of Korean local firms have over 300 employees, about 70–80 per cent of foreign subsidiaries have less than 300 employees. While more than 40 per cent of the foreign companies have been running their business less than ten years in Korea, most Korean local firms are over ten years old. The majority of the sample firms have an independent HRM department, with the exception of the Japanese cases. As a whole, 75 (54.3 per cent) out of 138 firms are unionized; and 48 (49 per cent) out of 98 foreign invested firms have unions. Union densities range from five to 100 per cent.

From survey results and case studies, several points are worthy of mention. First, the three foreign groups studied had, in general, different HRM policies. American firms had relatively 'high integration' with those of their parent companies; Japanese subsidiaries had a 'partly integrated model'; and the majority of European firms in Korea had the so-called 'segregation model' by leaving all personnel issues to Korean managers. The survey data showed similar patterns. To the question regarding 'the degree of the parent company's influence on HRM issues in subsidiaries', while about 52 per cent of US subsidiaries in Korea responded positively, only 40 per cent and 28 per cent of Japanese and European firms, respectively, answered positively.

In the case of Japanese firms, although they choose expatriates as HRM managers, their policies are unlike those of typical Japanese HRM systems in that they show short-term perspectives with little in-house training. Increasing labour costs and tough environments for investment probably influenced Japanese firms to have a 'ready-to-leave' mind set. In the case of European firms, there are at least two reasons for a segregation model. First, they wanted to overcome national differences through local responsiveness. Second, perhaps more critically, they have gained their competitive advantage through advanced technologies and financial capabilities, leaving human resources as relatively less important. According to HRM managers, such firms are most likely to adapt parent company knowledge and capabilities to rationalize existing HRM practices.

The second point to be emphasized is that the differences are declining between wages and work conditions at Korean and foreign firms. Several HRM managers in foreign banks commented that the levels of wages and working conditions at some Korean local banks are even higher – a reversal of the pre-1990 situation. A carpeted office was once a symbol of foreign firms. Nowadays, there is little difference between foreign firms and 'excellent' Korean firms in terms of working conditions and wages, primarily due to the improvement in Korean firms.

Finally, some organizational characteristics have affected HRM practices. On average, while JVs had more 'personnel management' style practices, wholly-owned foreign subsidiaries marked more practices as

HRM-type approaches. Beyond national and ownership differences, there are also some organizational characteristics that affect HRM practices. As Kochan *et al.* (1986) argued, management values and strategies played a significant role in explaining HRM practices. That is, firms with high scores for management values on HRM and 'differentiation' *vis-a-vis* cost leadership (Porter 1985) had more HRM-type practices.

DISCUSSION

Korean firms are transforming their HRM configurations. Including both firms that have transformed their HRM configurations and those that are considering changing, about 30 per cent of the firms surveyed were affected by these trends either partly or heavily (Ahn, 1996). Two major issues relevant to the current trends are the 'seniority versus performance' dimension and the 'job security versus flexibility' dimension. In each dimension, the matter is not the 'kind' but the 'extent' to which firms adopt HRM configurations with each aspect. These two dimensions are critical issues which can shake the traditional seniority/stability systems.

Seniority versus Performance

What can be the next configuration of Korean HRM on this dimension? Four possible scenarios, borrowed from Guest's (1995) framework in analyzing the HRM, can be developed: traditional 'seniorityism' (high priority on seniority without ability/performance factor); seniority-based system with some performance factor; performance-based system with some seniority factor; and performance-based model.

(1) *Traditional 'seniorityism': high priority on seniority without ability/performance factor.* One possibility is to remain with the traditional seniority systems. This may be the case at least for small companies for some period of time. As Kim (1994) pointed out, there are still many 'X business groups' which need to emphasize a rational and Tayloristic approach in the early stages of industrialization. According to human resource managers interviewed by the author in small firms, they usually borrow HRM practices from large firms on an *ad hoc* basis. This anecdotal evidence implies that the future configurations of small firms are dependent upon the contemporary configuration of large firms. After experimenting with performance-based systems, it seems unlikely that a firm will go back to a traditional system.

(2) *Seniority-based system with some performance factor.* As shown in Table 3, many firms have already introduced promotion by selection beyond seniority and performance-based bonuses. However, most firms that introduced performance-based pay and promotions did not ignore seniority (Ahn, 1996). Most firms that introduced NHRM practices are at this stage now. This scenario will remain as a dominant configuration in the near

future. There are at best some mixed evaluations of the NHRM systems. Since, in the past, changes such as 'business process reengineering' have spread rapidly in Korean business groups, NHRM practices are also expected to spread rapidly. However, so far the degree of change in each company has been incremental.

(3) *Performance-based system with some seniority factor.* This model is a possible future scenario. Western foreign firms will especially be likely 'pioneers' of this movement because the trends have a good fit with the HRM practices of their parent firms. Survey results showed that Western foreign firms now have more performance-based promotion and pay systems than Korean local firms. For example, 63 per cent of Korean firms, 76 per cent of American firms, 81 per cent of European firms, and 13 per cent of Japanese firms agreed with the statement: 'Pay for non-managerial employees is tied to individual or group performance in our firm', and the means of each group are 3.68, 4.24, 4.31, and 2.07, respectively, on a six-point scale.

(4) *Ability/performance-based model: high priority on individualized performance without seniority.* This option is unlikely to happen, at least in the near future. To discuss this option, we may need to distinguish the proportion of companies that have introduced performance-based practices from the proportion of performance as a basis of HRM practices within a company. Even if we focus only on the firms that have adopted performance-based practices, we can not regard these HRM practices as based purely on performance. When we look into each firm, the application of the performance factor to promotion and payment is limited to certain groups of employees, such as managers and salespersons. In short, the ability/performance factor is only adopted by a limited number of firms, for a restricted number of employees within each company, and to a constrained degree. These present circumstances, and strong resisting force based on the Confucian tradition, imply that it is difficult for this scenario to be actualized in the near future.

Stability versus Flexibility

Two catalysts of the current changes towards numerical flexibility are the 'honorary' retirement system and the recent revision of labour laws. During the 1990s, about one third of the large Korean companies adopted the honorary retirement system (Ahn, 1996). This type of system has been called by various names in different firms, including: early (which perhaps represents its true meaning most accurately), optional, and voluntary retirement systems. Few regard honorary retirement as an 'honor', rather it is considered as a 'shame' by Korean social norms. Some possible problems include the unintentional loss of competent workers, increasing distrust and conflicts between labour and management, and the decrease in loyalty of the remaining employees (Kim, 1996). Another factor that catalyzed the move towards flexibility was the aforementioned revision of labour laws, which included a clause of 'discharge upon critical business crisis'.

The 'stability-flexibility' issue can likewise be categorized into four options: traditional 'long termism' (high priority on job security with little flexibility); stability-based system with some flexibility; flexibility-based system with some stability; and flexible model (high priority on flexibility with little job security).

Unfortunately, during the process of change, social cohesion and trust between labour and management do not seem to be maintained. The driving force for change seems very strong as does the resisting force, as we witnessed during the recent general strikes in Korea. In Japan, in contrast, companies pursued change with care in order to maintain the social cohesion and the implicit mutual contract. Furthermore, Taira and Levine (1985) highly attributed the successful transition of the Japanese industrial relations system in the 1970s and early 1980s to management. During the 1960s the rate of economic growth was, according to them, unusually high. At the same time, the rate of inflation was high and accelerating. Inflated expectations and a tight labour market brought an escalation of wage demands and disputes. When the situation was completely reversed, '[i]nstead of seizing upon that golden opportunity to avenge the 1960s, employers ... have wooed workers' participation in joint efforts to face and overcome ... "national crises" bred of external shocks' (ibid.: 297). Unlike their Japanese counterparts, Korean managers had no chance to show such behaviour towards labour. As a result, the level of trust is generally low, even after high wage increases during the last decade. Steers *et al.* (1989: 141) concisely described the situation that Korean management encountered:

> managers are under increasing pressure to view employees as part of the production process instead of as a member of the corporate family. As a result of these forces, increasing emphasis is being placed on ensuring efficiency and productivity on the shop floor.

In addition, since traditional Korean managerial style can be characterized as 'top-down decision making' (Kang, 1989; Lee and You, 1987; Steers *et al.*, 1989), it is hard to expect that Korean management would have consensus decision making with labour on such an important issue as flexibility. Since most Korean *chaebols* are also family-driven, family members are significant share holders and many are still actively involved in management (Kang, 1989; Steers *et al.*, 1989). All these factors would affect firms' tendencies to have a more 'short-term' perspective that emphasizes efficiency and flexibility.

At this point, the configurations of Korean HRM can be best characterized by a 'seniority-based system with some degree of performance factor' and a 'stability-based system with some flexibility'. What will be the future configurations? Since the recent changes occurred as a desperate measure due to both internal and external pressures, it is very unlikely to reverse. Rather, the trends are moving towards performance and flexibility, though the speed of the changes seems slow. However, these two factors may have conflicting goals. NHRM emphasizes performance and skill development with in-house training, which can be achieved through HRM systems based on an internal labour market with a long-term perspective (Choi, 1994). However, these goals can not be achieved with high numerical flexibility. Hence, one question remains: 'is it really feasible to pursue both ability/performance-based systems and numerical flexibility at the same time in Korean contexts?' This is a critical task that Korean firms need to resolve in the future.

CONCLUSION

The current transformation of the HRM system in Korea can be characterized by the following four features. First, under pressure from internal and external factors, traditional seniority-based HRM practices with job stability are slowly breaking down. Well-working traditional practices have been challenged to move towards a system emphasizing ability and performance on the one hand, and flexibility on the other. Traditional HRM configurations were near to 'long termism'. Today we see a trend towards 'shorter termism' configurations, but still on the long term side of the spectrum.

Second, there is a wide gap between management and labour. While there is now general agreement between management and labour regarding performance-based systems, there still remains a wide gap in the case of moving away from job stability towards flexibility (Bae *et al.*, 1997). Management groups have a sense of crisis from global competition, and they also realize that current employment systems are not productive enough with respect to current production costs. Employees also have a sense of crisis due to job insecurity. Management was challenged by labour after the Democratization Declaration of 1987 as trade unions became actively involved in collective bargaining and strikes (Park and Lee, 1995). Given Korea's family-driven structure, with family ownership and top-down decision making traditions, management is most likely to continue to pursue change without much consensus.

Third, human resource managers are slowly gaining more autonomy and significance. In foreign subsidiaries, such managers have a higher sense of professionalism. Several of these pointed out that they tend to stay in HRM positions when they move to other organizations. However, their counterparts in Korean local firms often take non-HRM positions in the same organization rather than take HRM jobs in other firms. In Korean local firms, human resource managers traditionally '[did] not see themselves as representing a distinct profession' (Koch *et al.*, 1995: 237). Recently, such managers have become actively involved in the process of introducing NHRM practices. In addition, the tradition of family-driven management is diminishing. In such circumstances, the move of management control from owners to professional managers is a natural course (Steers *et al.,* 1989).

Finally, Korean companies are still seeking the 'best' Korean-type HRM configurations. This is a hot debate that is not easily resolved. As a country of 'late industrialization', Korea did not have enough opportunity to adopt Tayloristic systems by emphasizing a 'human relations approach' which was the dominant school at the time of its economic development (Kim, 1994). Therefore, Korean workplaces did not experience the whole process that companies in developed countries did. Without having long-established institutional traditions, Korean firms have been challenged to transform to other configurations. In the past, the Korean economy had a chance to leapfrog as a good 'learner' (Amsden, 1989; Kim, 1997). That is, 'the unique blend of traditional culture and pragmatic ability to adapt to changing environmental conditions have made the difference for Korea' (Steers *et al.,* 1989: 130). Is it possible that the Korean economy can again 'wisely learn' HRM systems from economically advanced countries? With that wisdom acquired during the industrialization process, now is perhaps the right time for Korean firms to 'invent' Korean-type HRM configurations rather than 'imitating' again.

ACKNOWLEDGEMENTS

I am grateful for the valuable comments and editorial help of Chris Rowley and John Lawler on earlier versions of this paper.

NOTES

1. This is in high contrast with the situation in Hong Kong; see Ng Sek Hong and Poon in this volume.
2. Much of the following can be usefully compared and contrasted with elements of Japanese HRM outlined in Benson and Debroux in this volume.

REFERENCES

Ahn, Hee-tak (1996) *The Current Situations and Future Directions of New Personnel Management Systems in Korean Firms.* Seoul, Korea: The Korea Employers' Federation.
Amsden, Alice H. (1989) *Asia's Next Giant: South Korea and Late Industrialization.* Oxford: Oxford University Press.
Appelbaum, Eileen and Rosemary Batt (1994) *The New American Workplace: Transforming Work Systems in the United States.* Ithaca, NY: ILR Press.
Bae, Johngseok, Chris Rowley, Dong-Heon Kim, and John J. Lawler (1997) 'Korean Industrial Relations at the Crossroads: The Recent Labour Troubles', *Asia Pacific Business Review,* Vol.3, No.3, pp.148–60.
Bae, Kyu Han and William Form (1986) 'Payment Strategy in South Korea's Advanced Economic Sector', *American Sociological Review,* Vol.51, No.1, pp.120–31.
Beer, Michael, Bert Spector, Paul R. Lawrence, D. Quinn Mills and Richard E. Walton (1985) *Human Resource Management: A General Manager's Perspective.* New York, NY: Free Press.
Bird, Allan and Schon Beechler (1994) 'Links Between Business Strategy and Human Resource Management Strategy in U.S.-Based Japanese Subsidiaries: An Empirical Investigation', *Journal of International Business Studies,* Vol.26, No.1, pp.23–46.
Choi, Jong-Tae (1994) 'The Adoption Strategy of New Ability Development System'. Paper, Conference on New Human Resource Management in Korea, Korea Personnel and Human

Resource Management Association, pp.39–51.

Deyo, Frederic C. (1989) *Beneath the Miracle: Labor Subordination in the New Asian Industrialism*. Berkeley, CA: University of California Press.

Duberley, Joanne P. and Paul Walley (1995) 'Assessing the Adoption of HRM by Small and Medium-Sized Manufacturing Organizations', *International Journal of Human Resource Management*, Vol.6, No.4, pp.891–909.

Ferris, Gerald R., Darold T. Barnum, Sherman D. Rosen, Lawrence P. Holleran, and James H. Dulebohn (1995) 'Toward Business–University Partnerships in Human Resource Management: Integration of Science and Practice' in Gerald R. Ferris, Sherman D. Rosen, and Darold T. Barnum (eds) *Handbook of Human Resource Management*, Cambridge, MA: Blackwell, pp.1–13.

Greenberg, Jerald (1990) 'Organizational Justice: Yesterday, Today, and Tomorrow', *Journal of Management*, Vol.16, No.2, pp.399–432.

Guest, David E. (1987) 'Human Resource Management and Industrial Relations', *Journal of Management Studies*, Vol.24, No.5, pp.503–21.

Guest, David E. (1995) 'Human Resource Management, Trade Unions and Industrial Relations' in John Storey (ed.) *Human Resource Management: A Critical Text*. London and New York: Routledge, pp.110–41.

Hirst, Paul Q. and Grahame Thompson (1996) *Globalization in Question: The International Economy and the Possibilities of Governance*. Cambridge, MA: Blackwell.

Kang, T.W. (1989) *Is Korea the Next Japan?: Understanding the Structure, Strategy, and Tactics of America's Next Competitor*. New York: Free Press.

Kaufman, Bruce E. (1994) *The Economics of Labor Markets*. Fourth edition. Fort Worth: Dryden Press.

Kerr, Clark, John T. Dunlop, Frederick Harbison and Charles A. Myers (1960) *Industrialism and Industrial Man: The Problems of Labor and Management in Economic Growth*. Cambridge, MA: Harvard University Press.

Kihl, Young Whan (1987) 'East Asia's Rise to Economic Prominence: Aspects of the Political Economy of Development', *Asian Perspective*, Vol.11, No.2, pp.248–63.

Kim, Kang-sik (1996) 'The Honorary Retirement System in Korean Enterprises and Measures for Improvement', *KEF Compensation Quarterly*, Vol.4, No.2, pp.184–98.

Kim, Linsu (1980) 'Stages of Development of Industrial Technology in a Developing Country: A Model', *Research Policy*, Vol.9, No.3, pp.254–77.

Kim, Linsu (1997) *Imitation to Innovation: The Dynamics of Korea's Technological Learning*. Boston: Harvard Business School Press.

Kim, Soo Kon (1994) 'The Direction and Future Tasks in the Introduction of New Human Resource Management Systems in Korean Firms'. Paper, Conference on New Human Resource Management in Korea, Korea Personnel and Human Resource Management Association, pp.17–34.

Koch, Marianne, Sang H. Nam and Richard M. Steers (1995) 'Human Resource Management in South Korea' in Larry F. Moore and P. Devereaux Jennings (eds) *Human Resource Management on the Pacific Rim: Institutions, Practices and Attitudes*. Berlin: de Gruyter, pp.217–42.

Kochan, Thomas A., Harry C. Katz and Robert B. McKersie (1986) *The Transformation of American Industrial Relations*. New York: Basic Books.

Korea Ministry of Labour (1995) *Reports on the Korean Labour Market and Policies*. Seoul: Korea Ministry of Labour.

Lawler, John J. and Johngseok Bae (1996) 'Overt Employment Discrimination by Multinational Firms: Cultural and Economic Influences in a Developing Country'. *Unpublished manuscript*, University of Illinois at Urbana-Champaign.

Lee, Changwook and Hyunseok Kim (1991) *Gainsharing and Pay Systems*. Seoul: Korea Productivity Center.

Lee, Michael Byungnam (1993) 'Korea' in Miriam Rothman, Dennis R. Briscoe and Raoul C. D. Nacamulli (eds) *Industrial Relations around the World: Labor Relations for Multinational Companies*. Berlin: de Gruyter, pp.245–69.

Lee, Sang M. and Sangjin Yoo (1987) 'The K-Type Management: A Driving Force of Korean Prosperity', *Management International Review*, Vol.27, No.4, pp.68–77.

Legge, Karen (1989) 'Human Resource Management: A Critical Analysis' in John Storey (ed.) *New Perspectives on Human Resource Management*. London: Routledge, pp.19–40.

Leipziger, Danny M. (1988) 'Editor's Introduction: Korea's Transition to Maturity', *World Development*, Vol.16, No.1, pp.1–5.

Lengnick-Hall, Cynthia A. and Mark L. Lengnick-Hall (1988) 'Strategic Human Resources Management: A Review of the Literature and a Proposed Typology', *Academy of Management Review*, Vol.13, No.3, pp. 454–70.

Lie, John (1990) 'Is Korean Management Just Like Japanese Management?', *Management International Review*, Vol.30, No.2, pp.113–18.

Lie, John (1991) 'The Prospect for Economic Democracy in South Korea', *Economic and Industrial Democracy*, Vol.12, pp.501–13.

Lim, Chang-hee (1995) 'The Adoption and Desirable Directions for the Improvement of the Team System in Korean Enterprises', *KEF Compensation Quarterly*, Vol.3, No.2, pp.164–73.

Mitchell, Daniel J.B. (1982) 'The Ownership of Jobs: Variations on a Theme by Meyers' in Walter Fogel (ed.) *Job Equity and Other Studies in Industrial Relations: Essays in Honor of Frederic Meyers*. Los Angeles, CA: Institute of Industrial Relations, UCLA, pp.99–154.

Moore, Robert W. and Samir T. Ishak (1989) 'The Influence of Culture on Recruitment and Training: Hofstede's Cultural Consequences as Applied to the Asian Pacific and Korea' in Gerald R. Ferris and Kendrith M. Rowland (eds) *Research in Personnel and Human Resources Management* (Supplement Vol.1). Greenwich, CT: JAI Press, pp. 277–300.

Morishima, Motohiro (1995) 'The Japanese Human Resource Management System: A Learning Bureaucracy' in Larry F. Moore and P. Devereaux Jennings (eds) *Human Resource Management on the Pacific Rim: Institutions, Practices and Attitudes*. Berlin: de Gruyter, pp.119–50.

Papanek, Gustav Fritz (1988) 'The New Asian Capitalism: An Economic Portrait' in Peter L. Berger and Hsin-Huang Michael Hsiao (eds) *In Search of an East Asian Development Model*. New Brunswick, NJ: Transaction Books, pp.27–80.

Park, Se-Il (1993) 'The Role of the State in Industrial Relations: The Case of Korea', *Comparative Labor Law Journal*, Vol.14, No.3, pp.321–38.

Park, Young-bum and Michael B. Lee (1995) 'Economic Development, Globalization, and Practices in Industrial Relations and Human Resource Management in Korea' in Anil Verma Thomas A. Kochan and Russell D. Lansbury (eds) *Employment Relations in the Growing Asian Economies*. London and New York: Routledge, pp.27–61.

Pfeffer, Jeffrey (1994) *Competitive Advantage Through People*. Boston, MA: Harvard Business School Press.

Porter, Michael E. (1985) *Competitive Advantage: Creating and Sustaining Superior Performance*. New York, NY: Free Press.

Sharma, Basu (1985) *Aspects of Industrial Relations in ASEAN*. Singapore: Institute of Southeast Asian Studies.

Schuler, Randall S. (1989) 'Strategic Human Resource Management and Industrial Relations', *Human Relations*, Vol.42, No.2, pp.157–84.

Schuler, Randall S. and Susan E. Jackson (1987) 'Linking Competitive Strategies with Human Resource Management Practices', *The Academy of Management Executive*, Vol.1, No.3, pp.207–19.

Sisson, Keith (1994) 'Personnel Management: Paradigms, Practice and Prospects' in Keith Sisson (ed.) *Personnel Management: A Comprehensive Guide to Theory and Practice in Britain*. Oxford: Blackwell, pp.3–50.

Steers, Richard M., You Keun Shin and Gerardo R. Ungson (1989) *The Chaebol: Korea's New Industrial Might*. New York, NY: Harper and Row.

Storey, John (1992) *Developments in the Management of Human Resources: An Analytical Review*. Oxford: Blackwell.

Taira, Koji (1996) 'Rejoinder to Open Peer Commentaries on Koji Taira's "Compatibility of Human Resource Management, Industrial Relations, and Engineering Under Mass Production and Lean Production"', *Applied Psychology: An International Review*, Vol.45, No.2, pp.146–52.

Taira, Koji and Solomon B. Levine (1985) 'Japan's Industrial Relations: A Social Compact Emerges' in Hervey Juris, Mark E. Thompson, and Wilbur Daniels (eds) *Industrial Relations in a Decade of Economic Change*. Madison, WI: Industrial Relations Research Association, pp.247–300.

Tichy, Noel M., Charles J. Fombrun and Mary Anne Devanna (1982) 'Strategic Human Resource Management', *Sloan Management Review*, Vol.23, No.2, pp.47–61.

US Department of Labor (1995) *Foreign Labor Trends: Korea*. Washington D.C.: Bureau of International Labor Affairs, US Department of Labor.

Von Glinow, Mary Ann and Byung Jae Chung (1989) 'Comparative Human Resource

Management Practices in the United States, Japan, Korea, and the People's Republic of China' in Gerald R. Ferris and Kendrith M. Rowland (eds) *Research in Personnel and Human Resources Management* (Supplement Vol.1), Greenwich, CT: JAI Press, pp.153–71.

Wall Street Journal, 30 December 1992, p.1.

Wilkinson, Barry (1994) *Labour and Industry in the Asia-Pacific: Lessons from the Newly-Industrialized Countries*. Berlin: de Gruyter.

Wright, Patrick M. and Gary C. McMahan (1992) 'Theoretical Perspectives for Strategic Human Resource Management', *Journal of Management*, Vol.18, No.2, pp.295–320.

Wright, Patrick M. and Scott A. Snell (1991) 'Toward an Integrative View of Strategic Human Resource Management', *Human Resource Management Review*, Vol.1, No.3, pp.203–25.

World Development (1988) 'Korea: Transition to Maturity', Vol.16, No.1.

Yang, Byung-Moo and Hee-tak Ahn (1992) *The Theory and Practice of Skill Grade Systems*. Seoul: KEF Institute of Labour Economics.

Yang, Byung-Moo, Hee-tak Ahn, Jae-Won Kim, and Joon-Sung Park, (1994) *Pay Systems in Korean Firms*. Seoul: Korea Employers' Federation.

Converging and Diverging Trends in HRM: The Philippine 'Halo-Halo' Approach

MARAGTAS S. V. AMANTE

In the Philippines, a diversity of historical, institutional, foreign and local influences provides the background for the entry of human resource management (HRM) strategies – summarized as the pragmatic ('best approach') model developed in the West. These trends tend to diverge from the traditional prototype of rigid labour standards and adversarial labour relations, which was an American post-colonial legacy. At the same time, the efforts by both employers and government policy makers to emphasize human resource development (HRD) tend to converge. At the firm level one venue for the convergence towards HRM strategies takes place in various labour–management co-operation schemes. Labor–Management Councils (LMCs) provide chances to accomodate local cultural values and sensitivities. These practices could be called the Philippine *meztizo* or *halo-halo* (blended or mixed) approach, which is most appropriate in the Philippine workplace but which may not work in other foreign contexts.

Through case studies this contribution analyzes trends in the convergence and divergence of employment practices in the Philippine workplace. The first section examines the current environment for HRM practices. The second section presents the most important elements of these work practices, through such aspects as compensation, hiring and recruitment, employment relations, and the like, concluding that benchmark practices in HRM bring about convergence, but in the final analysis the difference is made by innovations in entrenched institutional and local work practices.

THE ENVIRONMENT FOR HRM

The Philippine government reported that Gross National Product (GNP) grew by 6.8 per cent in 1996, while Gross Domestic Product (GDP) grew at 5.5 per cent (*Philippine Daily Inquirer,* 1997). These figures gave the Philippines 'Tiger' status among the Asian newly industrializing countries (NICs). At the same time, political leaders acknowledge that the effective utilization of human resources (HRs) is a strategic element in the sustainability of Philippine economic growth. The Philippine GNP *per capita* is now US$ 1,130; with GDP larger at $2,935 *per capita*, due mainly to the remittances from the large number of overseas Filipino workers (*Asia Week Magazine,* 1997). This is a major improvement considering that

Maragtas S.V. Amante, University of the Philippines System

between 1980 and 1985 average Philippine *per capita* GNP was $520 (*World Development Report*, 1995).

The Philippines had a population of 69.3 million in 1996, with a growth rate of 2.3 per cent. In 1996, the labour force was 29.7 million: 46 per cent in agriculture; 15 per cent in industry; and 37 per cent in services (*Yearbook of Labor Statistics*, 1995). The unemployment rate decreased to 7.5 per cent in 1996, from 9.8 per cent in 1995, and 11 per cent in 1985. Nearly one million Filipinos work abroad as professionals, sailors, domestic helpers or factory workers, mostly in the Middle East. They remitted more than $7 billion in 1996, which is, interestingly, more than what the export sector contributed to the balance of payments.

Alongside comparable Asian countries, the HR advantages in the Philippines are usually cited as: a relatively large percentage of the population with higher education (93 per cent literacy rate); a surplus of flexible, English-speaking skilled workers, and relatively low wage rates. For instance, the current minimum wage in the national capital region (Metro Manila) in 1996 is US$193 a month, or US$6.35 daily. However, there has been some increased emphasis on moving towards a more competitive and globalized economy. Some of the by-products of this are: employment restructuring (analyzed by Ofreneo, 1993a); changes in labour laws and policies; and more diversity in work practices. Other results include the further weakening of trade unions (Ofreneo, 1993b), with less than ten per cent unionization and less emphasis on collective bargaining in the conduct of labour relations.

Although distinct in terms of both approach and content there is a tendency in the Philippines to view industrial relations (IR) and HRM as two sides of the same coin. There are hints, however, that HRM is the primary means for work innovation. Philippine IR is a post-colonial legacy as both the government bureaucracy and the major utility and manufacturing firms were established when still a US colony. Furthermore, from the 1950s US multinational enterprises (MNEs) established the main patterns for recruitment, training, job design, pay systems, as well as labour relations. Tripartism is the declared state policy. Most government agencies dealing with wages and disputes settlement, including the social security agencies, are nominally tripartite. The President appoints representatives from trade unions, employers, and government. However, the participation of constituencies in the appointment process and accountability (especially for union leaders) are undefined, and hence, mainly political.

Labour relations revolves around a Labor Code enacted by President Marcos through martial rule in the mid-1970s. Amended several times since, the code regulates hiring, employment, minimum wages, work standards, termination, labour relations, and even training. To support their decisions on compensation, employee discipline and labour disputes, Filipino personnel managers usually refer to existing labour laws. As enterprises attempt to be competitive with regard to both pay and employment, managers must deal with work rules and jurisprudence which

FIGURE 1
STRATEGIC CHOICES IN PHILIPPINE HRM

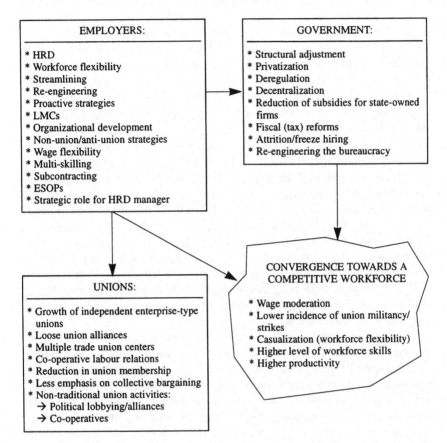

are designed to protect minimum work standards, but which dampen innovative (flexible) practices. Filipino HR managers often express the need to provide training to 're-tool' the workforce. The desired goals are the acquisition of multi-skilled employees, and a flexible work and pay structure. Yet, the Basic Law (the 1987 Philippine Constitution), mandates the government to safeguard workers' rights to self-organization, concerted activities such as the right to strike, job security, a living wage, and participation in decision making.

The increasing use of the HRM approach comes along with the state's policy of encouraging non-adversarial, voluntary modes to labour dispute settlement – conciliation, mediation and arbitration. A new specific government agency, the National Conciliation and Mediation Board (NCMB), organized in 1989, is tasked to promote such disputes settlement and LMCs. These LMCs serve both as a mechanism, and a venue, for joint confidence-building between employers and employees for better work conditions, health and safety, productivity, and the like. Government officials often explain the continuous decline in strikes and work stoppages as due to the promotion of mediation, conciliation and voluntary arbitration in unionized establishments. For example, in his Labor Day speech on 1 May 1997 President Ramos noted the declining frequency of strikes and concerted action. An interpretation of this decreased militancy emphasizes the argument that 'stakeholders' in the work relationship have made their strategic choices, instead of the usual resort to adversarial modes of dispute settlement. Figure 1 is a summary of the current strategic choices by stakeholders in Philippine HRM.

Since the mid-1980s privatization of state enterprises has turned around the government's budget deficit. Along with structural adjustment, positive fiscal balances provided signals to foreign investors of the government's commitment to a competitive business environment. The reduction in the size of the state bureaucracy, from 1.2 million employees to around 900,000, allowed government pay levels to gradually rise to competitive levels. Government tightly controlled the hiring of new employees, and salaries were pegged to standardized rates. Government policy is not to intervene in the determination of minimum wage rates. An amendment of the Labor Code in 1989 relegated this function to Regional Tripartite Wage and Productivity Boards, composed of representatives from unions, employers and government.

Among employers, various forms of intervention through HRM strategies include 'rightsizing' the workforce, which calls for flexibility. This requires a flatter job structure and the use of subcontractors, casuals, temporary employees, part-timers, and so on (Ofreneo, 1993a; Soriano, 1993). However, protests concerning these labour cost-saving measures have not spread widely, partly due to a reserve army of young unemployed workers fresh from school. Also, managers sought to 'reorient' their workforce through seminars on 'positive work values', especially of the Japanese variety, such as 5-S (*seiri, seiton, seiso, seiketsu, shitsuke*), *kaizen*, *kairyo*, Total Quality Management (TQM), zero-defect, and the like (Amante *et al.*, 1992; Amante, 1994, 1995; Aganon, 1994). Large firms also initiated benefits such as employee stock ownership plans (ESOPs), but with limited impact upon the transformation of internal IR.

Historically, unions and collective bargaining have never been a dominant feature (as shown by Ofreneo, 1993a). Furthermore, new enterprises established by foreign investors usually hire managers who advise them on how to prevent unionization. In unionized establishments, 'pro-active strategies' dampened militancy, as managers resolve disputes and misunderstandings through such schemes as LMCs and more open communication. HR strategies effectively wrestled away the initiative from union leaders. Previously, unionists acted as the 'voice' of the workforce by representing their grievances. Plant-level and federation-level union leaders are now threatened with the withering away of their traditional focus, especially on wages and job security. Despite this, however, most large enterprises are still unionized, and national labour leaders continue to articulate key concerns on pay and employment.

Subcontracting and numerically flexible employment (casual, temporary workers) further reduced the normal base for unionizing workers. The strategic choice for union leaders is to venture into new forms of organizing, while attempting the usual collective bargaining. New organizational thrusts may include housing and credit co-operatives, community or area political alliances where workers and their families live, and the like. Most large enterprises (such as the case studies) have independent 'enterprise unions' with loose alliances with a variety of national union federations. The continuing reduction in union membership, however, means a further erosion of trade unionism. This threatens workers' rights, as well as the viability of tripartism. With this trend, Filipinos will eventually have an IR structure where government regulators and employers dominate the strategic choices for the other role players.

Many HRD strategies (that is, skills formation) are the lynchpin around which key practices at the workplace converge. These strategies are initiated mostly by employers through managers who were either educated and trained abroad, or experienced in the latest pro-active techniques. In the past local managers were preoccupied with local cultural elements which motivated the futile search for the 'Asian way' of working. The canon of global competition, however, emerged to justify the use of 'best practices'. In the Philippines, 'best practice' refers mainly to the combination of Western and Japanese-style experiences blended with local cultural values and sensibilities. To a limited extent, government leaders involved in education, economic policy and labour regulation, also advocate HRD.

In the past, labour standards, legislation, rules and institutions provided the set-up for the adversarial relationship between unions and employers (Ofreneo, 1995). Since the 1980s, however, the source of tensions shifted to strategies over interventions designed to promote HR and organizational development. Yet, due precisely to these HR strategies, the usual adversarial approach is giving way to co-operative employment relations – LMCs, total quality commitment (TQC), and the like.

HRM IN SEVEN COMPANIES

The following section presents case studies of seven large companies in the Philippines. The focus is upon the convergence and divergence of practices in the workplace. The key point is that benchmark practices in HRD bring about convergence, but innovations with entrenched local work practices spell the difference on the bottom line. The firms are industry leaders: three are in manufacturing, while the rest are in services such as telecommunications, energy distribution, airlines, and banking (see Table 1 for details), and are listed in the top 12 corporations (except RAMCAR, which ranked 205 in 1995), influencing other firms in their HRM practices. However, these firms have been influenced themselves by environmental changes. For

TABLE 1
COMPANY CHARACTERISTICS

Company	Years of operation	Industry and characteristics	1995 Revenues ($)*
SMC	100+	Food/beverage manufacturing 13% are international sales	3.0 billion
MERALCO	94	Energy distribution Pure domestic monopoly	1.75 billion
CALTEX	75	Oil/gas refining and domestic distribution	936 million
PAL	50	Airline (national flag carrier); privatized but still 33% state-owned	1.06 billion
PLDT	67	Telecommunications 100% private ownership	222 million
PNB	79	State-owned bank Being privatized	121 million **
RAMCAR	75	Car batteries 100% private ownership 40% for export	44 million

Key:
SMC: San Miguel Corporation
MERALCO: Manila Electric Company
CALTEX: Caltex Philippines
PAL: Philippine Airlines
PLDT: Philippine Long Distance Telephone Company
PNB: Philippine National Bank
RAMCAR: Ramcar, Incorporated

* Revenues based on US$1 = Pesos 25 in 1995.
** PNB for 1994.

Source: The following tables are based on interviews with managers and published company reports.

example, the deregulation of the oil industry, operation of powerful foreign banks, and entry into the World Trade Organization meant stiff competition in several sectors, such as with battery brands from other neighbouring Asian countries.

The author visited these firms in the first half of 1996, and interviewed their personnel managers and union leaders. Company reports and publications were also examined. All the firms are located within, or in the outskirts of, Metro Manila, and all have been in operation for more than 50 years (many were established during the late colonial period). Entrenched work practices in most include: job positions with a rigid description of duties and responsibilities; dominance of supervisors in the work process (referred to as 'bos' or 'cabo'); and, in unionized enterprises, collective bargaining focusing on pay increases, benefits and job security. Also, the work of personnel managers stresses administrative aspects, minimization of payroll costs, keeping records or files, adherence to work rules, discipline, and the like. These practices differ significantly from mainstream American delineation of the HRM function (see, for example, Tracey, 1994), which stresses the effective management, direction and utilization of people.

MERALCO and PAL were state-owned enterprises. MERALCO was returned to its private owners in 1986 after the fall of the Marcos regime. PAL's privatization started in 1992 (after more than four decades of state control), but the government still retains 33 per cent ownership. PNB is in the process of privatization. All firms registered a positive income at the time of the study, reflecting Philippine economic recovery and growth. PAL, however, had reported severe income losses in 1993 and 1994, due in part to acquisition of new aircraft for long haul flights to keep up with international competition.

There are distinct departments and managers for IR and HRM – the best evidence of divergence, one might argue. What managers do, and what actually happens in the workplace in relation to the worker and the work environment, however, is another issue altogether. In the past, most companies had lawyers as managers for IR. This requirement has changed somewhat, although a legal background is still considered advantageous. Collective bargaining and strikes are managed by the firm's legal counsel or law firm. In SMC, line managers had leading roles in the bargaining panels, with lawyers advising them on legal implications. Strikes and other labour disputes in these firms are almost always reported in the news media. Thus, firms require that IR managers and their staff have strong media connections. In contrast, the HR managers focus attention upon training and skills formation. For instance, an advertisement by an executive 'head hunter' required the HR manager to: 'institutionalize and computerize personnel systems, reinforce innovative programmes for optimizing productivity, enhance the quality of work life and strengthen partnerships with the local communities'. Most important, it stated that: 'the applicant must be attuned to current technologies in culture building, total quality management, and productivity'. In SMC the HR manager is responsible for the whole spectrum of work related matters, including IR, skills training, compensation, and culture management.

The size of the workforce ranges from 632 in RAMCAR to 28,544 in SMC (see Table 2). In the case studies, between 60 and 85 per cent of employees are union members. Non-union members include those in the flexible workforce (temporary or casual employees), 'confidential' employees like the drivers and clerical staff of managers and executives, security personnel, payroll and finance staff, and so on. Almost all of the 31 subsidiaries of SMC are unionized, and collective bargaining negotiations take place in every season of the year. The same is true for RAMCAR, which has 14 subsidiaries engaged in separate activities such as raw

TABLE 2
WORKFORCE CHARACTERISTICS

Company	Workforce size	Average pay *($)**	Unionization (%)
SMC	28,544	520	66
MERALCO	7,997	680	70
CALTEX	940	640	81
PAL	14,000	415	85
PLDT	19,048	400	80
PNB	8,073	320	60
RAMCAR	632	248	75

* Does not include the non-monetary benefits, allowances, and bonuses.
** Based on US$1=Peso 25 in 1996.

material processing, production, marketing and the distribution. The workforce in only two of its manufacturing plants are unionized. In MERALCO, the supervisory employees have a separate union.

Three key aspects in comparing work practices were selected: skills development, compensation, and the determination of work rules. These aspects summarize what are often considered (see Storey, 1992) as critical dimensions in comparing IR with HRM. These dimensions, however, are constrained by the prevailing technical and economic environment.

COMPARING SELECTED HRM PRACTICES

Skills Development

Rank and file employees for entry level positions are usually hired with a minimum age requirement – between 20 and 30 years of age. There are mixed demands between fresh graduates and those with relevant work experience (usually between three and five years). Technical and professional jobs usually require work experience in other companies. Firms specify the male gender for certain jobs which require physical strength, and females for secretarial/clerical jobs. Jobs which require 'frontline' services with customers (accounts staff, clerks), even specify a 'pleasing personality'.

Firms engaged intensively in skills development to 're-tool' their workforce for competition. The strategy emphasized in-house training. Personnel departments have training officers assigned to identify and set-up internal training programmes. In all the case studies, trainers are managers

TABLE 3
SKILLS DEVELOPMENT PRACTICES

SMC	• Management Training Center programmes on basic supervision, marketing, finance and manufacturing management; international business and management of change; values and process management.
MERALCO	• Post-recruitment education programme: 'general-, job-based-, management, and process based-training'. • Adoption of TQM as a corporate philosophy. • Seminars on *kaizen*, *kairyo*, 5-S, etc.
CALTEX	• Multi-tasking and job enlargement programmes. • Subcontracting and work flexibility.
PAL	• Five TPCs as corporate goals: 'totally pleased customers'; 'time-management, productivity and cost-effectiveness'; 'teamwork, participation and communication'; 'total passenger care'; total personal commitment. • Allotment of $60 million for a world class training centre for pilots, cabin crew and staff.
PLDT	• Employee Development Division undertakes commercial training services, professional values education, management training, technical training, productivity, and teambuilding.
PNB	• Institute of Banking handles training for junior executives and management.
RAMCAR	• Employee training programmes for total quality and productivity; customer satisfaction; and process improvement. New employees required to complete TQC training.

and supervisors from other divisions within the firm. Company 'vision' or 'mission' statements uniformly echo a 'commitment to advance technological and human resources by investing in leading edge technology and adopting the best practices whenever possible'. These are costly statements – companies allocated large budgets for their training programmes at the expense of increases in pay and employment. The trade-off against pay increases triggered strikes in MERALCO, PAL, and PLDT.

Table 3 outlines the important features in skills development. They have a common emphasis on training to enhance competitiveness. The usual themes of the training programmes include: TQC, productivity, positive work values and attitudes, customer service, and the like. Most firms consider training a management prerogative. In RAMCAR the collective bargaining agreement (CBA) provides that 'it is management's exclusive right' to train employees and improve their ability. SMC created a training centre in 1989 to 'upgrade knowledge and skills of managers and employees'. The 2,700 retrenched employees in 1992 were provided with a financial package which included training for new skills and placement. The training centre has since focused upon management, leadership skills and functional development. SMC has also implemented a strategy to transform all employees from 'managed shopfloor operators' to 'self-directed, quality-conscious teams'. Training aims to 'foster a climate where teams of employees, fewer but more skilled, have greater ownership and responsibility for the desired results'. In addition to technical training, employees are provided with 'leadership and process management skills to enable the teams to have greater capability, ownership and responsibility for the desired results'. The training centre has programmes on basic supervision, marketing, finance and manufacturing management. There are also seminars on international business and the management of change. The operating divisions invest in technical training to acquire and enhance core competencies. There are also seminars on values, and process management to strengthen the total quality orientation of employees.

Firms also emphasized programmes which created positive work values. Seminars on Japanese-style work practices are especially popular – *kaizen* (continuous improvement), TQC, 5-S, informal preliminary discussions (*nemawashii*), informal consultation (*dango*), documented approval (*ringi*), and the like (see Sano, 1995). The Japanese concept of 5-S is introduced to Filipinos to roughly mean 'sort, systematize, sanitize, standardize housekeeping routines, and self-discipline'. The fashionable introduction of Japanese-style practices without any consideration of the social value systems behind them may, however, limit their effectiveness. Nevertheless, there are elements in Filipino work values which approximate these Japanese approaches.

In MERALCO, company philosophy states that employees will be provided 'with opportunities for professional growth and advancement on the basis of performance, integrity and loyalty to the company'. This meant a significant outlay in their training budget. In PAL, the CBA provides that 'the company shall adopt and maintain training programmes...to develop the skills of employees in order to meet requirements...and for job enrichment'. As early as 1989 RAMCAR prioritized training of employees in TQC, and productivity improvement. CALTEX introduced flexible work practices such as multi-skilling, multi-tasking, and job subcontracting. Extra job shifts with new technology required operators to perform additional tasks, to which the union protested by staging a strike. In the firm's view, the extra job shifts upgraded employee skills and versatility. In PLDT, PAL and PNB, an entire section in the HRD division is assigned to promote 'Productivity and Teambuilding'. The division even handles career development, aside from technical training. In PNB, current training emphasizes: decision making, junior executive development, leadership skills, social graces, personality development, foreign languages, empowerment of the sales force, and so on. After training, PNB requires two to four years of service from employees. The recent reorganization due to privatization resulted in a great number of 'voluntary retirees'; which also created a problem of a skills gap between newly promoted officers vacated by the retirees, and newly hired employees who have more banking skills since they were recruited from other banks. In PAL, the introduction of new technology meant changes in job descriptions. The union-management agreement provides that when new equipment is put into service, affected employees, if qualified in accordance with company rules and regulations, are given priority to familiarize themselves with it within a reasonable period of time. During such familiarization (or 'on the job training'), the job classification and rate of pay of the affected employee stays the same. When the manager certifies that the employee has acquired the skills related to the new equipment, the job and pay classification is upgraded. In case of new requirements for professional and technical licenses related to the new technology, the PAL agreement provides further that affected employees have the opportunity to comply within one year.

Compensation Practices

The average basic pay in these firms is definitely higher than the regional minimum monthly rate. Allowances, bonuses and other non-monetary benefits are in the vicinity of 50–100 per cent of basic pay in these companies. Compensation issues are summarized in Table 4. Although job based compensation is the norm, extra factors, based on job evaluation, influence pay rates. The usual practice is to award job points mainly for qualifications, skills, experience, responsibility, authority and work hazards. Extra factors include position in the job hierarchy, which is determined more by the power context and personal connections in the organization. Therefore, while managers conduct performance appraisals of their

TABLE 4
COMPENSATION ISSUES

SMC	Leads the pay rates in industries where it has operations. Emphasis is on performance based pay; ESOP instituted in 1988.
MERALCO	Pay increases arbitrated by the labour ministry due to deadlock with the union; management protested pay awards in Supreme Court. ESOP started in 1987.
CALTEX	Union protested the job evaluation plan; pay adjustments due to multi-skilling and multi-tasking deemed inadequate by the union.
PAL	Key issue in 1996 strike was the deadlock over pay increases, due to acquisition of new planes. Strong union demands for pay changes.
PLDT	16% of income for pay increases, while union demands 50% – the strike issue in 1996. ESOP a benefit plan.
PNB	Privatization aligns pay with higher rates in private banks; ESOP.
RAMCAR	Started productivity based pay in 1988, which is outside scope of agreement with union.

subordinates as a basis for promotion and merit pay, personal relations and even kinship eventually determine actual pay.

Since the firms are unionized, CBAs determine increases in pay. Wage increases are provided annually, lasting three to five years. The determination of wages is influenced mostly by changes in the cost of living due to consumer price increases. Decisions by firms to increase pay are also influenced by regional minimum wage rates. Wage increases under CBAs may be credited as compliance with the increases in such minimum rates. Usually, increases in minimum wage rates are integrated or credited with existing rates. Wage distortion due to mandated wage increases is a very common problem for compensation officers. The distortion often occurs when the new mandated wage rates – applicable mostly for the below minimum pay brackets in entry job positions, usually probationary or temporary employees – overtake pay rates of regular employees. Compensation practices reflect the general thrust to hold down payroll costs. However, the Constitution provides workers will be guaranteed their 'living wage'. At the same time, state policy encourages productivity-based pay schemes, but on which very few firms and unions are able to agree. Indeed, disputes over pay are the main reason behind strikes and other concerted action by unions in PAL and PLDT.

Firms continue to develop appropriate principles in fixing pay. In MERALCO, company philosophy reflects the personalistic style of its owners: employees are provided with 'just and reasonable compensation and benefits and attend to their personal well being.' It instituted a salary structure through job evaluation, which provided pay rates based on equivalent position grades. In 1996, both management and the union arrived at a new CBA. At the time of writing, the pay increases ordered by the Department of Labor and Employment in their arbitration decision is being contested and delayed in the Supreme Court by management.

Another pay practice concerns ESOPs, found in SMC, MERALCO and PLDT. Recent research (Sedano *et al.*, 1995; Aganon, 1997) on the Philippines shows that employee commitment increased in companies with ESOPs, even though workers view these simply as another benefit plan. However, while US-based research also indicates 'benefits' from ESOPs, this is a problematic area and research elsewhere is equivocal. RAMCAR started a productivity based pay plan in 1988, but constraints in plant and equipment dampened employee enthusiasm. Many RAMCAR workers opted for a day-off after satisfying target production quotas rather than devote more hours to work. The productivity plan is outside the scope of the CBA.

Determination of Work Rules

The determination of work rules through labour relations is summarized in Table 5. Under labour law, workers have the right to engage in concerted activities (strikes, pickets) for the purposes of collective bargaining. The protection of the right to strike and picket, and that of employers to lock out workers, has an established jurisprudence with clear procedures and

TABLE 5
KEY ISSUES IN COLLECTIVE BARGAINING

SMC	Union security and recognition; regular pay increases; job subcontracting; employee welfare, i.e. expanded medical and housing benefits.
MERALCO	Deadlock over amount and schedule of pay increases; coverage of benefits; exclusion of probationary employees; ESOP; dental and optical loans; financial assistance for childbirth; educational assistance; seniority/loyalty bonuses expanded retirement benefits.
CALTEX	Creation of additional shifts; work overloading; more overtime; hiring of more contractuals; limited pay increases and lesser benefits.
PAL	Pay increases based upon industry rates; modified hiring scheme for additional crew for long-haul flights for re-fleeting programme; reinstatement of strike leaders.
PLDT	Union security through automatic membership; union recognition despite inter-factional conflict; pay increases based upon inflation; expanded benefits for fieldwork; job evaluation to update 962 job positions.
PNB	Pay increases based on private sector industry rates; ESOP offering; representation in management reorganization and privatization committees; clearer dispute settlement procedures; higher premium pay for additional work hours.
RAMCAR	Deadlock in 1995 negotiations over proposed pay adjustments and benefits, but eventually resolved; functioning LMC scheme.

regulations.

Since the case studies are all unionized, collective bargaining determines many of their work rules. The trend, however, shows that many HRM strategies are excluded from collective bargaining. Analysis of most of the agreements regarding skills formation (that is, training) reveals that these are areas for management prerogative in most firms. At the same time, management recognition of the winning union faction's set of officers as a partner in the negotiations is also a frequent source of tension, as at SMC, PLDT and MERALCO.

Actual practices and procedures in resolving disputes reflect the American adversarial pattern. Once recognized, the union negotiations panel requests a meeting with management. Lawyers advise both panels in the timing and wording of offers for pay increases and benefits. It is almost always the case that lawyers eventually lead the discussions, especially in court, with union and management representatives reduced to the sidelines. Since wide gaps exist between union demands and management counter-offers, especially with respect to pay increases, deadlock almost always occurs. This results in the filing a strike notice. The Labor Secretary is eventually asked to arbitrate when both conciliation and mediation efforts fail, and is required to act upon the dispute with dispatch, or submit it to the National Labor Relations Commission (NLRC), a quasi-court with representatives from labour and management, for compulsory arbitration. The decision by the Labor Secretary or the NLRC is often eventually questioned by management in the highest court. These proceedings delay resolution (to the advantage of the lawyers), and the usual resort to adversarial, legalistic labour relations contributes to tensions.

In 1995–96 strikes attracted attention from the national media in PLDT, PAL and CALTEX. In MERALCO, PNB and SMC, union strike notices hastened the resolution of pay and employment issues. Only RAMCAR observed more stability and harmonious IR, except for a brief deadlock in the negotiations when both union and management asked the Labor Secretary to arbitrate. The firms facing the most pressure from competitiveness arising from deregulation policies, PLDT, PAL and PNB, have higher tension levels in employment relations. In contrast, firms which early on established coping mechanisms (LMCs) with high levels of trust, such as RAMCAR and SMC, enjoy relatively stable labour relations. In PAL, the company modified its hiring scheme for additional crew for long-haul international flights as well as for its programme to acquire new aircraft. Eventually, the pilots union supported this programme, but there was still resistance from ground staff union and cabin crew. Like MERALCO, PAL management took the issue of pay increases to the Supreme Court, effectively delaying resolution of the issue and contributing to continuing tension and mistrust.

Collective bargaining negotiations start first with the issue of union recognition, as well as the workforce to be covered. Then, substantial issues are discussed, focusing upon the schedule of pay increases, benefits and subsidies (for uniforms, food, housing, transport, education, and the like). The usual agreement starts off with a statement that both union and management: 'intend to promote and improve industrial, economic and social relations within the firm; and arrive at a better common understanding relative to rates of pay, vacation/sick leaves, hours of work, etc.; and to provide the means for the amicable settlement of all disputes and grievances to guarantee peace and harmony'. Table 5 provides a summary of the important items negotiated via CBAs. All agreements always contain a 'no strike, no lock-out' commitment clause.

In RAMCAR, the union must recognize management prerogatives, that is, 'the company's rights to the exclusive control over all functions and facilities, and to the direction of the entire workforce', that 'the company is the sole judge of the competency of an employee in the performance of his assigned work', and management's exclusive right 'to train employees and improve their ability, to make rules and regulations governing conduct and safety, and to decide on personnel movements and disciplinary action; and to create new or additional classification of jobs, or eliminate them'. In SMC, several union bargaining units have pending negotiations with management. At the time of the author's visit, labour issues being negotiated included the forced retirement of employees and factional leadership conflicts within the union. In one SMC subsidiary, issues for negotiations included: the amount and schedule of wage increases; cost of living allowances; subsidies for rice; improvement in sick and vacation leave; emergency and paternity leave with pay, and so on. In another subsidiary, regularization of contractual workers; schedule of wage increases; retention of across the board pay increases; and improvements in bonuses and paid leave were issues.

RAMCAR is an interesting case study in how IR and HRM strategies interact and converge. Tensions which led to a strike in the 1991 CBA negotiations provided lessons to both managers and union leaders. The Vice President for HRs was tasked to implement strategies for TQC and productivity improvement, which the union vehemently opposed. In 1991 there was deadlock over wage increases and benefits. The union organized a month-long strike. In the end, both sides requested the conciliation and mediation of labour ministry officials. In the renegotiations RAMCAR management adopted a paternalistic or patronizing attitude to provide the union with a face-saving 'winning edge', which provided an incentive to union leaders to continue negotiations. In issuing a return to work order, the Secretary of Labor emphasized that:

> A prolonged work stoppage will result in a shortage of car batteries, and will affect both the transport and mining industries which heavily use these products. It will affect the national interest – the country's ability to generate foreign exchange from the timely delivery of its exports.

Management granted the union's demands for recognition and security, pay increases, and the like. In return, the union committed itself to assist in the implementation of the productivity improvement programmes. With productivity incentives in place, the union agreed not to ask or negotiate for wage adjustments.

EMPLOYMENT AND CO-OPERATION SCHEMES

Employment

It is a common management prerogative 'to decide on personnel movements and disciplinary action, and to create new or additional job classifications, or eliminate them', as provided in many collective work contracts. In the case firms, labour flexibility is a contentious issue. CBAs usually provide for a 'last-in, first-out' principle in laying off workers. There are also relevant labour laws on the hiring and dismissal of employees. Employees undergo a probationary period of six months before they are 'regularized'. Applicants undergo a screening process which includes aptitude tests. Usually, new recruits are hired based on their qualifications and experience. Employees may be reassigned to fill job vacancies. In the case of termination of employment due to new technology, labour law provides that workers must be 'paid a separation pay equivalent

TABLE 6
COMMON EMPLOYMENT ISSUES

SMC	Retrenchment of 2,700 employees in 1992. Contracting out jobs; spin-offs of divisions into separate subsidiaries; retirement of redundant employees.
MERALCO	Reengineering and decentralization. Reduction of personnel through attrition. Job subcontracting through subsidiaries.
CALTEX	New production techniques required creation of new job shifts, multi-skilling and more tasks (job enlargement).
PAL	Hiring of new pilots and cabin crew for new aircraft, and for international flights; retrenchment/reassignment of redundant staff.
PLDT	Redundant workers due to computerized operations. 5,000 casuals; expansion of contractual jobs. Reduction of regular staff by 50% through voluntary retirement.
PNB	Voluntary, early retirement programme. Staff reorganization/reassignment due to privatization. Attrition and frozen hiring policy.
RAMCAR	Newly hired employees undergo six months probation before regularization. On the job training programmes extensive, which emphasize quality commitment.

to at least one month pay for every year of service'. Despite these laws, most of the firms were able to 'downsize' their workforce. The firms resorted to a flexible workforce strategy by hiring more casuals, temporary and probationary employees. Firms also offered early retirement programmes, and stopped hiring new employees. These are the most common employment issues (see Table 6).

Many firms reduced their workforce in the 1991–93 recession. They hired more casual workers, and subcontracted jobs when production peaked. The loss of job security due to casualization was the main issue in strikes during the period. In SMC, an example of issues related to employment is the retirement of employees affected by the 'rightsizing' programme, such as the subcontracting of the firm's warehouse units. A union from one affected subsidiary presented a key strike demand for the regularization of contractual workers, among others. Indeed, downsizing is a continuous strategy in many firms. SMC, for instance, laid off 2,700 employees in 1992, but with a financial package (higher in value than the normal retirement plan), including medical insurance, entrepreneurial skills training, job placements, assistance to business opportunities with SMC as dealers, distributors, and the like. PAL purchased new aircraft and temporarily hired foreign pilots and cabin crew but the union decried what it saw as management's attempt at 'union busting'. The CBA defined temporary hiring as not more than one year in length, and which could be filled by rescheduling regular pilots. If there are not sufficient regular pilots, the company may hire temporary replacements.

Labour–Management Co-operation Schemes

HR strategies take place in various LMCs, which are also the venue for the transformation of plant-level IR. LMCs provide a broad and flexible environment for both management and union representatives (Gatchalian, 1990). Under labour law, LMCs include 'any arrangement, mechanism, activity or process made up of workers and management, whether unionized or not, to improve work relations, work conditions, increase productivity, and enhance the quality of worklife'. The case studies show the importance of LMC dialogues not only as a means for communication, but also as a mechanism to integrate local cultural idiosyncracies with foreign (Western and Japanese) management techniques. Analysis of LMC agenda shows that it is a suitable venue to negotiate problems related to workplace adjustments – reorganization, productivity improvement schemes, and the like (see Table 7).

TABLE 7
LMC AGENDA

SMC	LMCs provided for in CBAs with unionized subsidiaries; LMCs functional, but not in all 31 subsidiaries.
MERALCO	LMCs, a prominent feature in the CBA with the supervisory union; provided for, but not prominent, in the agreement with the rank and file union; regular labour–management dialogues.
CALTEX	Strike incidence indicate the limits of LMCs to resolve issues on multi-skilling and multi-tasking in 1995.
PAL	Failure of LMCs to play a role in labour disputes; heavy reliance upon government arbitration and court decisions. LMCs formally established by CBA.
PLDT	No provision for LMCs aside from a grievance procedure; the 1996 strike demonstrated failure of labour–management communication.
PNB	Regular labour–management meetings before privatization; company reorganization froze communication lines; no provision for LMCs. No formal LMCs.
RAMCAR	Functional LMCs, with sincerity on both sides; meets monthly to discuss issues related to productivity and quality improvement.

Many unions in the 1980s initially resisted LMCs, viewing them as a threat. Indeed, in many instances (but not in the case studies), LMCs replaced the role of the union. In SMC, MERALCO and RAMCAR, the LMC meetings provided a positive environment for higher value-added, productivity and more harmonious employee relations, rather than a focus upon pay levels, the usual focus of collective bargaining. In the rest of the companies, however, the incidence of strikes in 1995 and 1996 show the non-relevance of LMCs when major issues require union participation. This included the introduction of: a fleet of new aircraft in PAL; technology in PLDT; job shifts and multi-tasking in CALTEX; and privatization in PNB. The lack of confidence building measures, as through LMCs, in these firms did not allow the unions to understand and contribute in efforts to improve productivity.

The LMC in RAMCAR is a significant case. Both union and management 'agree to hold regular (monthly) meetings of the LMC', which is composed of seven union officers and seven management representatives. The LMC considers any and all matters which could bring about effective and substantial implementation of the CBA, to produce a more harmonious relationship. Furthermore, matters discussed in the LMCs do not imply renegotiation of the CBA.

In PAL, the agreement provides that through the LMC both union and management 'shall exert efforts to attain high levels of productivity and efficiency, quality of service and promote goodwill among its employees and the public'. The LMC is composed of four representatives each from both union and management. There is, however, a relatively high level of tension concerning substantial pay increases, the dismissal of union strike leaders, and disputes over hiring and skills development for new aircraft. Under such circumstances, legal procedures initiated in court by management dominate over the promotion of the LMC.

Only the grievance procedure is the venue for labour–management communication in PLDT and PNB, where LMCs are not provided for. Grievances raised in PNB include 'problems related to any discharge, lay-off, disciplinary or personnel action affecting any regular employee or union member. Both parties agree to settle all disputes through friendly negotiation.' In many cases deadlock occurs and both union and management agree to seek the assistance of a mediator or conciliator from the Labor Ministry.

CONVERGENCE OR DIVERGENCE?

This contribution has provided evidence about the divergence in HRM in relation to personnel management and IR. Yet, trends also indicate a convergence towards the increasing emphasis on HRD strategies. Furthermore, advertisements for executive or managerial positions increasingly emphasize skills which combine the IR and HR functions. There is a premium for managers who can initiate innovations with entrenched local work practices. These managers must work within the organizational and cultural constraints, and find ways to motivate the local workforce.

Philippine HR strategies are mainly pragmatic responses to opportunities in the technological and economic environment. While still an incoherent principle with a limited consensus, HR strategies are clearly setting the trends among local personnel managers and professional practitioners. The case studies show that in the Philippine workplace there is a pragmatic combination of both foreign and local HRM methods which could be best described as the 'best practice' approach. These practices could be called the Philippine *meztizo* or *halo-halo* (mixed) approach – best in the Philippines, but which may not work in other foreign contexts. There are limitations on the universalistic view on how employment relations arise. Basic enterprise rationality with respect to the bottom line (profitability) mainly motivates the pragmatic use of what is considered as best practice. Managers are under pressure to produce and sell goods and services in the market. These pressures require the use of whatever strategies work to motivate the workforce. Definitely, culturalist and institutional explanations alongside basic enterprise rationality, partly provide the theoretical support for these HRM strategies.

An example of how work strategies must blend with local culture is in the building-up of mutual trust and confidence ('*tiwala*' in Filipino) in flexibility and adjustment measures. Consensus and consultation in decision-making, through continous information sharing mechanisms, such as LMCs, are very consistent with the basic Filipino cultural mindset. Consensus should involve not only the formal agents (managers and union officers) but also other influential, senior employees who are behind the scene. Among Filipino–Chinese owned firms (not part of these case studies), the older generation of entrepreneurs still emphasize trust and loyalty among the essential and senior – hence loyal – workforce. At the same time, there is stress upon rationality and risk minimization. In contrast, the newer generation of Filipino–Chinese managers emphasize management professionalization, ability and performance, while maintaining the basic values of trust and loyalty emphasized by their elders. Most of the younger Filipino–Chinese managers taking over from their elders are educated abroad, often in North American management schools. They are torn between the rational and traditional norms and practices insisted upon by their Confucian-oriented elders, and the demands of a competitive and ever changing technology.

The case studies can only hint at whether or not variations in HRM practices are due to differences in patterns of capital ownership, as well as the industrial and organizational structure. Clear differences could be observed in terms of the size of the enterprise. Large firms and conglomerates, as well as large-scale joint ventures tend to be unionized. In these firms there are distinct managers for both the HR function and IR. Small and medium firms, in contrast, tend to emphasize the non-union approach in their HRM strategies.

Given this diversity, what is the future of HRM approaches in the Philippines? Obviously, the Filipino *halo-halo* approach would not look like the American, Anglo-Saxon, German, Swedish, or even Japanese, models. Foreign investment brings along managers, technologies and work patterns which may, or may not, be effective in producing results from the local workforce. What is sure is that local managers, in coping with increasing pressures from global and regional competition, the entry of more foreign investors, and in respecting local sensitivities and cultural values, will be more motivated to use the *halo-halo* approach. This implies that the role of the nation-state, in particular its shared cultural norms and values, continues to be significant even as new technology homogenizes work practices. For example, even as union militancy declines (as observed by Ofreneo, 1995), there is still a need to observe labour standards.

However, the Filipino employer's 'wish list' (see, for example, PMAP, 1990) of desirable work practices hints at the pressures for convergence. For example, it is argued that HR managers must: align work values and ethics of employees with corporate thrust; have a firm grasp of the latest technology in office and factory automation; innovate with existing work and pay systems; emphasize ability, skills and performance regardless of personal relations, ethnic or linguistic background; and introduce flexible pay schemes which emphasize productivity through contingent rewards, rather than basic monetary components. Similarly, in the area of employee relations, managers must be familiar with techniques to achieve non-adversarial relations and satisfy demands to create a 'lean' and flexible workforce, rather than guarantee secure jobs. Finally, Philippine HR managers must justify their very existence, even as they design flatter work organizations which emphasizes teamwork rather than a rigid hierarchy of managers and supervisors who manage rank and file employees.

CONCLUSION

In many large Philippine firms HRM is distinct from both personnel management and IR – the key evidence for divergence. There are clear distinctions in the work of HR and personnel managers, whose qualifications, skills, and job descriptions are different from each other. The job title 'personnel manager' is still dominant among local firms. Yet, this divergence is weakening. The managerial job market indicates that firms tend to require their personnel managers to integrate HRD strategies in their work. Many new firms prefer to use the job title 'HR manager', instead of personnel manager for those people handling their workforce.

The case studies show that market competition can transform the traditional functions of personnel managers. Filipino personnel managers usually handle administrative functions such as recruitment, discipline, compensation, employee welfare, and records. Aside from these tasks, the same managers increasingly must satisfy demands arising from their inclusion in executive decision making – a role not so pronounced before. In employee welfare and communication, especially in non-unionized firms, HR officers assume a dual role as advocates for employees, as well as implementors of management policies. However, this can be difficult – as with the announcement of lay-offs, limited pay increases, or non-availability of funds for certain benefits. While in the past many IR managers were lawyers, the trend is shifting to a non-legal approach by hiring managers with a greater background in the behavioural sciences.

Both IR and HR managers are expected to handle the usual functions related to employee relations and collective bargaining. At the same time, they must be responsible for skills development and handling organization changes, such as worker retrenchment. HR managers are expected to be responsible for training and skills formation, as well as in the upskilling of employees for new technology. The job descriptions of HR managers usually include being able to: 'institutionalize and computerize personnel systems, reinforce innovative programmes for optimizing productivity, enhance the quality of work life and strengthen partnerships with the local communities'. Most important, they 'must be attuned to current technologies in culture building, total quality management, and productivity'.

The Filipino *halo-halo* or *meztizo* approach may be a derivative of the observed trends emerging in the Western workplace which focus on flexibility and skill development, among others (see Locke *et al.*, 1995). At the same time, the diffusion of Japanese-style work practices in the Philippines illustrates the spillover of foreign investment in HRM (as argued by Taira, 1992). These claims, however, require more evidence. The search for an alternative 'Asian way' in handling HRM is still pervasive (see, for instance, Lee 1996).

ACKNOWLEDGEMENTS

The author is most grateful to Chris Rowley for his editorial surgery, suggestions and comments. Thanks also to the anonymous referees for the critique; and to faculty colleagues, especially Dean Rene E. Ofreneo, and graduate students and seminar participants at the SOLAIR, University of the Philippines, who helped to clarify ideas. I am most grateful to managers and union leaders who provided an opportunity for discussions and interviews – Roel C. Sedano, Lucy C. Tarriela, Roger Tarriela, Rey Elbo, Dolores Pascual, Ben Claudio, Cel Gonzales, Myrna Rillera, Ivy Formoso, Alex Fabian, Levi Marquez, Joey Molina, Virgilo Pena, Arthur Florentin, Leony dela Llana, and many others. Errors and omissions are solely my own.

REFERENCES

Aganon, Marie E. (1994) 'Human Resource Management – a Comparative Analysis of Japanese, Chinese and Western Models in the Philippines', in Maragtas S.V. Amante (ed.) *Human Resource Approaches in the Philippines: A Study of Japanese, Filipino–Chinese and Western Owned Firms*. Quezon City: SOLAIR, University of the Philippines, pp.18–52.

Aganon, Kristine E. (1997) *Employee Ownership Programs and Employee Outcomes (Productivity, Commitment and Motivation)*,Unpublished Master of Industrial Relations Thesis, Quezon City: SOLAIR, University of the Philippines.

Amante, Maragtas S.V. (1995) 'Employment and Wage Practices of Japanese Firms in the Philippines: Convergence with Filipino–Chinese and Western-owned Firms', *International Journal of Human Resource Management* , Vol.6, No.3, pp.642–55.

Amante, Maragtas S.V., Marie E. Aganon and Rene E. Ofreneo (1992) *Japanese Industrial Relations Interface in the Philippines*. Quezon City: SOLAIR, University of the Philippines.

Asia Week Magazine (1997), March 7.

Department of Labor and Employment (DOLE) (1995) *Yearbook of Labor Statistics 1995*. Manila, Philippines: DOLE.

Gatchalian, Jose C. (1990) *Labor Management Councils (LMCs) as Organizational Communication Mechanisms – An Assessment*, Unpublished PhD Thesis, Quezon City:

College of Mass Communications, University of the Philippines.

Lee, Hyo Soo (1996) 'The Interaction of Production, Distribution and Rule-making Systems in Industrial Relations', *Relations Industrielles/Industrial Relations*, Vol.51, No.2, pp.302–30.

Locke, Ronald, Thomas A. Kochan and Michael Piore (1995) 'Reconceptualizing Comparative Industrial Relations: Lessons from International Research', *International Labour Review*, Vol.134, No.2, pp.139–62.

Ofreneo, Rene E. (1993a) 'Decline of Labor Militance in the Philippines', *Philippine Journal of Labor and Industrial Relations*, Vol.15, Nos.1/2, pp.67–96.

Ofreneo, Rene E. (1993b) 'The Dynamics of Structural Adjustments and Industrial Relations', *Philippine Labor Review*, Vol.17, No.1, pp.23–51.

Ofreneo, Rene E. (1995) 'Labor Standards and Philippine Economic Development', *Philippine Journal of Labor and Industrial Relations* , Vol.16, Nos.1/2, pp.50–68.

Personnel Management Association of the Philippines (PMAP) (1990) *Human Resources Management Practices and Issues Survey*. Manila: PMAP.

Philippine Daily Enquirer (1997), 30 January.

Sano, Yoko (1995) *Human Resource Management in Japan*. Tokyo: Keio University Press.

Sedano, Roel, Kristine Anne E. Aganon and Leni Lebrilla (1996) 'Employee Stock Ownership in the Philippines: Case Studies of Three Private Corporations', *Working Paper, School of Labor and Industrial Relations*, Quezon City: SOLAIR, University of the Philippines.

Storey, John (1992) *Developments in the Management of Human Resources*. Oxford: Blackwell

Soriano, Teresa (1993) *Flexible Work Arrangements in the Philippine Manufacturing Sector: Implications for Labor Relations*, Unpublished Master of Industrial Relations Thesis, Quezon City: SOLAIR, University of the Philippines.

Taira, Koji (1992) 'The End of Convergence Theories: Japanization of US Human Resource Management and Industrial Relations', *Research in International Business and International Relations*, Vol.5, pp.241–58.

Tracey, William E. (1994) 'HRM in Perspective' in William Tracey (ed.) *Human Resources Management and Development Handbook*. New York: American Management Association, pp.3–18.

World Bank (1995) *World Development Report 1995*. Washington, DC: The World Bank.

Yearbook of Labor Statistics (1985).

HRM Under Guided Economic Development:
The Singapore Experience

YUEN CHI-CHING

This contribution is organized into two sections, with the first section on labour–management relations in Singapore providing the background for a subsequent section on human resource management (HRM). Labour–management relations in Singapore is a controversial issue among academics. In reviewing the literature, the author felt that much of the strong sentiments attached to the subject matter arose from: (1) the use of Western theoretical perspectives to analyze an Asian system, a practice which at times has resulted in judgmental comments; (2) the tendency to adhere to a specific theoretical perspective, which in some cases resulted in the selective presentation of information; (3) conclusions being drawn from the analysis of one or two aspects of a system, for example labour law, which may not do justice to the system as a whole; and (4) defensiveness on the part of some local writers. In view of the above, the author deliberately refrained from adopting a specific theoretical perspective, and instead of dealing with one or two aspects of the system in detail, took a broad view of the system as a whole. It is only in the discussion sections that theoretical issues are addressed.

STAGES OF ECONOMIC DEVELOPMENT

The economic achievement of Singapore over the past three decades is widely acknowledged. Singapore became a self-governing state in 1959, and an independent nation in 1965. At the time of its independence, Singapore was little more than a poor seaport with a transient migrant population of coolies, merchants, and colonial administrators. By the mid-1990s the city-state had become a major financial and commercial centre for the region with an established manufacturing sector comprising relatively high-technology industries such as electronics, pharmaceutical/ chemical products, precision equipment, ship building and repair, as well as oil refineries. With a per capita Gross National Product (GNP) of US$25000, a land area of 648 sq. km., and a population of three million, Singapore is close to its long-cherished hope of becoming a 'developed country' (Ministry of Labour, 1995). In the 1996 Global Competitiveness Report compiled by the Geneva-based World Economic Forum, Singapore was

Yuen Chi-Ching, The National University of Singapore

TABLE I
KEY ECONOMIC INDICATORS

Year	Unemployment Rate (%)	Employed Persons (Number)	Real Wage Increase (%)	GDP Growth Rate (%)	Person-days Lost due to Industrial Stoppages (Number)	Labour Productivity (%)
1965	8.9	524	–	6.6	45,800	–
1970	10.2	644	–	13.4	2,514	6.3
1975	4.4	684	–	4.0	4,853	2.8
1980	3.5	1,073	–	9.7	0	5.7
1981	2.9	1,095	–	9.9	0	–
1982	2.6	1,122	–	6.4	0	–
1983	3.3	1,148	8.9	8.2	0	5.3
1984	2.7	1,156	7.9	8.3	0	6.9
1985	4.1	1,235	7.5	-1.6	0	3.1
1986	6.5	1,215	2.2	2.3	122	6.8
1987	4.7	1,267	2.6	9.7	0	5.1
1988	3.3	1,332	6.5	11.6	0	5.0
1989	2.2	1,394	7.4	9.6	0	5.2
1990	1.7	1,537	5.7	9.0	0	4.1
1991	1.9	1,524	5.6	7.3	0	1.8
1992	2.7	1,576	5.6	6.2	0	2.9
1993	2.7	1,592	4.0	10.4	0	7.0
1994	2.6	1,649	5.6	10.1	0	5.4
1995	2.7	1,701	4.5	8.8	0	3.7

Sources: Yearbook of Statistics, various issues; Department of Statistics (1995).

ranked the most competitive country, ahead of the US, Luxumbourg, and Switzerland; and in a separate competitiveness rating compiled by the International Institute of Management Development (IMD) in Lausanne, Singapore was ranked second, after the US (*Time Magazine*, 1996). The economic development of the city-state is summarized in Table 1.

Three stages of economic development can be easily discerned as they were marked by well publicized shifts in government economic policies. A description of the three stages will provide the background for the subsequent sections on industrial structure, labour force, industrial legislation and labour relations in Singapore.[1]

Industrialization and Basic Infrastructure Development, 1965–1979

With separation from the Federation of Malaysia in 1965, Singapore was reduced to a port without a hinterland. The government was faced with the problems of high unemployment and population growth rates, a lack of a manufacturing base, and a largely uneducated, migrant population. Hence, the immediate task was to create employment through industrialization, and so government turned to foreign capital. To attract foreign companies to establish manufacturing operations, not only were tax concessions and other incentives offered, the government also focused on infrastructure development such as roads, industrial estates, telecommunication, port and airport facilities. Foreign investments attracted during this period were mostly in low-skilled, labour-intensive industries. In addition to economic development, the government also embarked on a large-scale project of rehousing the population from unhygienic living conditions in traditional *'atap huts'*, to high-rise blocks in public housing estates. Basic medical care and an education system were also introduced.

Moves to High-Technology, Higher Value-added Industries/Services, 1979–Early 1990s

By 1979 the objectives of providing employment, hygienic living conditions, basic health-care and education were by and large achieved. With unemployment dropping to 3.4 per cent and the labour market getting tight, the government decided to restructure the economy by phasing out low-skilled, labour-intensive industries and moving to capital intensive, high-technology, higher value-added industries/services. The government also wanted to encourage a more efficient use of its limited workforce through automation. To achieve these objectives, labour costs were deliberately raised so that labour-intensive industries with low profit margins would have no alternative but to relocate elsewhere. Those with higher profit margins were encouraged to automate their operations by tax incentives and technical assistance from the National Productivity Board (NPB). Once again, attractive incentives were offered to entice high-technology companies to set up manufacturing bases in Singapore. To support the move to higher-value added industries/services, the government also stepped up its efforts in education and training.

'Going Regional', 1992 Onwards

By the early 1990s, while the pursuit for more advanced, newer technologies continued, the government introduced new initiatives to 'go regional'. Constrained by its limited size, natural resources, and domestic market, the government figured that Singapore had more or less reached its limit for development. Following the path of the developed nations, it seemed Singapore would settle into a slower growth rate as its economy 'matured'. The way to sustain its high growth rate was to ride on the developmental momentum of its fast developing neighbours: China, Malaysia, Indonesia, India, the Philippines, Vietnam, and so on. To this end, not only did the government lead in direct investments in the region, it also urged and supported local companies to 'go regional' (*Business Times*, 1993). Through various statutory boards the government provides information, advice, contact and other support to private enterprises. The education system is being revamped to prepare Singaporeans to be more entrepreneurial and mentally ready for challenging overseas assignments. At the same time, the Ministry of Education oversees the establishment of 'Singapore schools' in major Asian cities to support expatriate Singaporean families.

THE LABOUR FORCE

In 1995 Singapore had a labour force of 1.7 million: 61.35 per cent males and 38.65 per cent females. The labour force participation rate was 78.4 per cent and 50.0 per cent for males and females respectively. Unemployment was at two per cent and, except for a brief period from 1985–87, has been hovering around two to three per cent for about a decade and a half (Department of Statistics, 1996). Employment and distribution of employed persons by sector and occupation is presented in Table 2.

TABLE 2
DISTRIBUTION OF EMPLOYED PERSONS

Employed Persons by Sector	(%)
Manufacturing	25.6
Commerce	22.9
Transport & Communications	10.6
Financial & Business Services	12.0
Community & Personal Services	21.4
Others	7.5
Total	100.0
Employed Persons by Occupation	
Professionals & Managers	17.3
Technical & Assoc. Professionals	15.2
Clerical Workers	14.8
Service & Sales Workers	13.4
Production Craftsmen, Operators, Cleaners & Labourers	35.4
Others	4.0
Total	100.0

Source: Ministry of Labour (1995).

Due to the tight labour market, employers often experience difficulty in recruiting and retaining skilled labour, and for many the solution is foreign workers. This is a similar strategy to that in Taiwan (see Chen in this volume). However, while the government encourages the recruitment of professionals from overseas, it is wary of the social effects of a large pool of unskilled foreign workers and has placed strict restrictions on their employment. As of 1994, there were around 300,000 foreign workers in Singapore, which is roughly equivalent to 17.6 per cent of the local workforce (Tan, 1996). Only those foreign employees who earn less than US$1,071 per month are classified as foreign workers. Hence the figure did not include those in professional or managerial categories. The government's preferred solution to the labour shortage is to increase productivity through automation and training.

COMPANY TYPES

For the present discussion, the following typology of companies is adopted: multinational enterprises (MNEs), large local companies (LLCs), and small local companies (SLCs) (Economic Development Board, 1993). MNEs include Singapore-based subsidiaries as well as joint venture companies with more than 70 per cent foreign capital. Considering the government's reliance on MNEs for capital, technology, management expertise and international markets (Ministry of Trade and Industry, 1986), it is hardly surprising that firms in this category made up 12.1 per cent of the companies in Singapore and employed 34.7 per cent of the workforce.

Although LLCs comprised only 1.1 per cent of the total companies, they employed 23 per cent of the workforce (Economic Development Board, 1993). Many LLCs were originally state-owned companies established by the government to spearhead the development of a specific sector. These government-linked companies are scattered in various industrial/business sectors: telecommunications, ship building/repair, finance and banking, airline, manufacturing industries, construction and infrastructure development, power supply, port facilities, oil refining, and so on. While many of the successful government-linked companies have become public-listed companies (with the government still holding controlling shares), there are plans for the privatization of the others. Beside government-related companies, most of the other LLCs are successful local family businesses which have grown in size.

In 1993 there were 69,452 SLCs, comprising 86.8 per cent of the total number of companies and employing 42.3 per cent of the workforce. Many of the SLCs are small businesses in the commerce and service sectors. In the manufacturing sector, SLCs serve as contractors providing support services or as suppliers of parts and components. With government assistance, the productivity and value-added per worker of SLCs have improved steadily since 1986. Many of the SLCs started off with limited capital and had to rely on the cheap labour of family members to survive their initial years. Even after they became established, they retained the characteristics of family enterprises in regard to the decision-making process, as well as personnel practices.

THE LABOUR–MANAGEMENT RELATIONS SYSTEM

Trade Union Organization

In the struggle against Japanese occupation and British colonial rule, the workers and Chinese-educated students/scholars played an important role. Both the workers' and students' liberation movements were led by left-wing politicians who used the union movement for the organization of the resistance movements and to recruit followers to their causes. As early as 1940, the British colonial government introduced the Trade Unions Ordinance (amended in 1948) which provided for the registration, dissolution and supervision of trade unions (Anantaraman, 1991). The Act empowered the Registrar of Trade Unions to deregister a trade union if it carried out activities which were not in line with its stated objectives: if its use of funds was unlawful or improper; if the funds were used against the interests of the workers concerned; or if the workers could be represented by another trade union. Furthermore, a union could order industrial action only if the majority of its affected members voted in support of it in a secret ballot. The Act, retained and amended by subsequent governments, proved to be powerful in preventing left-wing union leaders from using the unions as a base of influence.

When Singapore became a self-governing state, the People Action Party (PAP) was elected to form the first government. A struggle between the social democrats and the pro-communist faction of the PAP resulted in the pro-communists forming their own political party, the Barisan Sosialis. This in turn led to the dissolution of the Singapore Trade Congress (formed in 1951) and the formation of the Singapore Association of Trade Unions (SATU) and the National Trade Union Congress (NTUC), which were associated with the Barisan Sosialis and the ruling PAP respectively. With the PAP winning complete control of the parliament in the 1968 election, all the trade unions came to be reorganized under the NTUC. This sequence of events accounted for the symbiotic relationship between the trade union movement under the NTUC and the ruling political party, PAP. Given this background, it is not surprising that in the 1982 amendment of the Trade Union Act, the objectives of trade unions were: to promote good industrial relations; to improve the working conditions of workers or enhance their economic and social status; and to increase productivity for the benefit of workers, employers and the economy.

As of 1994, there were 79 trade unions affiliated to the NTUC, which remained the only union federation. These unions, consisting of industrial, general, craft, staff, and house unions, had a total membership of 236,118 workers (Tan, 1995) and represented roughly 14 per cent of the workforce. To maintain the close relationship between the government/ruling party and the trade unions, there is a frequent exchange of key personnel between the two. For example, the present President of the Republic was the former Secretary-General of the NTUC, and the present Secretary of the NTUC was formerly a Minister of State for Trade and Industries.

At the firm level, trade unions perform the traditional functions of handling members' grievances, representing workers in cases of unfair treatment, and providing social welfare and recreational activities. At the national level, the NTUC represents workers in national wage negotiations, provides inputs to government policy-making bodies on issues such as industrial safety, training and development of workers, retirement age, and so forth. The NTUC also operates a wide range of services, most of which are available to non-members as well, although members usually enjoy discounts or priority in accessing the services. The NTUC operates the largest supermarket chain, the largest local taxi service, and was the third largest insurer in Singapore. In addition, it operates dental clinics, child-care cooperatives, holiday resorts, and radio stations. As the objective of the NTUC is not profit-maximization, it offers efficient services at reasonable prices targeted at the ordinary citizen. It therefore plays an important role in moderating the prices of essential services to the community. Through the Consumers' Association of Singapore, the NTUC also plays a role in protecting consumers' interests.

Employment Relations

With the need to enlist the help of foreign capital to bring about rapid industrialization, it was important that the government delivered a workforce that was hard working, disciplined and trained well enough to meet employers' needs. Singaporean workers were regularly rated the best in the 'Labour Force Evaluation Measure' compiled by BERI (the US-based Business Environment Risk Intelligence). The sub-scales which Singapore scored consistently high in were workforce characteristics and workforce organization (National Productivity Board, 1992).

The Employment Act, passed in 1968, set down basic legislation regarding working hours, various types of leave entitlement, contracts, termination of employment, retrenchment and retrenchment benefits, while the Industrial Relations (Amendment) Act of 1968, and the Trade Disputes Act of 1960 and 1981, laid down the rules and procedures for dealing with disputes between employers and employees/unions. The Industrial Relations Act excluded specific issues, such as promotion, internal transfer, retirement, retrenchment, dismissal and work assignment from collective agreements/bargaining. The duration of collective agreements was also extended from half a year to three years, thus the frequency of collective agreements was reduced. In the event of management and labour representatives failing to reach an agreement, the legislation mandated that the dispute be referred to the Industrial Arbitration Court (IAC). By making the referral of disputes to the IAC compulsory, by making it illegal to resort to industrial action after a trade dispute has been submitted to the IAC for arbitration, and by making decisions by the IAC final, the Industrial Relations Act and the Trade Disputes Act effectively made industrial actions illegal. Partly as a result of the above measures, the number of work stoppages fell drastically. The number of worker-days lost due to strikes or lockouts hit a high of 946,354 days in 1955, and between 1960 and 1963 averaged 279,059 days. However, in the 17 years between 1978 and 1994, only 122 worker-days were lost (Chew and Chew, 1995).

Wage Settlement

The establishment of the National Wage Council (NWC) in 1972 represented another crucial step towards orderly labour management relations. The NWC, a tripartite body, was to ensure orderly wage increases by setting annual national guidelines to reflect the state of the economy. The Council consists of four to six representatives each from employer organizations, trade unions, and the government, and is headed by a neutral chairperson. Under its operating principles, wage guidelines are to be reached by a consensus. It refrains from providing sectoral guidelines, arguing that employers draw their workforce from the same labour pool. Although not mandatory, the guidelines were followed closely by both public and private establishments. In 1985, the percentage of private and public sector employees who benefited from the NWC guidelines increase was 84.2 per cent and 99.5 per cent respectively (ibid.). One of the reasons for the high enforcement rate was that the IAC had in the past consistently followed the recommended guidelines when it settled disputes.

Besides ensuring orderly wage transitions, the NWC also played an important role in helping the government implement its economic policies. In response to the government's 1979 policy to phase out low value-added, labour-intensive industries, the NWC recommended a cumulative wage increase of around 36 per cent in the three years between 1979–81. Although NWC recommendations for 1982–84 were more moderate, wages nonetheless went up by 17.6 per cent due to the tight labour market. On top of the wage hikes, employers' compulsory contributions to the employees' Central Providence Fund (CPF) was increased to 25 per cent of the employee's basic wage, and employers also had to contribute 4 per cent of their basic wage to the Skills Development Fund (SDF), a national training scheme (this will be elaborated on in the following section).

The NWC had, however, gone too far in its wage adjustment. In 1985, Singapore experienced its first negative growth rate (–1.8 per cent) and went through a recession. Unemployment, which was at 2.7 per cent in 1984, rose to 4.1 per cent in 1985 and 6.5 per cent in 1986. The committee appointed by the government to look into the state of the economy attributed the recession to high business and labour costs. While real earnings went up by 7.3 per cent annually between 1979–85, productivity growth lagged behind at four per cent. By 1985, Singapore's labour costs were about 50 per cent higher than those of the 'newly industrialised countries' in the region (Tan, 1995).

The government took speedy action to help restore competitiveness. Business costs were decreased through the reduction of a range of business taxes and charges. In 1986 and 1987, not only did the NWC announced a freeze in wage increases, but it reduced the employers' contributions to the CPF to ten per cent and to the SDF to one per cent. The measures were effective and the economy bounced back. By 1987, Singapore registered a 9.4 per cent GDP growth rate, and between 1987–95 the country was able to sustain an average of eight per cent annual growth in GDP. With the economy on track, the NWC gradually restored employers' contributions to the CPF to 25 per cent.

Since the recession in the 1980s, the NWC has moved away from a national wage guideline in fixed percentages. Instead, it adopted a flexible system whereby a wage is broken down into several components (basic pay, annual variable component, monthly variable component, special bonus, etc.), with the components reflecting individual career progression, and performance of the national economy, company, and individual. In principle, the NWC would not allow salary raises to out-strip increases in productivity.

Training and Development

The government plays an active role in the training and development of the nation's human resources. Since 1979, employers have had to contribute a percentage of the basic wage of employees who earn less than S$1,000 to the SDF. The fund was utilized by the government to establish training centres, subsidize employers' training costs, and provide training for retrenched workers. While the SDF Board handles the administration of training subsidies, it was supported by a host of government bodies which provide training programmes, such as the Institute of Technical Education, Productivity and Standards Board, Vocational and Industrial Training Board, Economic Development Board, and the NTUC.

In 1994, the SDF supported 526,486 training places, each averaging 34 hours (SDF Board, 1995). About 85 per cent of the training places were allocated to employees with 'A' level qualifications and below. Heavy emphasis was placed on promoting training activities among SLCs, as training was most inadequate among the small companies. Recent initiatives introduced by the SDF Board to improve training in small companies include the Partners in Training Scheme, the Training Voucher Scheme, the On-the-Job Training (OJT) Scheme (under which NPB-trained OJT instructors were sent to small companies to help them set up OJT systems), the Retraining Voucher Scheme (to provide incentives for retrenched workers to upgrade their skills for further employment), Training Needs Analysis Consultancy Grant Scheme, and the Management Development Grant Scheme. Another area of training which the SDF Board is actively promoting involves high-end skills training (SDF Board, 1995). The role played by the government in industrial and management training is important as the bulk of companies in Singapore are either MNEs or small businesses. The former may lack the commitment and the latter the resources, to seriously invest in the long-term development of their employees.

In the 1960s and 1970s the emphasis of the government's education policy was on technical training, and primary and secondary education. In the 1980s, tertiary education was expanded and by 1993, combined polytechnic and university enrolment rose to about 42 per cent of each year's cohort (Department of Statistics, 1993). Since the late 1980s, the government has turned its attention to primary, secondary and pre-university education again, and this time the emphasis is more on quality: upgrading buildings and facilities, improving teachers' training and salaries, and so on. At the tertiary level, the push for quality is also on, with greater emphasis on research, and curricula development to support the government's 'go regional' drive.

Social Insurance

The CPF is a compulsory scheme that requires employees and employers to contribute equally to a total of 50 per cent of an employee's salary. In the early years, the government borrowed from the CPF (with interest) to fund infrastructure developments. Over the years, fund contributors were allowed greater control of their savings. While required to keep fixed amounts to provide for medical expenditure and retirement, they could use the remaining for home purchase, life insurance, investment in relatively secure stocks, children's education, etc.

On the whole, Singaporean workers have not fared badly in terms of social insurance. Unemployment, at two to three per cent, is low; and with a tight labour market, employment security is generally good. Some 90 per cent of Singaporeans own the home they live in (Ministry of Labour, 1995). Education, up to pre-university, is affordable even for low income groups, while university education can be financed through loans. In the private sector, 90 per cent of the companies provide health care (NPB-SILS, 1993), and in the public sector, employees can opt for either full medical benefits or the co-payment of medical bills (in the latter case, employees receive additional pay in lieu of full medical coverage). The reason behind the introduction of the co-payment scheme was that the government wanted Singaporeans to take more responsibility for their health and medical expenditure.

The government has candidly rejected social welfarism, noting the many problems associated with socialist and welfare states. Hence, there is no provision for unemployment benefit, nor for old-age pensions. Retired persons support themselves from their provident fund, and as is the case in many Oriental societies, most of them do receive support from their extended family. Welfare support is available only for hardship cases.

THE SINGAPORE INDUSTRIAL RELATIONS MODEL

The success of the Singapore economy depended on an efficient and forward-looking government which micro-managed and orchestrated different parts of the system to achieve social and economic objectives. The labour–management relations system was an integral part. However, assessment of the system varied considerably, depending on the perspective one adopts.

The Singapore industrial relations system has been described by Deyo (1981) as 'bureaucratic-authoritarian corporatist labour relations', an elite response to the imperatives of dependent development; and by Anantaraman (1991) as 'state corporatism'. Wilkinson (1994) described Singapore as a dependent developer which attempted to engineer an orderly society and a disciplined workforce 'in part on behalf of multinational capital'. If one were to look at the terms of the Trade Union Act, the Industrial Relations Act and the Trade Disputes Act, one is likely to agree that Singapore's system is 'pro-capital'. However, to do so is to ignore the vast improvement in workers' lives in the past 30 years.

Faced with high unemployment and high birth rates in 1965, Singapore did turn to foreign capital to help bring about rapid industrialization. To attract and retain foreign capital, the government delivered, among other things, a disciplined workforce. However, while Singapore did embark on the course of 'dependent development', the government has, to some extent, managed to steer the course of development of the nation. Through wage increase recommendations by the NWC, and compulsory employer contributions to the employees' CPF and to the SDF, the government has mandated businesses to give a share of their profits to the workers. Such measures resulted in a vast improvement in terms of living standards, housing, health, education, employment opportunities, public transport, provident fund, skills upgrading opportunities, and so on. In fact, by 1985, the government drove business and labour costs so high that many MNEs, and some local ones as well, decided to relocate elsewhere. Since then, the government has been monitoring the system to try to maintain a delicate balance between providing sufficient incentives to attract the right kind of foreign investment and taxing foreign capital to make them contribute to the nation.

Another indication that the government took control of the state's economic development was reflected in its selectivity in choosing foreign investors. Singapore has all along been selective in the type of foreign investment it wanted to attract. In 1979, with the economy approaching full employment, the government decided that it no longer needed labour-intensive investment and was rather ruthless in driving this sort of investment out. To date, Singapore still needs foreign investment for market access (due to its small domestic market and export-oriented economy) and technology transfer. However, since the early 1990s, the government has led local businesses to take on the role of investors (capitalists) in order to take advantage of the vast market and cheap labour in the developing economies of the region. In 1995 alone, Singapore companies invested at least US$8.06 billion in Asian countries (*Business Times*, 1997), which amounted to a *per capita* investment of US$2866.

As to whether trade unions in Singapore have performed their roles in society, the answer depends very much on how their role is defined. Trade unions in Singapore have always been described as mild and non-combative. Such descriptions are certainly true. Thus, if one takes a Marxist view that labour is always exploited under capitalism and the mission of trade unions is to destroy capitalism and return to the idyllic life of fishing and farming in the day and reading poetry in the evening, then trade unions in Singapore have failed. However, if the role of trade unions is defined as protecting the interests of the workers against capitalists and improving their life, then tripartism in Singapore has not fared badly.

Challenges Ahead

Although tripartism has operated effectively in the past decades, it may have to cope with a few challenges ahead. Firstly, the success of the economy depends to a large extent on the government's ability to micro-manage the system, which in turns depends on the existence of a single, dominant political party (Chew and Chew, 1996) *and* a unified labour movement behind it. The emergence of an effective opposition may bring about the splintering of the union movement. Alternatively, a split within the labour movement may provide the power base for the emergence of an effective opposition. In the past, the PAP was able to secure over 70 per cent of the electoral votes and almost complete control of the parliament. However, with the population becoming more educated, Westernized and well-travelled, voters' expectations have become more sophisticated, and their desire for the representation of alternative views has increased.

Second, in the constant push for development, an ideology of economic development has evolved in the society. The industrial relations system in Singapore has, to a large extent, been legitimized by past achievements in economic and social development. However, with the economy approaching maturity and with neighbouring economies competing fiercely for markets and foreign investment, it will be more difficult for the government to continue achieving a high growth rate in the future. If this scenario occurs, it may weaken the legitimacy of such a system.

Another challenge for the government is managing the distribution of wealth in society as well as perceived social equity. The system was accepted by workers because they benefited from it and their life/living standard improved significantly under it. However, with an open economy and the growing importance of managerial and professional workers, the gap between the rich and the poor is widening. Due to the government's omnipresence and its micro-management of the economy, as well as many aspects of the life of its citizenry, the electorate has come to perceive that the government is responsible for the 'fair' distribution of wealth in society. While managing this is by no means a simple task, managing perceived equity is a more complex dimension of the issue.

HRM PRACTICES IN SINGAPORE: AN OVERVIEW

A 1990 survey conducted by the National Productivity Board and the Singapore Institute of Personnel Management (NPB-SIPM, 1991) provided a broad view of human resource (HR) practices in Singapore. The survey covered 408 companies of various sizes and in different sectors. Of these, 47 per cent had a HR manager. The person in charge of the HR function could be a Chief Executive Officer (CEO), a HR manager/executive, or a non-HR manager/executive. The existence of a HR department was generally related to company size: almost 80 per cent of companies with 200 and more employees had a HR department.

The six most commonly practised HR activities were recruitment and selection, welfare and benefits administration, wage administration, performance appraisal, employee communication, and training and development. Among the least practised activities were industrial relations, productivity promotion, transfer and rotation, job evaluation, and personnel planning. However, in terms of current priorities, training and development was given the top priority, while personnel planning, although not commonly practised was ranked the sixth most important activity. In terms of the importance of HR activities 'in the next three years', the top-ranking items were, in order of importance, training and development, recruitment and selection, wage administration, personnel planning, performance appraisal, and welfare and benefits. Details of the ranking of HR activities are given in Table 3.

The same survey also reported that about 70 per cent practised promotion from within the organization. Performance appraisal was usually carried out once a year, and 78 per cent of the companies had performance appraisal for their managers as compared to 77 per cent for supervisors and 83 per cent for rank-and-file employees. Some 81 per cent had some sort of formal training programmes, while 60 per cent utilized a combination of external and internal training programmes. Personnel planning was carried out in about 70 per cent, the remaining 30 per cent were mainly small companies. Of the companies which implemented planning, 50 per cent did so jointly with other departments, while another 34 per cent of the companies had line departments doing their own planning independently.

The above findings show that in Singapore the HR function is still a mix between personnel/industrial relations and HRM models. However, there are indications – for example, the move towards a flexible wage system linking rewards to performance, the heavy emphasis on training and development, and teamwork – that the function is moving towards a HRM model. In the ranking of HR activities by their 'importance in the next three years', most of the items at the bottom of the list were traditional personnel items pertaining to standardization and formalization, while developmental activities such as training and development, promotion and career planning, personnel planning, and performance appraisal, were given high priority.

TABLE 3
RANKING OF HRM ACTIVITIES

Extent Practised		Current Priority		Priority in next 3 years	
Recruitment & Selection	92	Recruitment & Selection	2.5	Training & Development	2.3
Welfare & Benefits	89	Training & Development	2.5	Recruitment & Selection	2.4
Wage Administration	87	Wage Administration	3.0	Wage Administration	3.2
Performance Appraisal	83	Performance Appraisal	3.5	Manpower Planning	3.4
Employee Communication	80	Welfare & Benefits	3.7	Performance Appraisal	3.6
Training & Development	75	Manpower Planning	4.0	Welfare & Benefits	3.8
HR Policy Formulation	71	Promotion & Career Planning	4.3	Promotion & Career Planning	4.1
Promotion & Career Planning	65	Employee Communication	4.3	Employee Communication	4.2
Manpower Planning	64	HR Policy Formulation	4.6	Job Evaluation	4.4
Job Evaluation	60	Job Evaluation	4.7	HR Policy Formulation	4.7
Transfer & Rotation	51	Industrial Relations	5.1	Productivity Promotion	5.0
Productivity Promotion	46	Productivity Promotion	5.3	Industrial Relations	5.4
Industrial Relations	32	Transfer & Rotation	6.2	Transfer & Rotation	6.0

Note: Factors rated first are awarded 1 point, second 2 points, and so on up to the 10th ranking. The total score of each activity is an aggregate of the points awarded.

Source: NPB-SIPM (1991).

FACTORS AFFECTING HRM PRACTICES

There is considerable variation in HR practices among companies in Singapore. Divergence in HR practices is due to the following reasons:

Organizational Type

In Singapore, where small business enterprises constitute 86.8 per cent of companies and employ 42.3 per cent of the workforce, size is an important factor which affects HR practices. The majority of small enterprises started off as local family businesses and relied on relatives and family members in their initial years for cheap, reliable labour. Typically, such companies do not have a personnel department or a HR system. Personnel records are kept by clerks and only a limited range of personnel activities are practised. In a report by Chew and Teo (1991), it was noted that local companies have more problems with recruitment and staff turnover. Compared with foreign and joint venture companies, local companies interviewed more candidates for every employee recruited. The rejection rate for job offers was also higher. The retention rate for new employees beyond the first year of service is also low among local companies.

Headquarters Influence

Yuen and Hui (1993) compared the HR practices of 187 Singaporean, American and Japanese companies operating in Singapore. The study found that although cultural influences in HRM styles and practices did exist, they were not imperative. Operating in an unfamiliar environment, overseas subsidiaries of MNEs made strategic choices on whether or not to adopt the HRM system/practices of their parent company. In the case of Japanese subsidiaries, the strategy was to abandon the Japanese HRM system in favour of a wholesale adoption of the local system. This strategic choice reflects the cautiousness of Japanese companies operating in a region where memories of past hostility and aggression were still fresh. On the other hand, American subsidiaries tended to adopt the HRM system/practices of their parent company which, in comparison with the local firms, placed greater emphasis on employee morale, communication and welfare, communication with the public, job counselling, and labour market and wage surveys. Furthermore, the HRM practices of American companies showed greater strategic orientation. They varied more with fluctuations in organizational contingencies.

Level of Technology

The HRM function is given greater recognition in high-technology firms (ibid.). All the high-technology firms in the sample had a formally established personnel department, compared to only 71 per cent of the medium-technology firms.[2] High technology firms also practise more extensively a wider range of personnel activities, and greater emphasis is placed on activities that contribute to employee morale and satisfaction –

the design of incentive systems and pay structures, and the proper selection and development of employees.

Line managers and personnel superiors[3] in high-technology firms also rated HR activities higher than their counterparts in medium-technology firms. Perhaps the most affirmative finding, from the point of view of personnel managers, is that personnel superiors in high-technology firms have a very positive and supportive attitude towards the personnel function, rating morale, developmental, planning, and pay structure activities as highly important.

Sectoral Development

The post-1987 flexibility in NWC wage guidelines implicitly acknowledged the existence of sectoral and organizational differences. In the construction and hotel sectors, with many part-time and foreign workers, HRM practices are inevitably different from others, such as the banking sector. Furthermore, since Singapore's economy is export oriented, its business/industrial sectors are highly sensitive to environmental changes. For example, the recent downturn in demand for PC drives sent manufacturers (who until recently were aggressively recruiting skilled workers) retrenching their workers.

CONCLUSION

With the influence of MNEs and the proactive policies of the government, the HRM function in Singapore has evolved over the past three decades. From the traditional Chinese family business, with the patriarch in charge and no personnel function (in the Western sense) to speak of, Western models of personnel/HRM are well in place in many organizations these days. Concepts like training and development, personnel planning, performance appraisal systems, and Quality Circles (which are foreign to traditional Chinese culture and Chinese management), have become common practice in Singapore.

HRM practices in Singapore have been, and will continue to be, influenced by state policies under the present tripartite arrangement. The state has actively intervened in national manpower planning, training and development, wage levels and employment relations. For example, the government decides each year on the number of students entering different disciplines, reasoning that with a labour force of only 1.7 million, it is too costly to allow oversupply, and hence wastage, of labour/skills. In training and development, the state has, through the NPB (now renamed Productivity and Standards Board, or PSB), provided generic as well as industry-specific training. The PSB also looks after the retraining of workers made redundant by technological developments. In the public sector, the Public Service Commission specifies the minimum number of training days which public organizations have to provide for employees at different levels of appointment. The government hoped to improve public sector efficiency by providing extensive training, and even if employees were to leave for the private sector, the nation overall would still benefit from the training provided.

Government policies often had far-reaching implications for HRM practices at the organizational level. For example, when the NWC adopted the flexible wage policy (by introducing different wage components reflecting basic wage, individual performance, performance of the organization, and growth of the national economy), the government pushed for the introduction/fine-tuning of performance appraisal in both public and private organizations so that performance-related bonus payments could be implemented effectively.

In addition to the state, other forces which affect HRM practices include the headquarters influences of MNEs, level of technology, organizational size, sectoral differences in HR requirements, and so on. However, the influences of these forces can be constrained by local values/culture, as well as by the 'realities' of the local labour market. An example of the constraining influences of local culture is the reluctance of local employees to accept Western-style open appraisal systems (as also occurs in other Asian countries). Due to their concern for 'face', their inclination to avoid situations where one or both parties may experience a 'loss of face', and their concern for 'power distance', Singaporeans are generally uncomfortable with open appraisal systems. As a result, attempts by HR departments to introduce open appraisal have met with stubborn resistance from employees.

The 'realities' of the local labour market can also affect the extent to which government/MNE initiated HR policy changes are implemented at the firm level. The local labour market is tight, and high turnover is a major problem which HR managers have to contend with. Given the tight labour market, many companies paid only 'lip service' to the government's urge to use performance bonuses to encourage individual productivity. In interviews with HR managers, many confided that their company paid uniform performance bonus to employees in the same job category, as differentiating bonus payments could cause dissatisfaction and trigger job-hopping. For the same reason, many private-sector companies did not respond to the government's initiative to make employees more responsible for their health and medical expenditure. After all, what could companies do if they could not recruit even with full medical benefits? High labour turnover has also made companies cautious about spending too much on training, in spite of the government's continual urge to step up training efforts.

Judging by current practices, HRM in Singapore is not a distinctive entity from personnel management. Towers Perrin (1997), a US-based management consultant firm, recently conducted a local survey on HR priorities and practices in Singapore. The survey covered 43 companies including local subsidiaries of MNEs (such as American Express, Citibank, Motorola, Sony and Philips), as well as major local companies (for example, Singapore Telecom and Singapore Power). It found that only 45 per cent of the companies fully incorporated HRM strategy into their business plan. 'For the majority of the remainder... HR strategy is at best only loosely linked to business strategy.' Almost half of the companies did not have a 'distinctive or differentiating' corporate culture to speak of. Reward programmes were also found to be poorly linked to the objectives and outcomes which companies sought to influence. Bearing in mind that the survey covered mainly MNEs and LLCs, the findings probably presented a rosier picture of current HRM practices in Singapore than it would have been if SLCs were also included. Hence, it is safe to say that HRM practices in Singapore are still fairly oriented towards personnel management.

Nevertheless, looking into the future, the trend of development is towards a HRM model. In the same survey conducted by Towers Perrin (ibid.), it was found that a gap existed between current HRM practices and the perceived importance of various HR activities by HR professionals. In terms of perceived importance, most of the companies surveyed did recognize the importance of incorporating HR strategies into business plans, implementing career planning, introducing cultural transformation and implementing reward systems that are properly linked to results. It appears that although current HR practices in Singapore were still some distance from the HRM model, it is a target which companies aimed for. Also, at the national level, the government places great emphasis on education and training and this will inevitably have an impact on firm-level HRM practices. However, given the pace of environmental changes and the large number of factors affecting HRM practices, HR activities will always vary among organizations, even among those operating in the same sector.

NOTES

1. Interestingly, these can be compared and contrasted with developments in other locations outlined elsewhere in this volume.
2. A full explanation of the classification of high, medium and low technology firms is provided in Appendix 1, 'Scheme for Classifying Companies According to Level of Technology' in Yuen and Hui (1990). The classification scheme follows closely the scheme used by the Economic Development Board in Singapore. High-technology firms include those engaged in petroleum and petrochemicals, oilfield equipment and services, chemical and pharmaceutical, bio-technology, communications equipment, ocean engineering and oil rig construction, aerospace and related industries, precision engineering, etc. Medium-technology firms include mainly mass-production companies using technologies that are relatively well established (for example, consumer electronics, office equipment, etc.).
3. 'Personnel superior' was the immediate superior of the person in charge of personnel/HRM in a firm. Personnel superiors in the study were often CEOs.

REFERENCES

Anantaraman, Venkatraman (1991) *Singapore Industrial Relations System*. Singapore: Singapore Institute of Management/McGraw-Hill.
Business Times (1993) 9–10 January, Singapore.
Business Times (1997) 22 January, Singapore.

Chew, Irene K. H. and Albert C. Y. Teo, (1991) 'Human Resource Practices in Singapore: A Survey of Local Firms and MNCs', *Asia Pacific Human Resource Management*, Autumn, 1991.
Chew Soon Beng and Rosalind Chew (1995) *Employment Driven IR Regimes: The Singapore Experience*. Aldershot: Avebury Press.
Chew Soon Beng and Rosalind Chew (1996) *Industrial Relations in Singapore Industry*. Singapore: Addison-Wesley.
Department of Statistics (1995) *Singapore, 1965–1995 Statistical Highlights, a Review of 30 Years' Development*. Singapore.
Department of Statistics, *Yearbook of Statistics, Singapore*, various issues.
Deyo, Frederick C. (1981) *Dependent Development and Industrial Order*. New York, NY: Praeger.
Economic Development Board (1989) *SME Master Plan: Report on Enterprise Development*. Singapore.
Economic Development Board (1993) *Growing with Enterprise: A National Effort*. Singapore: Economic Development Board.
Lee Hsien Loong (1994) 'Training for Workforce 2000', May Day Message delivered by Deputy Prime Minister, *Productivity and Quality Statement, 1994*, Singapore: National Productivity and Quality Council.
Leggett, Chris (1993) 'Corporatist Trade Unionism in Singapore' in Stephen Frenkel (ed.) *Organized Labor in the Asia-Pacific Region*. Ithaca, NY: ILR Press, pp.223–46.
Leggett, Chris (1993) 'Singapore' in Stephen Deery and Richard J. Mitchell (eds.) *Labour Law and Industrial Relations in Asia*. Australia: Longman, pp.96–136.
Ministry of Labour, *Singapore Yearbook of Labour Statistics*, various issues.
Ministry of Trade and Industry (1986) NPB Report of the Economic Committee, Singapore.
National Productivity Board (1992) *Productivity Statement: A Document of the National Productivity Council*. Singapore: National Productivity Board.
NPB-SILS (1993) *Survey on Employee Benefits, Singapore*: National Productivity Board [and] Singapore Institute of Labour Studies.
NPB-SIPM (1991) *1990 Survey on Human Resource Management Practices in Singapore*. Singapore: National Productivity Board [and] Singapore Institute of Personnel Management.
Skills Development Fund Board (1995) *Skills Development Fund Annual Report 1994/1995*. Singapore: Singapore National Printers.
Storey, John (1992) *Developments in the Management of Human Resources*. Oxford: Blackwell.
Tan Chwee Huat (1995) *Labour Management Relations in Singapore*. Singapore: Prentice Hall.
Tan Chwee Huat (1996) 'Employee Relations in Singapore – Current Issues and Problems', *Employee Relations*, Vol.18, No.3.
Time Magazine, Asian Edition, 10 June 1996.
Towers Perrin (1997) *Human Resources – Priorities and Challenges*. Singapore: Towers Perin.
Wilkinson, Barry (1994) *Labour and Industry in the Asia-Pacific: Lessons from the Newly Industrialized Countries*. Berlin: de Gruyter.
Yuen Chi Ching (1990) 'Human Resource Management in High- and Medium- Technology Companies', *Personnel Review*, Vol.19, No.4, pp.36–46.
Yuen Chi Ching and Hui Tak Kee (1993) 'Headquarters, Host-Culture and Organizational Influences on HRM Policies and Practices', *Management International Review*, Vol. 33, 1993/4.

The Development of HRM Practices in Taiwan

SHYH-JER CHEN

More than 60 per cent of the paid employees in Taiwan are employed by small and medium-sized, mostly family-owned enterprises, which traditionally do not have distinct human resource management (HRM) functions. State-owned and large-sized private enterprises, in contrast, have gradually established human resource (HR) systems and learned HR techniques from foreign-owned companies during the past few decades (Farh, 1995). This piece first examines employment structure and labour market developments in Taiwan, then evaluates employment legislation and the development of HRM functions, and finally identifies several major challenges for future HRM, such as employee participation and employment security.

LABOUR MARKET DEVELOPMENT

Taiwan has experienced rapid economic growth and egalitarian income distribution in recent decades. The annual average rate of economic growth between 1952 and 1990 was 8.9 per cent. Gini coefficients declined significantly from 0.58 in 1953 to 0.303 in 1990. Unemployment remains low, with the annual unemployment rate, on average, 2.1 per cent from 1960 to 1995. Table 1 presents data on macro-economic and labour statistics for selected years.

Development strategy shifted from import substitution to export-led growth (Deyo, 1989). In order to utilize relatively abundant HRs, the Taiwanese government encouraged labour-intensive industries, such as textile and food, in the early stages of economic development (Galenson, 1979, see Bae on Korea, in this volume). In addition to private enterprises, the Taiwanese government took over many monopolistic state-owned enterprises (SOEs), such as in the petroleum, transportation, sugar, and electronics industries, from the Japanese government after 1945.

The labour force has grown from 3.6 million in 1960 to 9.04 million in 1995. In 1995, some 5.4 per cent of the labour force listed themselves as employers; 17.1 per cent as self-employed workers; 8.8 per cent as unpaid family workers; and 68.6 per cent as paid employees (working for both public and private sectors) (DGBAS, 1996). In addition, the labour force participation rate has continuously declined over the last five years. The

Shyh-jer Chen, National Sun Yat-sen University, Taiwan

TABLE 1
MACRO-ECONOMIC AND LABOUR STATISTICS FOR SELECTED YEARS

	1960	1965	1970	1975	1980	1985	1990	1995
GNP per capita (US$)	143	203	360	890	2,155	2,992	7,413	11,315
Economic growth rate (GNP) (%)	6.4	11.0	11.3	4.4	7.1	5.6	5.5	5.9
Consumer Price Index (1991=100)	19.04	21.42	26.51	47.14	71.45	86.57	96.50	116.06
Unemployment rates (%)	3.98	3.29	1.70	2.40	1.23%	2.91	1.67	1.79
Gini Coefficient	–	–	0.294	–	0.277	0.290	0.303	–
Total labour force (000s)	3,637	3,891	4,654	5,656	6,629	7,651	8,423	9,040
Male LFPR* (%)	–	–	–	–	77.11	75.47	73.96	72.03
Female LFPR* (%)	–	–	–	–	39.25	43.46	44.50	45.34

* labour force participation rate

Sources: Council for Economic Planning and Development, 1996; Directorate General of Budget, Accounting and Statistics, 1996.

labour force participation rate was 60.9 per cent in 1987, but dropped to 58.71 per cent in 1995. The decline was especially rapid for male workers as they declined from 76.4 per cent in 1983 to 72.03 per cent in 1995. In contrast, the female labour force participation rate actually grew in the 1980s, although it declined slightly in the early 1990s (ibid.).

The labour force employed in the manufacturing sector was 14.8 per cent in 1960, a figure which increased steadily through the 1960s and 1970s, and peaked at 35.17 per cent in 1987. Since 1988 the manufacturing work force has decreased, to 27.08 per cent as of 1995. In contrast, workers employed by the service industry increased from 29.3 per cent of the labour force in 1960 to 50.71 per cent as of 1995.

Due to the adoption of labour-intensive policies and rapid economic development over the past several decades, the demand for labour gradually surpassed its supply, especially for lower-skilled workers. The labour shortage began to prevail in many industries, such as manufacturing and construction in the mid-1980s. In 1989 the government began to encourage the migration of foreign workers from South East Asia to relieve labour shortages (see Yuen on Singapore, in this volume). Although there is a heated debate on the effects of foreign workers on the Taiwanese economy, the total number of foreign workers increased rapidly in the past few years. There were more than 220,000 legal foreign workers in mid-1996. It is expected that the total number will be twice by the end of this century (Ay et al., 1996).

ORGANIZATIONAL CHARACTERISTICS

There are variously-sized enterprises, both indigenous and foreign-owned, as well as joint ventures (JVs).

Types of Enterprise

Small and medium-sized enterprises (SMEs) are the major type of enterprise in Taiwan. Of the 5.2 million paid employees in the private sector in 1995, some 64.7 per cent were employed by companies which had less than 30 employees. Only 5.5 per cent were employed by companies which had more than 500 employees. There are several interesting characteristics to these SMEs. First, owners often also serve as managing directors and perform key functions, such as purchasing and handling finances. Higher-level managers are usually relatives and/or close friends. The owners can be considered the Chief Executive Officer or the entire board of directors. In other words, ownership and entrepreneurship are not separated in these companies. Second, the economy of SMEs is limited in scope and its financial structure is quite weak. They are run by their own family members who do not want to absorb outside capital because they worry about the dilution of ownership. Third, many SMEs are short-lived. The average life span of companies is only 12 years. San (1991) estimates that only about 4.5 per cent of companies in Taiwan remain in existence more than 26 years after their establishment. Fourth, SMEs employ low-skilled workers and pay less than large-sized companies for comparable workers. Crucially, workers have a low commitment to their job resulting in a high level of turnover and lack of attachment to the firms (Huang, 1994).

Large-sized enterprises have been protected by the Taiwanese government since the early stage of economic growth. Importantly, the owners of large-sized companies have maintained good relationships with the ruling party, the Koumintang (KMT). For example, the KMT usually recruits the owners of large-sized enterprises to be members of the Standing Committee, the highest decision-making group within the KMT. SOEs, such as Taiwan Electronic Power Company and Chinese Petroleum Company, are the largest companies. Workers employed in SOEs have a lower turnover rate, and enjoy higher labour standards, than in private companies. Personnel policies, such as hiring, promotion, benefits, and salary, are regulated by the government. However, since the 1990s, the government has moved to privatize these SOEs, such as China Steel Company.

The privatization of SOEs has been a serious challenge to HR/personnel departments. As these companies did not usually resort to layoffs to adjust their employment, how to utilize HRs more efficiently in response to market competition after privatization became a major issue. For example, China Steel Company used some methods to re-deploy HRs. On the one hand, the company encouraged people to retire earlier with higher retirement payments. On the other hand, the company established several new subsidiaries. This allowed the company to 'rearrange' its original labour force more efficiently. Generally, workers in the SOEs do not support the privatization policy because they worry about losing their higher labour standards and even their jobs.

The Style and Role of Management

Researchers have noted the importance of Confucianism in Taiwanese economic success (Wilkinson, 1994 and elsewhere) (see Bae on Korea, this volume). Confucianism tries to build up a value system which helps to maintain social order. Its philosophy originates with people's behaviour in accordance with family ethics; 'well-behaved' people manage their family well (Chen, 1990). As mentioned earlier, the traditional Chinese culture has also been 'generalized' into ethnic labour relations in companies.

Chen (ibid.) proposes six principles which a good manager should follow in traditional Chinese literature: be morally upright; behave properly in order to be a model for their subordinates; establish rules for their subordinates to follow; have authority and power; be 'just' in providing rewards and punishment; create an atmosphere of harmony in their department. These principles strongly emphasize authority, obedience, loyalty, and harmony in organizations. Wilkinson (1994) points out further that there are no standardized rules for management practices in Confucianism. Rather, there are highly personal and particular relationships between employers and employees. Furthermore, employers' authority stems from moral superiority rather than competence.

HR managers usually play a minor role in organizations, in comparison to other line managers in finance, marketing, and so forth. In general, the HR department is put in the lower rank in the hierarchy of companies, and people usually treat HR departments as a secondary function in the organization (Farh, 1995).

THE IMPACT OF EMPLOYMENT LEGISLATION ON HRM PRACTICES

HRM practices are affected by several employment laws, such as the Labour Standards Law (LSL), the Labour Union Law (LUL), the Collective Agreement Law (CAL), the Employee Welfare Fund Law, and The Settlement of Labour Dispute Law.

Labour Standards Law

The LSL, which replaced the Factory Law, was promulgated by the Legislative Yuan and enacted in 1984. This law is applicable to seven types of business, such as agriculture, mining and quarrying, manufacturing, transportation, and construction (Article 3). The Council of Labour Affairs (CLA) (1996) reported that the coverage of the LSL was 3.6 million of Taiwan's 6.2 million paid employees in the private sector, accounting for 58 per cent of all paid employees in 1995. The CLA is now trying to further expand the LSL's coverage. For example, in 1996 the CLA chair, Shen-shan

Hsieh, made an effort to spread its coverage to include service occupations. In spite of the opposition from employers' associations and other government agencies, such as the Ministry of Finance, this was partly successful. The LSL was revised by the Legislation Yuan in December 1996, and coverage of the LSL expanded towards fresh sectors, such as banking. It is worth noting that one revised provision states that all sectors should be included by the LSL by the end of 1998. The purpose of the law is to provide minimum standards for labour conditions, to protect workers rights and interests, to strengthen labour-management relations and to promote social and economic development (Article 1). This law provides a comprehensive framework of rules to govern labour-management relations. Matters covered by this law include wages, retirement pensions, severance pay, overtime and holiday wages, child and female workers, the circumstances of terminating a labour contract, and labour-management conferences. It is obvious that issues in this law are widespread and critically affect HRM practices.

Some scholars point out that the standards of the law are significantly higher than in other well-developed countries, except for the 'basic wage'.[1] Many employers argue that it is hard for small companies to comply with the law due to its high standards (San, 1993; Lee and Wu, 1996). There are many controversial provisions in the LSL, such as the meaning of the term 'wage' and the items that should be included in its computation, which in turn affect the calculation of retirement and severance payments (Articles 2 and 55). In addition, according to Article 53, an employee who has worked for the same business entity for more than 25 years may apply for voluntary retirement. However, this article has been criticized for not considering the nature of small businesses in Taiwan; considering that more than 95 per cent of Taiwan's businesses do not operate for more than 25 years, there is very little chance for a worker to qualify for the retirement pension provisions.

Kleingartner and Peng (1991: 430) point out that 'the most serious problem with the Labour Standards Law lies in its comprehensiveness coupled with poor enforcement.' For example, the LSL states that an employer shall deduct a certain sum of money every month and deposit it in a special account as the reserve fund of retirement payment for workers (Article 56). However, in 1995 the coverage rate for such retirement funds was only 12.93 per cent of the number of establishments (CLA, 1996). In fact, inadequate enforcement of this aspect of the LSL has led to increased labour disputes.

Labour Unions Law and Collective Agreement Law

Trade unions in Taiwan are regulated by the LUL, enacted in 1929 and last amended in 1975. The law sets forth the structure, formation, and obligations of trade unions. In addition, collective bargaining is governed by the CAL, first promulgated in the early 1930s in wartime China. The law stipulates the rights of collective bargaining between unions and employers. There are several characteristics of trade unions and collective bargaining in Taiwan that are worthy of further detail.

First, a union should be organized when there are a minimum of 30 workers in the workplace (Article 6) and union membership is mandatory. All workers within the jurisdiction of a union who are at least 16 years old have the right and obligation to join and become members (Article 12). According to the Enforcement Rules of the LUL, a worker may be suspended from employment for a prescribed period of time by the relevant union for refusing to join (Article 13). However, many workers do not join because the union is not able, in reality, to suspend their employment. Table 2 shows the number of unions and membership in selected years.

TABLE 2
UNIONS AND UNION MEMBERSHIP IN TAIWAN, 1987–95

Year	Union* Density (%)	Industrial Unions		Craft Unions	
		Membership (000s)	Unionization Rate (%)	Membership (000s)	Unionization Rate (%)
1987	23.4	703	30.72	1,396	36.27
1988	27.0	696	29.52	1,564	42.78
1989	30.6	698	30.57	1,721	42.79
1990	33.3	699	31.30	2,057	50.65
1991	34.9	692	29.29	2,259	59.73
1992	35.4	669	28.88	2,389	59.70
1993	36.3	651	28.51	2,521	61.19
1994	36.3	637	27.38	2,640	60.26
1995	33.8	598	25.35	2,537	58.05

*Union density is calculated by the author as the ratio of the number of union members to the number of employed persons. The number of employed persons is total labour force minus unemployed workers; therefore, it includes workers who are not allowed to join unions, such as police officers, public employees etc.

Source: CLA (1996: Tables 3–1)

Second, trade unions are divided into two categories: industrial unions and craft unions. Craft unions play a less active role in industrial relations because the major reason for a worker to join is to participate in government-subsidized labour insurance programmes. Consequently, craft unions are usually called 'labour insurance unions' (San, 1988; Lan, 1992; Frenkel et al., 1993; Chen and Taira, 1995).

Third, sources of operational funds for unions are admission and regular membership fees, special funds, special contributions, and government subsidies (Article 22). The LUL also sets out that government subsidies shall be granted only to those general federations of unions above the municipal level. In fact, unions in Taiwan have been called 'company unions' or 'employer-sponsored unions', because many local unions receive special contributions and subsidies from employers (Frenkel et al., 1993; Freeman, 1994). Therefore, it is difficult for such unions to become independent and autonomous.

Fourth, it is uncommon for unions and employers to bargain collectively. The CLA (1996) reported that only 292 out of 3,689 unions signed collective agreements with their employers, accounting for less than eight per cent of unions. Researchers have pointed out one of the reasons is that many provisions in the CLA restrain bilateral negotiations between two parties (Kleingartner and Peng, 1991). For example, every collective agreement must be submitted by either or both parities to the authorities for approval. The competent authority can cancel or amend the agreement if it is contrary to the law or regulation (Article 4). The other reason might be the 'substitution effect' from the LSL. The high labour standards give little room for both parties to bargain (San, 1993). Thus, most collective agreements repeat and duplicate the working conditions specified in the labour laws.

The trade union movement's development in Taiwan can be divided into two major periods. The watershed was the mid-1980s, when martial law was lifted and the LSL was passed. Before this, unions served only as an auxiliary instrument in helping the government promote economic development, and it has been documented that industrial peace contributed significantly to Taiwan's economic growth in the past several decades (Lee, 1988; 1995). In addition, despite the fact that there was no 'organic' connection between the unions and the KMT, a major function of unions is to mobilize workers to help KMT candidates win elections (Chen and Taira, 1995).

After lifting martial law, strikes became legal. Although the LUL allows only 'one plant, one union' (Article 8), many illegal unions were formed against this provision. Unions began to concern themselves much more with the welfare issues of workers. These developments resulted in the establishment of labour relations departments in many large-sized companies, especially SOEs, such as Chinese Petroleum Company and China Steel Company. HR managers assumed greater responsibility for dealing with the demands of unions and workers.

The Settlement of Labour Dispute Law

Labour disputes are governed by the Settlement of Labour Dispute Law, promulgated in 1928 and last amended in 1988. Labour disputes in this law are categorized into rights disputes or adjustment (interests) disputes. Rights disputes concern those between workers and employers regarding their rights and obligations arising from laws or regulations, collective agreements, or labour contracts. In contrast, adjustments disputes arise between workers and employers when they cannot agree whether to continue employment or to change the terms and conditions of employment (Article 4). The disputes can be resolved by conciliation or/and arbitration, depending on the nature of the dispute. Rights disputes can either be settled by conciliation procedures or by the courts. Adjustment disputes can either be resolved by conciliation or arbitration procedures (Article 5 and 6).

The conciliation and arbitration committees in labour disputes are composed of members appointed by the competent authority and disputing parties under the chairmanship of the representative appointed by the competent authority. In spite of formal procedures in the Settlement of Labour Dispute Law, most labour disputes in Taiwan are resolved using informal conciliation procedures between workers and employers without direct government intervention. This contrasts with such procedures in other countries, such as the Philippines (see Amante in this collection).

SELECTED HRM PRACTICES

This section reviews selected HRM practices in Taiwan, including staffing, training and development, and compensation. As stated previously, most SMEs do not have a distinct HR or personnel department. In contrast, large-sized and some SOEs have gradually established HRM systems, using, for instance, job analysis, job evaluation, performance appraisal, and compensation practices.

Staffing

The major positions in SMEs are nearly all held exclusively by close family members, since non-family members are usually not trusted by the owner. This fact is reflected in staffing practices; these enterprises hire close relatives or close friends as workers to ensure loyalty. Also, some employers believe that hiring close relatives and friends contributes to reduced turnover rates. The value placed on loyalty is not only restricted to these enterprises, however. Loyalty and the 'right' personality qualities, such as being an easy-going and hard-working employee, are also major concerns for staffing large-sized enterprises. For example, President Enterprise, the biggest food company in Taiwan, puts loyalty and personality as its first priorities when hiring.

As far as selection procedures are concerned, different types of enterprises use different methods. SOEs select their candidates by using competitive written examinations. Farh (1995) points out that using written examinations as the sole criterion for staffing is done not because it is valid but because it is seen as objective and fair in the mind of the public. In contrast, private enterprises combine various methods to select their employees, such as physical examinations, interviews, written examinations and educational qualifications.

According to research by the DGBAS (1996), about 28 per cent of interviewed employees reported they found their current job through an newspaper or magazine advertisement. Importantly, more than 58 per cent reported that it was via referrals (by relatives or friends). This is consistent with the view that close relatives and friends are hired by small-sized, family-owned companies.

Training and Development

Training in Taiwan is viewed by employers as a personnel cost rather than an investment in HR (Farh, 1995). Employers are reluctant to spend much on training employees because of high turnover rates, especially for small-sized enterprises. When comparing training and development between large and small-sized companies, Jean (1994) finds that around 60 per cent of large-sized companies have an independent training department; however, less than one per cent of small-sized companies have one. Only 21.3 per cent of small-sized companies had held training programmes. Most training in small-sized companies is sub-contracted to business consulting companies or co-sponsored with the government. In addition, only 18.6 per cent of the total labour force in Taiwan reports they have attended a training programme. Of these, 72.4 per cent paid the training fee themselves and 27.6 per cent were assigned and supported by their employers (ibid).

In order to improve workers' skill levels, the government has passed several training laws to encourage employers' investment in training. In the early 1960s, a large proportion of the labour force was employed in the agricultural sector and workers lacked industrial skills. The government passed the Law for Occupational Training Fund in 1972. This law requested enterprises employing more than 40 workers to deduct at least 1.5 per cent of all workers' compensation for an occupational training fund. However, the law was repealed in 1974 due to the oil crisis (ibid). Similarly, in 1983 the Law for Occupational Training was passed in order to encourage enterprises to develop HRs. This law offered enterprises tax reductions if they initiated training programmes (see Yuen, this volume).

Compensation

Compensation is one of the most important HRM issues for both workers and employers (CAL, 1995). At the national level, the increase in real wages has nearly paralleled the increase in productivity over the past several decades. For example, the increase in annual labour productivity was, on average, around 5.94 per cent from 1952 to 1986; while the growth in annual real wages was 5.30 per cent (Lee, 1988). Thus, it is argued that 'workers in Taiwan enjoyed their share of the fruits of economic development' (ibid.: 193).

At the firm level, the compensation package includes base pay and various types of bonuses, such as year-end, competition, invention, long-service, spring festival and mid-autumn festival gifts, and so forth. There are several reasons for employers to use different types of bonuses instead of paying a higher base wage. First, the LSL prescribes that employers allocate retirement and severance payment according to the years of a worker's service. Second, both the Labour Insurance Law and the Health Insurance Law request employers to pay the insurance and health insurance fees for their workers. The computation of the two payments by employers is based on a worker's base wage. Therefore, employers pay higher bonuses and benefits to reduce their levels of responsibility for such benefits.

According to the report from the CLA (1995:3), the ratio of base wage to total compensation was 68.98 per cent in 1994. Around ten per cent of the entire compensation figure was paid by employers for employees' protection programmes (for example, medical care, life insurance and pensions). The ratio of payments to employees' protection programmes to the entire compensation has increased during the past few years. More than 90 per cent of enterprises provide year-end bonuses. Even when the enterprise did not make a profit in the previous year, many employers still paid a bonus. The amount depends on the balance of profits. Over the past few years, employees working for high-tech and monopolistic enterprises have enjoyed higher bonuses. For example, Chinese American Petrochemical Company (CAPCO), a Taiwanese-American JV, gave a 14-month-base-wage year-end bonus in 1995.[2] In addition, Formosa Plastics Corporation, a most successful private company, usually provides about 4.5-month-base-wage year-end bonus. Public employees receive 1.5 months wages as a year-end bonus. Yet, since there is no commonly acceptable formula for the amount of year-end bonus, many disputes erupted over this issue during the past decade. For example, the CAPCO union asked for a 4-month-base-wage year-end bonus in 1996; however, the company agreed to pay 3.5-month-base-wage because of the economic recession. Therefore, the union tried to call a sit-down strike in early 1997.

Most SMEs in Taiwan do not use job analysis and job evaluation to price their workers. However, large-sized and SOEs do use such systems. Due to a higher turnover rate, small companies rely heavily upon external competitiveness to develop their compensation practices. To acquire the market wage level, personnel managers often meet regularly and informally to exchange pay information (Farh, 1995).

Despite the complexity of the composition of compensation packages, base pay is traditionally seniority-based (Lee, 1995). With the traditional culture of avoiding conflict between management and employees, most workers can be promoted along the grades of their job titles if their annual performances are classified as 'above-average'. That is, their base pay increases with their tenure. At the end of the year most workers can receive a performance bonus based on their performance evaluation, although the proportion of qualifying workers varies in different companies. For example, more than 80 per cent of employees in SOEs and the public sector can be ranked as grade A in their performance evaluation and receive one-month-base-wage performance bonus. If they are ranked as grade B, they can receive a half-month-base-wage performance bonus. It is not common for the employees to receive a 'below-average' (grade C or below) evaluation.

Comparing Personnel/IR with HRM between SMEs and SOEs

This section makes a summary in comparing Personnel/Industrial Relations with HRM between SMEs and SOEs. The aspects include rules, behaviour, managerial role, key manager, personnel selection, payments system, work conditions, labour management, job design and in-house training. By using the ticks, crosses and percentage marks to indicate level of presence of HRM practices, the researcher's subjective judgment is presented in Table 3.

COMPARATIVE AND INTERNATIONAL HRM PRACTICES: A FIELD

TABLE 3
PERSONNEL/IR VERSUS HRM IN TAIWANESE SMEs AND SOEs

Dimensions	SMEs	SOEs
Rules	x	x
Behaviour	x	%
Managerial role	%	%
Key managers	x	%
Personnel selection	x	%
Payments system	x	%
Work Conditions	✓	%
Labour management	✓	✓
Job design	x	%
In-house training	x	✓

Key:
✓   all
%   some
x   none

Source: Adapted from Storey (1992), see for explanations of the dimensions.

STUDY

To compare larger Taiwanese-owned firms with foreign subsidiaries and JVs, we use a questionnaire collecting data from 26 Taiwanese-owned firms and 26 subsidiaries and JVs (14 from the US, seven from Holland, two from Japan, two from Germany and one from Australia). Most companies investigated are located in the Taipei or Kaohsiung areas. Several of the main characteristics of the firms are presented in Table 4. We use 27 items,

TABLE 4
CHARACTERISTICS OF TAIWANESE-OWNED FIRMS AND FOREIGN SUBSIDIARIES

Factors		Foreign subsidiaries and joint ventures	Taiwanise-owned firms
Independent	yes	23	23
HR Department	no	2	3
Age of firm	0–10	13	8
(in years)	11–20	5	6
	20–30	7	7
	over 30	0	4
Size of firm	0–100	3	2
(employees)	101–300	13	3
	301–500	1	3
	over 500	8	17
Unionized	yes	17	13
	no	8	11

TABLE 5
COMPARISON OF HRM PRACTICES BETWEEN FOREIGN SUBSIDIARIES AND
TAIWANESE-OWNED FIRMS

HRM Practices	Foreign subsidiaries and joint ventures	Taiwanise-owned firms	F-value
Recruitment and Selection	4.36 (0.57)	4.38 (0.58)	0.03
Training and Development	3.50 (0.49)	3.22 (0.56)	3.59*
Employment Security	4.61 (1.17)	5.04 (1.04)	1.90
Tasks and Assignment	4.35 (0.93)	4.27 (0.66)	0.16
Job Redesign	3.83 (1.00)	3.54 (0.89)	1.20
Control	4.69 (0.88)	4.44 (1.12)	0.80
Wage Level	3.73 (1.25)	4.08 (1.09)	1.13
Performance-based Pay	4.19 (0.60)	4.43 (0.60)	2.09
Performance Appraisal	4.50 (0.89)	4.10 (1.03)	2.24
Employee Participation	4.35 (1.16)	3.77 (1.48)	2.45
Employee Ownership	3.07 (1.55)	4.15 (1.38)	7.03**
Culture	4.42 (1.03)	4.21 (0.99)	0.09

1. HRM practices are measured from the 27-item questionnaire assessed on a six-point scale. 1 means 'strongly disagree,' and 6 means 'strongly agree.' Standard deviations are given in parentheses.
2. Approaching 1 means HRM practices are more like a cost-minimizing type, while approaching 6 means more like commitment-maximizing type. (see Tables 7 and 8 of Bae's article in this volume for definitions of the variables.)
3. * $p<.05$; ** $p<.01$

(a condensed form of the 38-item questionnaire used by Bae in this volume).

A six-point scale is used to measure the 12 HRM practices. These are: recruitment and selection; training and development; employment security; tasks and assignment; job redesign; control; wage level; performance-based pay; performance appraisal; employee participation; employee ownership, and culture. The results of the survey are shown in Table 5. From the results, it seems there is no significant difference in most aspects of the HRM practices between Taiwanese-owned firms and foreign subsidiaries and JVs. Only training and development and employee ownership show significant differences in the HRM practices between them. Farh (1995:280) points out that in the 1960s large American and Japanese multinationals, such as IBM, Matsushita and Mitsubishi, began to influence personnel management practices in Taiwan. From the results, we can observe the emergence of some convergence in HRM practices between Taiwanese-owned firms and foreign subsidiaries.

To further investigate whether there are differences in HRM practices between these firms, a logit regression model is used. Dependent variable is dichotomous. Foreign subsidiaries or JVs are represented by 1, and 0 represents Taiwanese-owned firms. Independent variables are four broad HRM areas which are summarized from the 12 HRM practices. They are: HR flow, work systems, rewards systems and employee influence (see the summary in Bae, in this volume).

The results of the logit analysis presented in Table 6 indicates that there is no significant difference in the four HRM areas between Taiwanese-owned enterprises and foreign subsidiaries and JVs.

MAJOR CHALLENGES IN HRM

There are several factors affecting the future development of HRM in Taiwan. First, the continuous movement of capital to mainland China and South East Asia has resulted in a serious problem of security of employment. Second, the process of privatization has caused workers in SOEs to fear for their jobs. This is reflected in the fact that workers have asked to participate on the board of directors and in the business strategy decision-making process. Third, people worry that foreign workers might be used as substitutes for domestic lower-skilled workers which will then raise the unemployment rate. This section summarizes two major challenges

TABLE 6
LOGIT RESULT

Variables	Coefficient	Standard Error
HR Flow	−0.594	0.791
Work Systems	1.067	0.619
Reward Systems	−0.719	0.815
Employee Influence	−0.114	0.467
Constant	1.479	2.73
−2 Log Likelihood	65.21	
n	52	

– employee participation and employment security – of future importance for HRM in Taiwan.

Employee Participation

As mentioned above, collective bargaining between employers and unions is not an important institution in Taiwan in determining the terms and conditions of employment. There are several channels specified in labour law for workers to participate in their workplace, such as the factory council and labour-management conferences, employee stock ownership and profit sharing, and employee welfare committees. Recently, as mentioned earlier, independent unions demanded the right to participate in managerial decisions, such as the distribution of year-end bonuses, and to be on the board of directors.

The factory council is prescribed in the Factory Law, promulgated in 1929. The monthly factory council meeting is composed of equal numbers of employer and worker representatives. The functions of the council are to promote work efficiency, mediate disputes, assist in the enforcement of collective agreements, improve safety and sanitary facilities in the factory, and make plans for workers' welfare (Article 50). In addition, the LSL states that a business entity shall convene monthly labour-management conferences to co-ordinate the relationship, and promote co-operation, between management and labour and to increase work efficiency (Article 83). Workers and employers each elect three to nine representatives to the conference. The functions of the conference are to: report on labour turnover, production plans and business conditions; discuss matters relating to the harmonization of labour relations and labour-management co-operation concerning labour welfare and increases in labour productivity; take suggestions (Article 13) (see Amante on the Philippines, pp.111–132).

The Taiwanese system of factory council and the labour-management conferences deal mainly with workplace-level matters, such as labour productivity and labour welfare. For example, China Steel Company holds labour-management conferences every month. The issues proposed by the workers include the reduction of working hours, the establishment of job rotation for operational workers, and so forth. However, since there is no penal provision to force workers and employers to hold the conference, the number of plants which actually hold conferences and council meetings is quite low. For example, at the end of 1995, only 980 out of 187,281 establishments held labour-management conferences, accounting for just 0.5 per cent of the total establishments covered by the LSL (CLA, 1996).

The employee welfare fund committee is prescribed in the Employee Welfare Fund Law, promulgated in 1943 and amended in 1948. The law states that every public or private factory, mine, or other undertaking should allocate employee welfare funds for the purpose of carrying out employee welfare activities (Article 1). A factory, mine, or other undertaking sets aside a sum of money for the fund. The sources of the welfare fund are: the capital at the time of establishment, monthly business income, and the monthly salary or wage of employees (Article 2). A factory, mine, or other undertaking should form the employee welfare committee to be responsible for the custody and the use of the welfare fund (Article 5), and composed of seven to 21 representatives, of which workers should be more than two-thirds.

In general, employee welfare fund committees are more popular in the workplace than labour-management conferences. At the end of 1995, some 9,310 enterprises, including most large-sized firms and SOEs, had established such committees (CLA, 1996). The welfare fund is usually used by the committees to run company facilities, such as those to provide cafeteria, barber shop, laundry service and library provision.

In current employment legislation, there is no mechanism for workers to participate in matters relating to the strategic business decision-making process, such as technological change and business investment. As we have noted, the issues discussed in the labour-management conference and the factory committee meetings are related to workplace-level matters. Nevertheless, over the past several years, the demand for workers' participation in managerial decisions and on the board of directors from trade unions in some SOEs has increased rapidly. In 1995, when Taiwan Telecommunication Company was about to be privatized, workers argued that 'The Three Laws on Telecommunication' should contain a provision on workers' participation, allowing for three worker representatives on the board of directors. The Chinese Petroleum Workers Union had the same request for the SOE, Chinese Petroleum Company.

Employment Security

Employment security was not an important issue in Taiwan's HRM practices before the 1980s. There are several reasons for this relative unimportance. Workers usually expect to run their own independent businesses; hence, they do not expect to be paid employees for their whole working life. Employees are interested in learning skills for their future, so when they first enter into the labour market they usually move among different companies. Therefore, a high turnover rate is an important characteristic of Taiwan's employment structure, especially for younger workers. Huang (1994) surveyed the top 1,000 companies and found that the annual turnover rate in those companies was, on average, 23.23 per cent. In addition, the labour turnover rate is much higher in small-sized enterprises: for companies employing between one and nine workers, the monthly turnover rate was more than 20 per cent. In other words, workers do not expect to develop their career at one company.

A second reason for the relative unimportance of employment security is that family-owned companies in Taiwan usually do not lay off employees to adjust employment. This policy seems to be embedded in traditional Chinese culture. The employer–employee relationship in Taiwan is seen as an extension of familism. Employees are usually treated by their employer as members of their family. Beyond just their employment relationship,

TABLE 7
A SUMMARY OF THE NUMBER OF INVOLUNTARY UNEMPLOYED WORKERS
FROM MID-1995 TO MID-1996

Industry	Number of workers who involuntarily lost jobs	Reason for job loss
Electronic company	306	Plant closure
Electronic company	685	Plant closure
Storage company	132	Plant closure
Plastics company	160	Plant closure
Textile company	105	Plant closure
Textile company	112	Plant closure
Textile company	150	Plant closure
Computer company	135	Layoff
Manufacturing company	147	Severance
Bicycle company	139	Plant closure
Textile company	120	Severance
Mechanics company	1,500	Plant closure
Paper company	107	Layoff
Manufacturing company	101	Severance
Manufacturing company	107	Plant closure
Steel company	200	Plant closure
Steel company	650	Plant closure
Electronics company	200	Plant closure
Auto company	500	Layoff
Airplane Research Center	4,006	Severance
Construction company	106	Plant closure

Source: Lee, Chi-Yang (1996)

employers are expected to take care of their employees almost like their own children (Huang, 1996). Furthermore, with low unemployment rates from the 1960s, if an employee did find themselves out of a job, it would not have been difficult to find another one.

Nevertheless, employment security for workers is prescribed in the LSL. An employer may, by advance notice to a worker, terminate a labour contract only where: the business is suspended or assigned; there is an operating loss because of business contraction; major forces necessitate a business suspension for more than one month; a change in business nature requires a reduction in the number of workers and they cannot be assigned to other proper positions; a particular worker is confirmed to be incompetent for the work being done by him or her (Article 11). The provision has restricted employers from laying off or firing their employees at will.

In recent years the crisis in the employment security of workers has been caused not only by economic difficulties, but also by the migration of capital to other countries. Some points about the outflow of capital and the 'hollowing-out' of industries are becoming more widespread in the area. Consequently, unemployed workers and disputes on employment security are increasing rapidly. Table 7 shows the numbers of workers who involuntarily left their current jobs between mid-1995 and mid-1996. The total number is nearly 10,000. According to research by the DGBAS (1996), the proportion of unemployed workers in the 30–49 age bracket (prime-aged workers) has increased rapidly. Due to a lack in training investment for a secondary specialty, unemployed workers have found it difficult to find alternative job opportunities in other companies. These incidences of downsizing have led the government to consider enacting a Law for Plant Closure to further protect workers.

CONCLUSION

This article has examined a range of HRM practices in Taiwan. There are several characteristics of HRM practices in small-sized firms. Such firms: (1) are without distinct HR/personnel departments; (2) use seniority-based reward practices; (3) spend very little money and effort on in-house training; (4) have high levels of employee turnover; (5) use referrals from relatives and friends in recruiting; (6) avoid conflict in labour-management relations; (7) are without written and explicit job descriptions.

From the field data set, it is shown that there are no significant differences in most aspects of HRM practices between larger Taiwanese-owned firms and foreign subsidiaries. Along with the increase in the subsidiaries and JVs from Japan and Western countries, large-sized and SOEs in Taiwan are, in fact, gradually establishing Western HRM practices. The results also show the emergence of convergence in HRM practices between the two groups. In addition, with the increase in international competition and the transformation of industrial structure from traditional labour-intensive to high-technology industries, the article proposes two major challenges affecting future HRM practices in Taiwan. These are employee participation and employment security.

NOTES

1. There is no minimum wage in Taiwan. The LSL prescribes that 'a worker shall be paid such wage as is determined through negotiations with his employers, provided, however, that it shall not fall below the basic wage. The basic wage referred to in the proceeding paragraph shall be prescribed by the central competent authority and submitted to the Executive Yuan for approval' (Article 21). Most provisions mentioned in this article are extracted from the Labour Laws and Regulations of the Republic of China (CLA, 1990).
2. The popular method which firms used to calculate the amount of year-end bonus is employees' monthly base-wage multiplied by a fixed number.

REFERENCES

Ay, Chang-Ruey, Pe-Song Chiu, and Lien-An Hsu (1996) 'Why Do Legally Imported Foreign Workers Escape?', *Proceedings of the Third Annual International Conference of Human Resource Management in the Asia-Pacific Region*, National Sun Yat-sen University, 24–26 November.
Chen, Chia-Shen (1990) 'Confucian Style of Management in Taiwan,' in Joseph M. Putti (ed.) *Management: Asian Context*. McGraw-Hill, pp.177–97.
Chen, Shyh-jer and Koji Taira (1995) 'Industrial Democracy, Economic Growth and Income Distribution in Taiwan', *American Asian Review*, Vol.13, No.4, pp.49–77.
Council for Economic Planning and Development (1996) *Taiwan Statistical Data Book*. Taiwan: Executive Yuan.
Council of Labor Affairs (CLA) (1990) *Labor Laws and Regulations of the Republic of China.*

Taiwan: Executive Yuan.
Council of Labor Affairs (CLA) (1995) *The Impact of the Compensation Structure on Business in Taiwan*. Taipei: Executive Yuan (in Chinese).
Council of Labor Affairs (CLA) (1996) *Monthly Bulletin of Labor Statistics, Taiwan Area, Republic of China, September 1996*. Taiwan: Executive Yuan.
Deyo, Frederic C. (1989) *Beneath the Miracle: Labor Subordination in the New Asian Industrialism*. Berkeley, CA: University of California Press.
Directorate-General of Budget, Accounting and Statistics (DGBAS) (1996) *Monthly Bulletin of Manpower Statistics, Taiwan Area, Republic of China, October 1996*. Taiwan: Executive Yuan.
Farh, Jiing-lih (1995) 'Human Resource Management in Taiwan, Republic of China,' in Larry F. Moore and P. Devereaux Jennings (eds) *Human Resource Management on the Pacific Rim: Institutions, Practices and Attitudes*. Berlin: de Gruyter, pp.265–94.
Freeman, Richard (1994) 'Repressive Labor Relations and New Unionism in East Asia' in Paula B. Voos (ed.) *Proceedings of the Forty-sixth Annual Meeting*, Industrial Relations Research Association Series, Boston, 3–5 January, pp.231–8.
Frenkel, Stephen, Jon-chao Hong and Bih-ling Lee (1993) 'The Resurgence and Fragility of Trade Unions in Taiwan,' in Stephen Frenkel (ed.) *Organized Labor in the Asia-Pacific Region*. Ithaca, NY: ILR Press, pp.162–86.
Galenson, Walter (1979) 'The Labor Force, Wages, and Living Standards' in Walter Galenson (ed.) *Economic Growth and Structure Change in Taiwan: The Postwar Experience of the Republic of China*. Ithaca, NY: Cornell University Press, pp.384–447.
Huang, Bin-Der (1996) 'The Development of Ethical Labor Relations in Industrial Internationalization', Paper presented at the Conference on Labor Relations and Industrial Internationalization, Council of Labor Affairs, Kaoshiung, 12–13 April (in Chinese).
Huang, Tung-Chung (1994) 'Employee Ownership and Organizational Effectiveness', *Paper presented in a seminar for research projects held by the National Science Commission*, Taiwan: Executive Yuan (in Chinese).
Jean, Chian-Chong (1994) 'Corporate HRD Practices in Taiwan, Republic of China', *Journal of Labor Studies*, Vol.1, pp.109–30 (in Chinese).
Kleingartner, Archie and Hsueh-yu Peng (1991) 'Taiwan: An Exploration of Labor Relations in Transition', *British Journal of Industrial Relations*, Vol.29, No.3, pp.427–45.
Lan, Ke-jeng (1992) 'An Analysis of Union Organization and Performance in Taiwan', *Journal of Labor*, Vol.1, pp.1–25 (in Chinese).
Lee, Chi-Yang (1996) 'How to Reduce Labor–Management Disputes in Taiwan', Paper presented at a seminar held by the Institute of Human Resource Management, National Sun Yat-sen University, Kaohsiung, Taiwan, 2 July (in Chinese).
Lee, Joseph S. (1988) 'Labor Relations and the Stages of Economic Development: The Case of the Republic of China', *Paper presented in the Conference on Labor and Economic Development*, Chung-Hua Institution for Economic Research Conference Series, No.11, Taipei, Taiwan, 21–23 December, pp.177–204.
Lee, Joseph S. (1995) 'Economic Development and the Evolution of Industrial Relations in Taiwan, 1950–1993' in Anil Verma, Thomas Kochan, and Rusell Lansbury (eds) *Employment Relations in the Growing Asian Economies*. New York: Routledge, pp.88–118.
Lee, Joseph and Hui-Lin Wu (1996) 'The 1984 Fair Labor Standards Law and its Impact on Industrial Development in the Republic of China on Taiwan' in Joseph Lee (ed.) *Labor Standards and Economic Development*. Taiwan, Chung-Hua Institution for Economic Research, pp.147–72.
San, Gee (1988) 'A Critical Review of the Labor Standards Law in Taiwan, ROC – with Emphasis on the Pension and Severance System', *paper presented in the Conference on Labor and Economic Development*, Chung-Hua Institution for Economic Research Conference Series, No.11, Taipei, Taiwan, 21–23 December, pp.343–66.
San, Gee (1991) 'Improvement of Retirement System in Labor Standards Law' in Hui-Lin Wu (ed.) *Taiwan's Labor Market*. Taiwan: Chung-Hua Institute for Economic Research, pp.357–92 (in Chinese).
San, Gee (1993) 'Taiwan' in Miriam Rothman, Dennis R. Briscoe and Raoul C.D. Nacamulli (eds) *Industrial Relations around the World*. Berlin: de Gruyter, pp.371–87.
Storey, John (1992) *Developments in the Management of Human Resources*. Oxford: Blackwell.
Wilkinson, Barry (1994) *Labor and Industry in the Asia-Pacific: Lessons from the Newly-Industrialized Countries*. Berlin: de Gruyter.

HRM in Thailand: Eroding Traditions

JOHN J. LAWLER, SUNUNTA SIENGTHAI
and VINITA ATMIYANANDANA

Thailand emerged in the late 1980s as a rapidly developing economy. Fuelled by extensive foreign investment and expanding world trade, the country continued to experience very high rates of economic growth, so that it ranked among the world's most dynamic economies during the past decade. This has been favoured by a relatively stable political situation, high literacy and increasing levels of education, and a fairly homogeneous population that is not plagued by ethnic conflict and internal divisiveness. It has succeeded at substantially reducing the rate of population growth, which, coupled with economic expansion, has led to significant increases in real per capita income.

Yet, the country is not without problems as the recent troubles have highlighted. Economic growth has been concentrated mainly in Bangkok and a few other large cities, resulting in substantial migration from rural areas and the overcrowding of cities, especially Bangkok. Its economic infrastructure has been severely taxed by rapid growth, as evidenced in notorious traffic jams. Parts of the country, particularly the North-East, remain impoverished, and over-development in many areas has led to serious environmental problems. The country now also confronts major AIDS problems, all of which have which implications for the sustainability of rapid development.

The study of human resource management (HRM) in Thailand is intriguing because, like so many other things, it has evolved very rapidly over the past ten to 20 years. The traditional employment management systems of Thai firms are increasingly giving way to sophisticated HRM methods, many of which have been imported from the West. Yet, Thai culture, influenced both by East and South Asia, also substantially impacts on HRM practices. Furthermore, while many traditions related to the employment relationship are eroding, others seem firmly grounded in the complex texture of Thai society.

THAI ORGANIZATIONAL FORMS

In Korea, Taiwan, and Japan, economic takeoff largely involved the activities of indigenous firms. In the Thai case, foreign multinational

John Lawler, Institute of Labor and Industrial Relations, University of Illinois at Urbana-Champaign; Sununta Siengthai, Thammasat University, Bangkok; Vinita Atmiyanandana, Urbana, Illinois school district.

enterprises (MNEs) initially played the leading role in promoting the country's development. However, indigenous firms, many of which are MNEs in their own right, are ever more dominant in the economy.

Within the set of foreign MNEs, the relevant distinction is between the policies pursued by Japanese subsidiaries and those pursued by subsidiaries of Western MNEs. In many ways, these systems are consistent with stereotypical notions of Western and Japanese styles of HRM, although there are modifications necessitated by the Thai environment. In addition, efforts by Western and Japanese MNEs to impose HRM systems in an ethnocentric fashion in their Thai operations have, on occasion, generated significant cultural clashes in the workplace.

Indigenous Thai firms also fall into at least two categories with respect to HRM policies. Most private sector firms began as family-owned enterprises closely tied to the Sino-Thai community. There are a number of large firms that continue to be managed in that manner, and the employment and personnel practices that these companies pursue are typically quite distinct from those companies with a broad base of investors, especially publicly traded firms (Thai corporations). A third category within the set of indigenous firms consists of numerous state-owned enterprises. However, this article is concerned with HRM in the private sector and will only mention HRM systems within the state enterprise sector in passing.[1] Another complication is that many of the larger firms in Thailand are joint ventures involving both Thai and foreign partners. HRM systems in such companies may be influenced by both the methods utilized by both foreign and Thai firms. This contribution will focus, however, on 'ideal types', recognizing that organizations in practice are likely to be an amalgam of the different HRM styles depicted here.

The descriptions presented below are based, in part, on the authors' earlier work (Lawler et al., 1989; Lawler and Atmiyanandana, 1995). This work involved personal interviews conducted with the heads of human resource (HR) or personnel departments in about 100 firms operating in and around the greater Bangkok area. The interviews focused on various aspects of the firms' HRM practices, and we use this article as an opportunity to relate the findings of this work to Schuler's (1988) notion of HR strategy. Our early work describes in detail the methodology employed in this research, as well as specific findings. Here we extend those findings by analysing them from a strategic HRM perspective.

HUMAN RESOURCE STRATEGY

Strategy has emerged as a leading framework for the analysis of HRM practices within organizations. As used here, HR strategy is taken to mean efforts within a firm to create some alignment between its set of employment and HRM practices and its broader, long-term organizational goals and objectives. The extensive HR strategy literature contains numerous typologies, sets of 'best practices', and so forth. The authors believe one such framework proposed by Schuler (1988) is particularly useful in helping us understand the various ways in which HR strategy may be pursued in Thailand. Schuler proposes five 'menus' corresponding to the traditional functional areas of personnel and from which managers might select practices. We will use this typology to analyse different HRM systems in firms operating in Thailand. The following summarizes the various components of four of Schuler's menus (we use his system only in part in order to conserve on space):

• *HR Strategic Planning:* Is the planning process formal versus informal? Is it tightly versus loosely integrated with the firm's organizational planning process? Is planning long-term versus short-term in focus?

• *Staffing*: Does the firm rely primarily on internal versus external sources in filling jobs? Are career paths broad versus narrow? Is there a single or are there multiple promotion ladders? Are the criteria used in making staffing decisions explicit versus implicit? Does the firm rely on extensive versus limited socialization? Are the staffing procedures generally open versus closed and secretive?

• *Compensation:* Does the firm pay generally low versus high wages in comparison to the market? Is there an emphasis on internal (task-based) versus external (market-based) equity in compensation decision? Are there few versus many fringe benefits? Does the company utilize many versus few performance incentives? Finally, does the firm offer high employment security, coupled with variable pay, versus low employment security, coupled with fixed pay (that is, does the firm lay people off rather than cut pay in times of adversity)?

• *Training and development:* To what extent does the firm engage in training and development efforts? If it does, are these short-term versus long-term in focus? Is training narrow versus broad and is the focus on enhancing productivity versus improving employee quality of life? Is training planned and systematic versus spontaneous?

THAI-OWNED FIRMS

We now present detailed descriptions of HRM systems, such as they exist, in the two principal types of modern sector, privately owned and Thai-controlled business firms. Needless to say, these observations represent a fairly stereotypical view of such systems and there is considerable variation around these norms.

The Family Enterprise

Organization and management. If one considers domestically owned firms in Thailand as a whole, most are family enterprises. With the exception of privatized state enterprises, most large scale businesses in Thailand began as family enterprises and many still operate in that manner. Also, although Thai corporations (see below) often utilize highly systematic and rationalized HRM systems, their HRM practices are still rooted, to some extent, in the more unstructured, though often highly effective, style of the family enterprise. Thus, an understanding of HRM practices in Thailand must begin with a consideration of the family enterprise system. Of course, we focus here on those family enterprises that operate with the 'modern sector' economy and are comparable in size and activity to Thai-owned corporations and MNE subsidiaries (all of the case study firms that were interviewed had at least 100 employees). Although a significant force even in this sector of the economy, family enterprises are not so dominant here as once was the case (for reasons discussed below).

These larger scale family enterprises are similar to family enterprises in other East and South East Asian countries because the entrepreneurial community in Thailand, like many of these other countries, has been primarily Chinese and thus utilized the traditional Chinese approach to management. As such, many are part of what has been dubbed the 'bamboo network'. While some of these companies are involved in a single line of business, many are comparable in size to very large corporations, though not so visible. The reason is that a particular family or family group may own dozens of separate companies, all relatively modest in size, each involved in specific business activities and run more or less as a profit centre. The upper management of each company is composed of family members or trusted friends. The activities of these separate entities is then generally co-ordinated by the family patriarch and a close circle of associates, again, mostly family members (although some of these organizations are now headed by women, including a couple of the largest of family-run organizations in Thailand). Isarangkun and Taira (1977), who provide perhaps the best general description of the personnel systems of traditional Thai family enterprises, aptly characterize control in such firms as 'management by entourage'.

The HRM function in traditional family enterprises is relatively unstructured and ill-defined (see Chen on Tawain, in this volume). In fact, the concept of a formal HRM function, as encountered in Western industrialized countries, is often completely absent in family enterprises. Many of these firms only have rudimentary personnel departments that often act as little more than payroll offices, although the larger family enterprises may find it necessary to elaborate the personnel function to some extent, adding perhaps some rudimentary HRM activities. In our early work (Lawler and Atmiyanandana, 1995: 310), we found that only about 40 per cent[2] of Thai family enterprises had what the authors described as 'relatively high' levels of professionalism in the HRM function (based on the credentials of HR/personnel managers and the organization of the HRM/personnel function). In contrast, about 60 per cent of Thai corporations, 74 per cent of subsidiaries of European MNEs and 96 per cent

174 HRM IN THE ASIA PACIFIC REGION

of subsidiaries of American MNEs fell into the relatively high category.[3]

Those interviewed generally indicated that the HRM or personnel function within family enterprises is not seen as especially critical and the chief personnel manager is likely to be a less significant family member or perhaps even an outsider. Most incumbents of such positions have only very limited professional training in HRM or personnel administration. That a family enterprise may be composed of numerous smaller, quasi-independent operations serves to minimize the need for an elaborate HRM function even in fairly large organizations, since personnel activities are decentralized.

Thai family enterprises are most similar to the indigenous firms characteristic of Taiwan, Singapore, Hong Kong (see Ng and Poon), Indonesia, and Malaysia. They are clearly very different from the large scale organizations that dominate in contemporary Japan and Korea. Ironically, the Chinese management system, as it is occurs in South East Asia, is very different from the emerging private-sector system of the People's Republic of China (PRC), as shown in Nyaw (1995) and Warner (in this volume). This involves joint ventures with Japanese and Western firms (although the heavy involvement of Taiwanese firms in the PRC may be altering this).

Strategy. The concept of 'strategy' often implies a fairly deliberate and intentional process, but, as Mintzberg (1989) notes in his classic exposition, this is not always the case. Rather than deliberate and planned, a strategy may be emergent; that is, the stance of the organization versus its environment evolves out of a series of decisions that may be only randomly related to one another. The notion of emergent strategy may be applied in the HRM area as well (Walker, 1992). This view of strategy development is quite applicable in the case of family enterprises in Thailand. Returning to Schuler's (1988) HR planning menu, we would consequently characterize the HR strategy formulation process in family enterprises as extremely informal, if indeed even present. Major shifts in personnel policy are most likely originated by the head of the firm on an *ad hoc* basis. While the head of a family enterprise might have a well-defined concept of organizational strategy, the idea of aligning this with HR strategy is not likely to be a concern and HR strategy, such as it exists, is emergent rather than deliberate (obviating the need to consider such linkages). Consequently, organizational and HR strategies are, at best, only loosely linked in such firms. Similarly, HR planning and strategic analysis, to the extent that it occurs, is likely to be fairly short-term in focus.

In organizations that develop HR strategies in a deliberate and purposeful manner, we would expect the formulation of some underlying strategic mission or ideology that serves to bind the organization together and guide employment practices. In the case of the enterprises, where HR strategy is not explicitly created, it would still seem that there has emerged an organizational ideology that underlies personnel practices. We earlier characterized this as 'social control' (Lawler *et al.*, 1989: 214), as contrasted with something like the rational control strategic theme often encountered in Western firms (see below). By this, we mean a system of control rooted largely in the Thai national social fabric. A pattern of hierarchy and authority that derives from Buddhism as practised in Thailand (Siengthai and Vadhanasindhu, 1991) serves to set role expectations in this manner (such as the Six Directions or *disha*). This translates into patterns of authority within organizations that reflect an individual's social standing. Status can also from such ascriptive factors as age, gender, regional origin,[4] and, to some extent, ethnicity. Individuals tend to be deferential to those whom they see as socially superior, and those in a superior position, in turn, have social obligations to their inferiors.

The Thai expression *kreing chai*, which refers to an important cultural norm (but is not readily translatable into English), denotes '...a set of unwritten but widely understood and rigid rules by which interpersonal behaviour is regulated' (Siengthai and Vadhanasindhu, 1991: 234). This would include conventional relationships between social inferiors and superiors.[5] Coupled with this is the tendency of Thais to be disinclined to confrontation and conflict. Thus, elaborate structures and formal systems of control, including those created or supported by a sophisticated HRM system, would not be seen as so necessary in traditional family enterprises. The external social system is imported and serves as a substitute control system. The Confucian traditions that have some influence on the Chinese entrepreneurial community in Thailand also help create a control mechanism, at least among family members and higher level employees from outside the family. The Confucian ethic, with its emphasis on loyalty to family and friends (Chen, 1991), as well as diligence and industriousness, also serves to maintain stability within the family enterprise.

Staffing. The staffing process in family enterprise organizations is simplified by its reliance on familial relationships. Thus, virtually all higher level positions in the organization are occupied by family members. Of course, the family is defined here as the extended, rather than immediate, family, so there is an extensive network from which to choose. Indeed, these companies might well draw on relatives in other countries (given linkages among the overseas Chinese communities) to establish operations elsewhere. One of the authors recalls a statement in a magazine article years ago (the reference is no longer available) in which a leading Hong Kong entrepreneur observed: 'Wherever in the world I have a relative, I have a branch office.'

While family members generally fill almost all of the upper-tier positions in these organizations, middle- and even lower-tier positions are typically filled by those who have connections with family members. Unless these organizations are rapidly expanding, recruiting is generally not a major problem, as turnover tends to be slight. When it is necessary to hire from outside the family, these firms rely almost exclusively on referrals from trusted individuals (family members, close family friends, influential business or government officials, or current employees). Indeed, lower-tier workers are often recruited from the relatives of current workers or domestic servants. This process of using personal or family connections to locate a job is referred to in Thai as *mee sen* (literally 'to have strings').

In terms of Schuler's (1988) typology, we would characterize staffing practices as largely internal. This expression must be qualified to some extent in relation to the way it is normally used in the case of Western organizations. Internal staffing refers here to within kinship and personal networks rather than primarily within the organization. Thus, we would characterize the staffing process as particularistic rather than universalistic (Trompenaars, 1994). Particularistic cultures legitimize different ways of responding to situations depending upon the people involved (for example, friends and family versus strangers) and thus reject the notion of universal rules and procedures (which would, for example, be in conflict with nepotism). Particularism is positively associated with collectivism and like many other East and South East Asian countries, Thailand is substantially higher on both of these dimensions than industrialized Western countries (ibid.). Both of these traits promote special treatment for those within the kinship group.

Career paths are potentially quite broad, especially at the higher levels of the organization. Individuals may engage in many different activities over the course of their work lives and these companies tend not to have rigidly defined job classifications. Promotion ladders likewise are not clearly defined, except that promotion beyond a given level within the organization usually necessitates family membership (thus, we characterize these as single promotion ladders). As far as staffing criteria are concerned, the notion of having some sort of family connection, as a principal factor, is fairly explicit. Socialization is normally quite limited, as family enterprises rely on the external and established social control mechanisms described above, coupled with familial or personal loyalty. Thus, extensive formal orientations are not common in such firms. Finally, procedures for making specific staffing decisions are fairly closed, given general secretiveness of decision making processes in family enterprises.

A traditional strength of the family enterprise has been that it is rather closely knit, thus fairly stable. In smaller organizations that serve niche markets, this style of management, coupled with the staffing practices described here, is likely to continue to be effective. Yet, such a style is likely to become much less viable for larger firms for a variety of reasons (many of which are discussed below). One important factor has to do with the availability of skilled managers and workers. The supply of siblings, children, cousins and in-laws may be insufficient to provide all of the sophisticated talents often required in larger organizations, especially those active in global pursuits. As firms move beyond kinship and personal networks to staff positions, it may be difficult to get the best talent if potential recruits for managerial and professional positions feel that opportunities for promotion for non-family members are non-existent. This has placed pressure on family enterprises regarding open upper-level opportunities for those from outside of the family, perhaps promoting the use of more sophisticated staffing practices in some of these firms. This is likely to be one of the continuing threats that will serve to lessen the viability of the traditional family enterprise in coming years and to promote the continued expansion of corporate forms of organization.

Compensation. In general, wages and salaries in family enterprises, certainly for non-family members, would be relatively low. This, however, is necessarily impressionistic, as firms in Thailand are quite reluctant to disclose any sort of financial data. This is also likely due in part to the fact that family enterprises are often relatively 'low tech' operations compared to Thai corporations and foreign firms. Also, the fact that Thailand is a surplus labour economy, especially when it comes to lower-skilled positions, means that family enterprises have generally encountered little in the way of competitive pressure for wage increases among lower-level employees. The close-knit nature of the family enterprise also reduces turnover among upper-level employees, especially those who are family members, so pressures to increase wages for such positions have typically not been high either.

The issue of wage equity within the family enterprise is really quite different from the way it is conceived of in the West. Within that framework, wages tend to be market driven and thus reflect some external equity influences. Yet, there is often also a strong internal component. In contrast to the Western, as well as the Japanese models, this component reflects particularistic and ascriptive criteria (ibid.). Thus wages depend on such factors as social background, gender, and age (not to mention family membership). The role of such factors in wage determination in family enterprises is also documented in the work of Isarangkun Na Ayuthaya and Taira (1977). Of course, systems such as job evaluation are not typically used. This approach is probably best characterized as idiosyncratic rather than based on conventional notions of internal and external equity.

Wage systems are not very complex, so fringe benefits are relatively few, except perhaps for family members. Family enterprises do seem to use many incentives, though these are much less formalized than would be the case in Western firms. The bonus system is widely used (see Chen on Taiwan, this volume) and employees may receive year-end bonuses equivalent to two or three month's salary (depending upon firm performance). However, such incentive systems are likely to have a strong particularistic component and are largely at the whim of the firm's owners (who are quite secretive regarding actual firm performance). Rewards are also often distributed on special occasions, such during the Chinese New Year celebration. Workers tend to see the likelihood of receiving such incentives as compensating for the relatively low wages paid by these firms.

Finally, employment security in family enterprises tends to be relatively high. The nature of social relationships in Thai culture is such that the loss of employment would be accompanied by significant 'loss of face'. Thai labour law also makes layoffs difficult and potentially costly. Thus culture, coupled with relatively low base wages, promotes high job security in family enterprises.

Training and development. Training seems to be a problematic issue in family enterprises, although they are not unique in this respect. That is, training is often seen as a cost with unclear future benefits. Family enterprises are often loath to assume the risks of such efforts, although technological change in certain industries may necessitate it. Of course, clear distinctions exist between training and development for family members, which might often include sending individuals to advanced academic programmes, and training and development for those outside of the family circle. Extensive training and development for non-family members is also limited as such individuals are not expected to move up a great deal in the organization. In applying the Schuler (1988) framework to non-family members, when any training takes place, it is likely to be narrow, spontaneous, and short-term in focus. The emphasis would generally tend towards productivity rather than relational and quality of life issues.

The limited emphasis on training and, especially, longer term management and professional development for non-family members is another HRM issue (like the decision generally to exclude non-family members from higher level positions) that reduces the viability of family enterprises, given the changing nature of economic conditions in Thailand. As we have noted, it is difficult to recruit the most talented and best educated managers and professionals into family enterprises because they see little hope for advancement to the top of the firm. Such individuals might be willing to work in family enterprises if they at least had the opportunity to acquire skills and work experiences that would prepare them for career opportunities elsewhere. However, that individuals might leave before the firm recoups its investment in the training or development effort is precisely the reason that the family enterprise is reluctant to incur such costs.

The Thai-Owned Corporation

Organization and management. There are now several hundred firms trading on the Stock Exchange of Thailand (SET). While foreign investors are certainly involved in these companies, the vast majority are controlled by Thai interests. As noted earlier, most of these companies evolved out of family enterprises, usually because they needed to raise capital to support rapidly expanding business activities. Many have now become MNEs in their own right. Despite being publicly traded, most of these firms continue to be controlled by the founding families. An example of such a firm that has evolved in this way is Bangkok Bank, which is one of the two or three largest banks in South East Asia. The Thai government's commitment to privatizing its many state enterprises has also spawned a number of publicly-held corporations, such as Thai Airways. Currently, the government is in process of privatizing the national electric and telephone companies. These firms lack the legacy of family control, though many inherit the bureaucratic systems of state enterprises. Finally, the Thai royal family has been instrumental in promoting economic development through the establishment of companies, most of which are now traded publicly (though the Crown Property Bureau continues to have some financial interest in many of these companies). An example of this type of firm is Siam Cement, which is generally seen as Thailand's leading corporation.

Structurally, these firms tend to look much like corporations in Western countries rather than Japanese corporations. Managers and executives in these companies are often graduates of MBA programmes that are patterned after the Western model. Indeed, Thailand has several MBA programmes and many of these are offered by its leading public and private universities (Siengthai and Vadhanasindhu, 1991). Furthermore, from the US, Northwestern University's Kellogg Graduate School of Management and Wharton School at the University of Pennsylvania offer MBA degrees through a residential programme in Bangkok in co-operation with Chulalongkorn University. Indeed, there would seem to have been a proliferation of MBA and other business programmes in Thailand in recent years and there may be something of a shake-out, at least for the weaker programmes, in coming years. There is also a substantial indigenous managerial cadre which has been trained in business schools in Western countries. Although the Western model is the dominant paradigm in Thai management education, it has been adapted in various ways to Thai cultural and social conditions and this is certainly true in the case of the HRM area.

The same professionalization of general management in Thailand has also occurred in the HRM area. Much of this change has occurred since the mid-1980s. Prior to then, the personnel function in such organizations had typically been carried out by individuals with legal training (see Amante on the Philippines, in this volume) or by graduates of political science programmes. This was in part because the function basically involved monitoring compliance with labour laws (as well as overseeing the payroll function). Moreover, most positions for personnel administrators were in state enterprises or government agencies (as there were few publicly held corporations, and positions in family enterprises were, of course, reserved for family members). The political science major, with its emphasis on public administration, was often the avenue to management positions for Thais from non-entrepreneurial families.

Interestingly, the Vietnam War would seem to have had something of a professionalizing impact on the personnel/HRM function in Thailand; a number of Thais who worked in administrative positions for the American military, which had an extensive presence in Thailand during the war, gained knowledge of basic personnel functions as practised in American organizations at the time. These individuals brought such skills to the Thai companies for which they later worked (mostly corporations rather than family enterprises). More recently, the HRM systems implemented by MNEs operating in Thailand have served as models for indigenous firms. Although certain aspects of the Japanese system, such as Quality Circles and some limited forms of participative management, have found their way into Thai corporations, the European and American approaches have been most readily followed. There has been the emergence of Western-style management programmes, there now are HRM concentrations within MBA programmes in Thai universities, and many professionals have obtained degrees from HRM and industrial relations programmes in Western countries. There are also several different management and professional associations in Thailand, such as the Personnel Management Association of Thailand (PMAT) which provide professional support for the HRM function, including seminars and related training and development activities for HRM practitioners (as do educational institutions with short courses and 'mini-MBA' programmes).

Strategy. The process of strategic decision making, both at the organizational level and within the HRM function, is much more extensively discussed among managers in Thai corporations. Thus, strategies, in Mintzberg's (1989) terms, are much more likely to be deliberate than emergent. There are, however, some environmental and cultural limitations. First, these corporations have often developed and expanded in a period of generally strong economic conditions, where strategies of growth have seemed fairly clearly warranted. Thailand's economy is not growing as rapidly as it once was and companies are facing more difficult times in the near term. If we think of strategy as a proactive process where managers and executives guide organizations through uncertain environments, the strategic decision-making processes of Thai corporations have not really been tested all that much in these circumstances. For example, Thailand's own 'bubble economy' in real estate is deflating, which has created problems for banks with extensive loans in this sector. Some have apparently done well in responding to this situation, while others are in serious trouble. The strategic responses of the banks to these difficulties will be a test of the strategic capabilities of Thai executives.

Second, certain aspects of Thai culture may run counter to the nature of strategic decision making, at least as it is conceived of in Western settings. Thais are rather fatalistic in outlook, a characteristic that Jaeger and Kanungo (1990) note is related to a general sense of the world as externally, rather than internally, controlled by managers (as well as others) in developing countries. In addition, the strategic change process, which may result in displacement of individuals through 'downsizing' and restructuring, runs counter to the Thai notion for the need to preserve harmony and avoid contention and conflict (Lawler and Atmiyanandana,

1995; Siengthai and Vadhanasindhu, 1991). Moreover, radical change associated with strategic transformation creates the potential for loss of face for those affected.

While there would seem to be a trend within publicly held Thai corporations for greater strategic action (see, for example, an examination of the banking industry in Thailand by Lawler and Siengthai, 1996), including in the HRM area, this is still an evolving process. Thus, within the Schuler (1988) framework, HR strategic planning, when used, may tend to be towards the long-term, formal, and relatively tightly integrated with the organization's objectives; the approach is not yet fully refined. Indeed, our survey data indicated that only slightly more than 25 per cent of Thai corporations substantially utilized even so simple an activity in this area as succession planning (about the same percentage as for family enterprises), while over half of Western MNEs operating in Thailand relied extensively on this method.

In terms of a strategic mission or ideology, it appears as though the Thai corporation is really an amalgam of the traditional style of Western firms – one of rational control – and the social control system characteristic of the Thai family enterprise. What is unclear at this point is how the strategic focus of Thai corporations will shift in the future. Western management style is moving towards greater reliance on decentralization, worker discretion, and work teams (Osterman, 1992). This approach is not very consistent with the hierarchical character of Thai culture, so we might anticipate some adaptation of these styles to the Thai context.

Staffing. Staffing practices in Thai corporations tend to rely on internal systems to the extent that this is possible. In this way, these firms are similar to family enterprises in that management endeavours to create a familial-like atmosphere to encourage employee commitment and loyalty towards the organization. However, more akin to Western firms, career paths tend to be relatively narrow and there are multiple promotion ladders which correspond to different organizational functions and activities. Unlike the family enterprise, there is a professional managerial cadre (typically educated in MBA or related professional programmes) organized largely along functional lines (marketing, finance, human resources, etc.). Even in corporations still controlled by the founding family, professional managers unrelated to the family occupy positions at all levels within the firm, and intra-firm mobility opportunities are fairly extensive. Managerial professionalization is typically expected by outside investors.

While Thai corporate executives may prefer relying on relatively structured internal labour markets, economic conditions do not always allow this. Turnover among staff at the managerial and professional levels is a chronic problem as rapid economic growth has engendered severe shortages in many key occupations. Companies compete with both other indigenous firms and MNE subsidiaries (which often pay higher salaries than Thai-owned firms) and 'job hopping', which has led to escalating salaries for managers, is pervasive. Thus, external recruiting for upper-level employees is a major issue in these companies. While standard recruiting methods, such as campus recruiting, newspaper advertising, and the use of 'head hunters', are relied upon to some degree, informal social networks are probably the most important recruiting device. As in family enterprises, 'having strings' is often the critical factor. Again, this is really a cultural trait, rooted in the collectivist nature of Thai society.

In the case of lower-level employees, staffing practices are not much different than those in family enterprises. Again, the substantial excess supply of semi-skilled and unskilled workers means that recruiting and selection are not significant concerns. Jobs may be posted at the factory gate and filled by those who live nearby. Networking is also important, as friends and relatives of current workers often have the upper hand.

Employment in Thai corporations tends to rely extensively on explicit criteria and these tend to be related more closely to performance relevant factors than is the case in family enterprises. However, somewhat implicit criteria related to personal connections are also quite important. Employment procedures tend to be more open than in family enterprises, though undoubtedly much less so than would be the case in the typical Western firm. One clear distinction between corporations and family enterprises is that the former tend to rely much more heavily on the use of testing in selecting at least upper-level employees; about 70 per cent of the corporations in which we conducted interviews indicated widespread use of testing for this purpose, while only about 35 per cent of the family enterprises indicated this to be the case (Lawler and Atmiyanandana, 1995). Finally, Thai corporations are more apt to use work orientations and other socialization techniques fairly extensively.

Compensation. Compensation levels would generally tend to be higher than in family enterprises, but have not typically been as high as in subsidiaries of Western MNEs. In the past, this was because Thai corporations did not have the same resources to compete in the labour market with foreign firms. A number of managers in these corporations specifically complained in the course of our interviews as to their inability to compete with the relatively high salaries offered by European and, especially, American firms. However, these companies generally offer relatively high employment security in return for lower wages and salaries, since, like family enterprises, employment is rarely terminated. This may well be changing as companies confront the job-hopping problem and continual shortages in certain higher level occupations, though the extent of change is not yet clear. The severe economic downturn now under way is also likely to promote lay-offs.

There appears to be an increasing use of job evaluation involving internal equity considerations based on job requirements. For example, only about 18 per cent of the family enterprises we surveyed (ibid.) used formal job evaluation systems to a substantial extent in establishing internal wage structures, though about 45 per cent of the family enterprises did so. As far as annual wage and salary adjustments are concerned, Thai corporations are increasingly utilizing performance-based, rather than seniority-based, criteria; seniority is still a much more significant component of compensation adjustments than appears to be the norm in Western firms operating in Thailand, though less the case than in Thai subsidiaries of Japanese firms (ibid.: 311). The managers we interviewed indicated that although seniority as a basis for pay adjustments is very much in line with Asian values, performance-based pay systems are becoming more common now, mainly as a result of competitive pressures. In addition, the annual bonus system serves as another means of providing performance incentives to workers, as in the case of family enterprises. Thus, a number of pay incentives are utilized. However, few fringe benefits and perks are offered by Thai corporations, except to higher-level managers and executives.

Training and development. Training and development activities are seemingly more pervasive in Thai corporations than family enterprises. Traditionally, this seems to be because these companies may have had difficulty competing for top quality employees with foreign firms and so must do more to develop their workers, though whether that is still the case is unclear. Training tends to be more extensive for managers and professionals than for lower-level workers. For example, about 85 per cent of Thai corporations were found to rely substantially on formal training programmes for managers and professional employees, while only 60 per cent did so in the case of lower-level workers (ibid.). A great deal of the training that is done involves management development activities. Thus, in the case of managers and professionals, the training seems to have a long-term focus, is planned, fairly broad, and concerned both with enhancing productivity and improving the quality of work life. Training for lower-level employees is typically more pragmatic (that is, emphasizing productivity enhancing) and often involves on-the-job activities. Thus, while planned, it is likely to be fairly narrow, and have perhaps a relatively short-term focus. As Deyo notes (1995), training efforts by Thai firms in response to competitive pressures have been limited. In general, the response to these conditions has often involved reductions in wages and fringe benefits, outsourcing, and increased use of temporary workers.

FOREIGN-OWNED FIRMS

Having provided a general description of the HRM practices and issues in indigenously-controlled firms, we will more briefly touch on HRM practices in subsidiaries of MNEs, differentiating between firms whose 'home' is based in Europe, America, Australia and New Zealand (Western firms) and Japan. To be sure, the distinction is somewhat artificial, as there are clearly important differences within the diverse set of Western firms. Yet, space does not allow an extensive treatment of the various sub-types we might encounter in this category and the Western firms tend to be more similar to one another than to the conventional Japanese model. Moreover, Japanese and American firms are the two leading investors in Thailand, hence a focus on the Japanese system and what is, as presented here, largely the American HRM system seems reasonable. The general characteristics of these two systems is well understood, so we concentrate on issues encountered in implementing these in the Thai context. Also, the following discussion is concerned exclusively with HRM practices as applied to Thai employees; the issue of expatriate management is not addressed.

Subsidiaries of Western MNEs

Organization and management. The structure and control of Western MNEs vary considerably. Applying the framework of Hennan and Perlmutter (1979), some subsidiaries are part of highly polycentric systems, where they enjoy considerable autonomy, while others are part of either ethnocentric or geocentric systems and much more extensively controlled by the parent company. In either case, the control of HRM practices tends to reflect the broader control system (subsidiaries of polycentric MNEs tend to have locally defined HRM systems, while subsidiaries of ethnocentric or geocentric MNEs tend to have more centrally controlled HRM systems). The common denominator would seem to be fairly high levels of professionalization within the HRM function. Subsidiaries of American MNEs and, to a lesser extent, European MNEs, were found to have significantly higher levels of HRM professionalism than either family enterprises or Thai-owned corporations (Lawler and Atmiyanandana, 1995).

Strategy. In the case of subsidiaries with centralized control systems, HR strategy formulation tends to have a long-term focus, to be fairly tightly integrated with organizational objectives, and to be relatively formal. In the case of more polycentric organizations, the degree to which strategic planning in the HRM area occurs really depends on the nature of the firm. Size would seem to be a critical factor, with smaller subsidiaries of this sort sometimes run in ways not unlike family enterprises, with rather *ad hoc* personnel management systems and limited HR strategic planning. In general, though, the strategic focus of Western subsidiaries generally tends to be one of rational control, which results in more systematic control systems that the Thais tend to characterize as 'bureaucratic' by comparison to indigenous and other Asian-based firms.

Staffing. In the main, Western firms operating in Thailand tend to emphasize external sources in filling positions. This does not mean that internal development is ignored and some of these companies have a strong development to such an approach. However, Western firms are likely to pay significantly above market wages with the intention of attracting more highly qualified workers. These companies tend to prefer workers with either experience in other MNEs or, in the case of managers and professionals, an academic degree from a Western country. For example, American firms tend to favour those with degrees from US universities. This concern is related to a firm's socialization objectives. By selecting individuals already oriented towards Western perspectives and values, these companies require limited internal socialization efforts and can rely more extensively on Thai managers rather than assigning an expatriate to these positions.

Although there is considerable variation across companies, Western firms tend to have fairly narrow career paths with multiple promotion ladders, again depending upon the employee's specific speciality. Most have fairly detailed and clearly defined job classifications and descriptions. Yet, there are signs that the growth of team-based management systems is starting to have an impact on staffing practices within these firms. In general, staffing decisions are made via fairly open and explicit criteria, much more so than in indigenous firms. Western firms tend to be quite suspicious of the particularism and networking that are seen to be pervasive in indigenous firms, though this perspective fails to recognize the importance of strong and trusting personal relationships fundamental to Asian cultures. Indeed, based on comments made during our interviews, it would seem that Thai workers are often uncomfortable with the rigid application of the universalistic criteria they encounter in staffing practices in subsidiaries of Western firms.

One example of the impact of the universalistic employment standards utilized by Western firms is on employment discrimination based on gender. Although discrimination against women in the labour market is less pervasive in Thailand than in countries such as Japan and Korea, opportunities for women, particularly in managerial and professional jobs, are limited (Siengthai and Leelakulthanit, 1994). Western firms, particularly subsidiaries of American MNEs, are less prone than Asian firms to engage in, for example, explicit discrimination based on gender (Lawler, 1996).

Compensation. As noted, compensation in Western firms tends to be high relative to the labour market, as is consistent with a policy of buying, rather than developing, talent. These firms tend to make rather extensive use of formal job evaluation systems, often imported directly from the parent company. About 90 per cent of the American firms studied, and 53 per cent of the European firms, used job evaluation systems in determining wage structures, so that compensation tends to reflect internal equity considerations (Lawler and Atmiyanandana, 1995). These rates are much higher than for indigenous firms (see above).

Performance incentives are also extensively utilized, though primarily in the form of performance-based salary adjustments (rather than bonuses or some form of profit sharing). In that sense, the incentives are relatively few in number, though clearly important. Conversely, seniority is not a particularly important factor. An important distinction between indigenous firms and Western subsidiaries is in regard to performance-based compensation, in that the latter tend to emphasize individual incentives, while the former tend to emphasize group incentives. Thai workers tend to find this emphasis on interpersonal competition somewhat disquieting and in conflict with collectivist cultural values.

Western subsidiaries seem to offer somewhat more in the way of fringe benefits than indigenous firms, though the extent of the difference is not that clear. As far as job security is concerned, it would seem that, at least in principal, these firms offer low employment security in relation to indigenous firms (although legal restrictions make terminations difficult), coupled with relatively high and fixed pay. However, until recently, economic conditions in Thailand have been very strong, so that significant lay-offs by these firms have not been an issue. As Thailand confronts lower growth rates, this may change and substantial terminations may begin to occur, which may have an important impact on employee relations.

Training and development. Again, consistent with the HR strategy of buying skills rather than developing them internally, training is not a high priority in Western firms, although that does not mean training is completely absent. Training is more significant in the case of upper-level employees and more limited in the case of production workers and other lower-level employees. In fact, the patterns here are rather similar to Thai corporations (though less extensively utilized). For upper-level employees, training and development tends to be long-term, broad, and systematic, with an emphasis on both quality of work life and productivity issues. Firms engage in some management development efforts, and Thai managers and professionals may be sent on temporary assignments to facilities in other countries. For lower-level workers, most training is on the job, relatively narrow, short-term, and productivity oriented, though planned. However, as these organizations introduce more team-based systems, the training requirements for lower-level employees are likely to increase.

Subsidiaries of Japanese MNEs

Organization and management. The substantial appreciation of the Japanese Yen during the late 1980s led many Japanese companies to move production facilities off-shore. Consequently, Japanese MNEs have been the major foreign investors in Thailand for more than a decade, accounting for the largest share of foreign direct investment. As is the norm with Japanese MNEs (Oddou *et al.*, 1995), subsidiaries in Thailand rely heavily on Japanese expatriate managers, at middle- as well as upper-level positions. This is in contrast to most Western MNEs, which tend to use expatriates sparingly (and some not at all). Thus, co-ordination and control in Japanese subsidiaries is achieved through the presence of Japanese staff, rather than through complex structural arrangements or the recruitment of employees with some prior exposure to Japanese culture. Also, as in Japan, the HRM function in Japanese subsidiaries is often integrated within the general management function and not clearly distinguished from it. In many of the Japanese subsidiaries in which we conducted interviews, the general manager also assumed the role of the chief HR manager.

Strategy. Japanese subsidiaries have well-developed HR strategies, although they do not completely replicate the systems used in Japan. Central to the Japanese system is a strategic focus emphasizing ideological commitment to the goals and values of the firm. These HR strategies of Japanese subsidiaries can be characterized as long-term and tightly integrated with overall organizational strategy.

Japanese subsidiaries endeavour to acculturate employees, using this as a basis for co-ordination and control. Some Thai managers and academics with whom we spoke in the course of our study said they felt that Japanese managers expected Thais, as Asians, to be culturally similar to Japanese workers. Yet, that is not the case, as work is not normally the central life interest of most Thai workers. For one thing, the Theravada Buddhism of Thailand emphasizes moderation – the 'middle path' – in dealing with life's issues. Moreover, a dominate Thai value is *sanuk* (literally 'fun'), which means, among other things, that people ought to take life with the proverbial 'grain of salt'. Although Thailand is a collectivist culture, Thais tend to think of themselves as being more individualistic than the Japanese.

This failure to recognize these cultural differences has created problems in some Japanese companies. Workers have complained to the government that Japanese firms are exploitive of workers in the demands that they place upon them for high performance and organizational loyalty, resulting in the formation of some inquiry commissions. Although Thai workers tend to be relatively passive and nonaggressive, and despite the fact that the labour movement is quite weak in Thailand (Brown and Frenkel, 1993), there have been protracted strikes against some Japanese firms. Recently, a Sanyo plant was burned to the ground by workers disturbed by a misunderstanding regarding the payment of annual bonuses.

Staffing. As expected, Japanese subsidiaries rely on internal staffing systems, with broad career paths, and a single (or few) promotion ladders. There is considerable job rotation, teamwork, and so forth, coupled with only a few job descriptions and an absence of detailed job descriptions. Employment criteria are more on the implicit side, with employers placing considerable emphasis on an individual's character as well as job performance. Hence, staffing procedures may be somewhat particularistic and network-based, like indigenous firms. While Thai workers often feel more comfortable with that aspect of these companies (relative to the staffing practices of Western MNE subsidiaries), they also seem to resent the 'bamboo ceiling' that exists for Thais regarding promotions to upper-level positions. The Thai government has, from time to time, placed political and legal pressure (for example, via limitations on work permits) on Japanese companies to reduce expatriate presence and open more of these jobs to Thai nationals.

'Fit' with the organization is a major concern, and performance evaluations seem to deal more with a worker's 'attitude' than specific performance. The staffing process is relatively secretive. Not surprisingly, Japanese subsidiaries engage in extensive socialization efforts. In one site we visited, the plant of a large electronic products manufacturer, even production workers were required to participate in an orientation programme lasting almost three months, and in which such subjects as Japanese culture and customs were taught. Some Thai HRM managers we interviewed said that they thought Thai workers resented, to some extent, the heavy dose of organizational indoctrination to which they are exposed, seeing it as a kind of cultural imposition.

Compensation. Japanese companies have a reputation for paying relatively low base wages. However, there are many performance incentives. In our earlier work, we found that nearly 57 per cent of the Japanese subsidiaries utilized profit sharing to a substantial extent, although this was the case in only about 24 per cent of Western MNE subsidiaries and 32 per cent of indigenous firms (Lawler and Amityanandana, 1995). Use of job evaluation by Japanese subsidiaries is almost non-existent, and factors such as age and seniority are important determinants of base pay. Indeed, about 90 per cent of the Japanese subsidiaries we studied relied heavily on seniority as a determinant of base pay (ibid.).

Seniority-based compensation, coupled with long-term employment is, of course, consistent with internal equity if a worker's contribution to the organization is averaged over their work life. Japanese subsidiaries, however, do not generally have the lifetime employment guarantees that at least certain workers have in Japan. As with other firms, continuing economic growth has meant that the need for massive 'downsizing' has not been an issue. Moreover, Thai workers believe that Japanese firms are less likely to fire workers (compared to Western, especially American, MNEs). This is one reason that individuals are prepared to work for Japanese companies despite low pay. Whether declining growth will allow these companies to continue to offer high job security is still an open question.

Training and development. Given the focus on internal development, training at all levels of the organization is considerably more prevalent in Japanese subsidiaries and is consistent with Japanese practice at home. Thus, training tends to be long-term, broad, and systematic. It involves both productivity and quality of life issues, the latter being related to socialization concerns. Thai employees are often sent to Japan for extended training, and this can include lower-level workers as well as managers and professionals. What is unclear at this point is the extent to which Japanese subsidiaries are now using such techniques as continuous improvement (*kaizen*) and lean production in Thailand.

DISCUSSION

Table 1 summarizes our analysis of HRM for Thai-owned and foreign-owned firms, indicating clearly different patterns for each of the four specific types of organizations considered. Of course, our analysis suggests general profiles and there is considerable variation within these categories.

TABLE 1

SUMMARY OF HR STRATEGY IN THAI-OWNED AND FOREIGN-OWNED FIRMS

HR Strategic Characteristics	Type of Firm			
	Family Enterprise	Thai-Owned Corporation	Western Subsidiaries	Japanese Subsidiaries
Strategic Planning				
– process	informal	formal	formal	formal
– integration	loose	tight	tight	tight
– temporal focus	short-term	long-term	long-term	long-term
Staffing				
– sources	internal	internal	external	internal
– career paths	broad	narrow	narrow	broad
– promotion ladders	few	multiple	multiple	few
– criteria	explicit	explicit	explicit	implicit
– socialisation	limited	extensive	limited	extensive
– procedures	closed	open	open	closed
Compensation				
– level	low	mid-range	high	low
– equity	idiosyncratic	internal	internal	internal
– fringe benefits	few	few	many	many
– incentives	many	many	mixed	many
– security	high	high	low	high
Training and Development				
– temporal focus	short-term	long-term	mixed	long-term
– breadth	narrow	broad	mixed	broad
– purpose	productivity-oriented	mixed	mixed	mixed
– planning	spontaneous	planned	planned	planned

Trends

We subtitled our article 'Eroding Traditions' for several reasons. Employment relations in Thailand are rooted in the highly traditional methods of the family enterprise. In such organizations, 'HRM' as it is practised in the advanced industrialized countries, is largely absent. This does not mean, of course, that there is neither rhyme nor reason to the systems these organizations have used. As we have shown, these methods are quite consistent with the traditional values and social arrangements of Thailand. Yet, these traditions are eroding as the country modernizes and as it participates ever more extensively in the world economy. Also, MNEs have imported techniques that have been adopted by indigenous firms, though not without modification in many instances. Thai corporations have professionalized the HRM function, and we would expect this trend to continue.

The methods historically employed by family enterprises are necessarily yielding to generally accepted HRM practices. Larger scale family enterprises will find it increasingly difficult to maintain the status quo, particularly if they intend to compete globally. Many of these companies are likely to 'go public' in the coming years, adding impetus to forces favouring change in their HRM systems. Of course, smaller-scale indigenous firms, most of which are family enterprises, are likely to maintain traditional employment management systems.

The context in which these changes have occurred has been very rapid economic expansion. However, like many other Pacific Rim countries, Thailand's economy, while not stagnant, has weakened somewhat in the past couple of years. It is expected by most observers of the Thai economy that economic growth will slow to less than the average of 8 per cent that it has been enjoying in the last decade. The National Economic and Social Development Board estimated that economic growth for 1996 was around 6.8 per cent. This may be high by world standards, but it represents a drop in what the economy has been experiencing. The major factor explaining this phenomenon is the slowdown of exports which have been the engine of economic growth. The Bank of Thailand expected that the 1996 export growth would be 0.5 per cent or zero compared with 23.6 per cent growth in 1995. While import growth has also declined, this has not been so drastic as that of export growth. Thus, the country's current account deficit cannot improve either.

The zero growth of exports has important implications for HRM. This is in particular a critical situation for those firms engaged in the manufacture of labour-intensive goods. Thailand has lost some competitive advantage in producing labour-intensive goods to China, Indonesia, Vietnam and South Asian countries. Thai labour-intensive industries, therefore, will have to improve competitiveness either by increasing productivity through improving HRs or by upgrading technology or both (similar problems confront other countries in the region (see Bae on Korea, and Chen on Taiwan in this volume). Improved competitiveness will certainly take time and involve both management system improvement and changes in employees' attitudes and firm's willingness to invest in human capital. Thus, more training and more sophisticated HRM systems will be required, particularly in the family enterprises that have been resistant to these changes.

The external pressures, due to changes in the world market situation, have also in recent years led to the need for manufacturing firms to shift to higher technology. This has created the tight labour market for skilled and professional manpower, as evidenced in the relatively frequent job-hopping problem mentioned above. The situation has generated a government call for a HR development plan, particularly for certain economic development areas, such as the Eastern and Southern seaboards.

In recent years, Thailand has been successful in attracting major manufacturing industries, such as electronics and automobile production, to set up bases. For example, both Ford and General Motors plan to build plants in Thailand and several Japanese automobile manufacturers already have plants there. Thus, the next decade will be a transitional period in a move from labour-intensive to more knowledge-intensive manufacturing. The industrial restructuring process will continue throughout this period. In achieving this, it has been acknowledged that the private sector and the government must invest more in research and development activities, as well as in HR development.

Anecdotal evidence suggests that greater team-based production is being practised in firms which use just-in-time production techniques to improve productivity. Many have started to rely more on performance-based compensation systems, particularly those faced with fierce competition in the world market. In the process, the HRM function is becoming more tied to business plans and strategies. Despite the trend towards HRM professionalization noted above, there continues to be a shortage of HRM practitioners. This has led to the practice of job rotation of staff from other areas to perform the HRM function. This is believed to promote an understanding of how HRM is critical to the success of business operations as line managers temporarily occupy these staff positions.

The professionalization of the HRM function tends to be greatest in the area of HR development. Thai firms appear to be more willing to invest in training and development activities. As noted, high growth has resulted in a tight the labour market, and personnel poaching and job hopping have led to increases in the wages and salaries of all levels of employees. Eventually, this has affected the production costs of firms and their competitiveness. In order to alleviate the problem, many industries have set up their own training centres to develop skilled and professional HRs at various levels of operation. Examples include Toyota in the automobile industry, various textile manufactures, and electronics firms.

Structural Influences

Although economic forces are apt to exert considerable impact on the HRM strategies pursued by firms operating in Thailand, longer-term social and organizational forces are also at work. Modernization and the breakdown of traditional societal forms tend to be associated with cultural shifts towards greater individualism and less hierarchical societies (Hofstede, 1980). Whether this is occurring in the rapidly developing economies of East and South East Asia as it did in Europe and America is hard to tell at this point, although there at least anecdotal evidence to this effect. Indeed, certain countries in the region have endeavoured to combat Western influences (that is, greater individualism and egalitarianism) associated with economic development by reinforcing traditional values. In this regard, Singapore promotes Confucianism as a core element of national culture (at least for the majority Chinese population), and economic growth in Malaysia has corresponded to efforts to strengthen the country's Islamic traditions. Thais, however, seem to be less concerned with changing values and culture and more willing to accept the natural flow of events. The HRM strategies typical of Western firms are, of course, relatively consistent with rational individualism and, to perhaps a lesser extent, egalitarianism. Thus, to the extent Thai culture moves in this direction, we might anticipate increased adoption of Western style HRM practices (as opposed to the maintenance of the status quo, the adoption of Japanese practices, or the evolution of some uniquely Thai system).

We might also consider the viability of different organizational theory perspectives for explaining the transformation of the Thai system of employee–management relations. One approach to consider is structural contingency theory. Although the strategic choice paradigm has seemingly displaced contingency theory, much of the applied strategy literature is still rooted in notions of organizational-environment fit. In many ways, the shifting approaches to HRM in Thai-owned companies reflect significant environmental changes. Traditional employment practices in family enterprises have given way to more structured and rationalized HRM practices in Thai-owned corporations as these firms confront changing cultural and economic patterns. Managers in these firms must deal with the demands of investors for more professionalized styles of dealing with employees. Moreover, the extensive social networks of traditional Thai society have begun to break down with modernization and as urban areas, particularly Bangkok, have grown very large and congested (thus limiting the opportunity for the social interaction necessary to build and reinforce such networks).

HRM systems in Thailand cannot, however, be understood just in terms of efforts by managers to achieve fit with changing environmental conditions. Notions of strategic choice and the exercise of managerial discretion are integral to perspectives such as the resource dependence model (Pfeffer and Salancik, 1978). In such a framework, key decision makers are seen as also endeavouring to shape the environment to fit the organization. Such a perspective seems especially appropriate in understanding the actions of MNEs, which tend to import systems from their home countries. As observed above, American firms rely on selecting individuals that have already been socialized into Western values (for example, Thai managers who have been educated abroad or who have previously worked for Western firms). Japanese firms use large numbers of expatriate managers and extensive intra-organizational socialization methods, along with extensive screening of job applicants, to achieve a similar effect. Within Thai-owned firms, the shift in the balance of political power away from family members towards professional managers has led to the introduction of management techniques, including those in the HRM area, with which these managers feel comfortable. This professionalization argument is also quite consistent with the institutional model (DiMaggio and Powell, 1983; Scott et al., 1994). Institutional perspectives argue that organizational fields tend to become isomorphic in part through the spread of professional standards. In addition, organizations often mimic one another (as in the pursuit of 'best practices'), perhaps as a means of dealing with uncertainty. This also seems to be at work in Thailand as evidenced by the partial convergence of HR strategies in Thai-owned corporations with those of subsidiaries of Western MNEs.

CONCLUSION

This contribution has examined different HR strategies typically encountered in larger-scale businesses operating in Thailand. We have compared and contrasted styles of HRM within indigenously owned companies as well as subsidiaries of MNEs. In concluding this work, we wish to relate what we have observed to the framework for comparing the HRM approaches in organizations with the more traditional personnel/industrial relations ten-point framework, (see Warner and others in this volume). While somewhat redundant of the Schuler (1988) framework, the purpose here is to allow our work to be compared to that of the other contributors. Building on such a framework, we offer the following observations:

- *Rules:* Rules within firms tend to be largely defined, certainly in the Thai-owned corporations and many of the Western MNEs, though less so in the Japanese subsidiaries. In family enterprises, rules tend to be flexible, but also rather *ad hoc*.
- *Behaviour:* Values and mission are starting to play a more significant role in Thai-owned corporations and Western MNEs, as they long have in the Japanese subsidiaries. Though also significant in family enterprises, the approach can be seen there as more emergent than deliberate.
- *Management Role:* Monitoring and controlling has been the dominant perception of their role on the part of managers in Thai-owned firms (given the traditional hierarchical nature of the society), as well as in subsidiaries of Western MNEs. This is quite consistent with the hierarchical nature of Thai society, though this may be undergoing change. Japanese subsidiaries have generally taken a more nurturing approach in some areas (for example, employee skill development), but they are still largely monitoring-style organizations (given the role of expatriate managers).
- *Key Managers:* This varies quite a bit across types of organizations. In Japanese subsidiaries, general and line managers dominate in the HRM area; this is also true in the family enterprises. HR managers dominate in Thai-owned corporations and Western subsidiaries.
- *Personnel Selection:* Hiring is clearly an integrated and key task in all of these types of firms, although for different reasons. In the family enterprise, personnel selection is integral to the social, as well as economic, role of the head of the company. In Western and Japanese subsidiaries, it is necessary to allow these firms to adapt HR strategies

from their home countries. In Thai-owned corporations, integration is driven mainly by efficiency considerations, although the aura of the manager as a kind of patron is also an aspect of this process (as in the family enterprise).

- *Payments System:* Pay is increasingly performance related and driven by the external market, although job evaluation-like processes are probably dominant in most organizations.
- *Work Conditions:* These are largely a matter of being separately negotiated, except in Japanese subsidiaries where there is greater reliance on harmonization.
- *Labour Management:* Union activity is quite limited in the Thai private sector, although as we noted, militancy is growing in some areas (a trend common in other parts of East and South East Asia). However, the absence of unions does not mean employment conditions are not influenced to some extent by the collective action of workers, as work groups and worker social networks often exercise informal influence within organizations.
- *Job Design:* Teamwork is dominant in Japanese subsidiaries, though not as widespread in other types of companies. However, team-based approaches seem to be on the increase, just as in other parts of the world.
- *In-House Training:* Except in Japanese subsidiaries, training has not be a key element in these organizations and would not generally be seen as part of an ongoing process. Again, this may be changing as Thai companies necessarily upgrade technology in order to compete internationally (the country can no longer thrive by relying on low-wage, labour intensive industries).

ACKNOWLEDGEMENTS

The research reported in this article was supported in part by the Office of International Programs and Studies of the University of Illinois at Urbana-Champaign.

NOTES

1. The Thai government is in the process of privatizing large numbers of state enterprises and this sector is diminishing in importance.
2. As noted above, the percentages cited here and below are based on a sample of about 100 firms.
3. As noted below, only about 38 per cent of the MNEs of Japanese companies in Thailand fell into the 'relatively high' category. This has in part to do with the structure of these firms, as discussed later.
4. For example, those born in the poorer North East part of the country ('Isan') are, other things equal, likely to have lower status than those born in Bangkok or some other regions of the country.
5. Illustrative of this would be that the Thai language contains numerous first and second person pronouns, and which are used in a conversation depends upon the relative social ranks of the individuals involved.

REFERENCES

Bangkok Post Economic Review: Year End 1996 (1996), pp.24–5.
Brown, Andrew and Stephen Frenkel (1993) 'Union Unevenness and Insecurity in Thailand' in Stephen Frenkel (ed.) *Organized Labor in the Asia-Pacific Region.* Ithaca, NY: ILR Press, pp.83–107.
Chen Chia-Shen (1991) 'Confucian Style of Management in Taiwan', in Joseph M. Putti (ed.) *Management: Asian Context.* Singapore: McGraw-Hill, pp.177–97.
Dawson, Alan (1996) 'Bangkok Post', Week in *Review* (distributed via e-mail), 22 December 1996.
Dawson, Alan (1997) 'Bangkok Post', Week in *Review* (distributed via e-mail), 5 January 1997.
Deyo, Frederic (1995) 'Human Resource Strategies and Industrial Restructuring in Thailand' in Stephen Frenkel and Jeffrey Harrod (eds) *Industrialization and Labor Relations: Contemporary Research in Seven Countries.* Ithaca, NY: ILR Press, pp.23–36.
DiMaggio, Paul J. and Walter W. Powell (1983) 'The Iron Cage Revisited: Institutional Isomorphism and Collective Rationality in Organizational Fields', *American Sociological Review*, Vol.48, No.1, pp.147–60.
Far Eastern Economic Review (1988), 30 June, pp.60–63. See 'The Jewels of the Crown'.
Heenan, David A. and Howard V. Perlmutter (1979) *Multinational Organizational Development.* Reading, MA: Addison-Wesley.
Hofstede, Geert (1980) *Culture's Consequences: International Differences in Work-Related Values.* Beverly Hills, CA: Sage.
Isarangkun Na Ayuthaya, Chirayu and Koji Taira (1977) 'The Organization and Behavior of the Factory Work Force in Thailand', *The Developing Economies*, Vol.15, No.1, pp.16–36.
Jaeger, Alfred M. and Rabindra N. Kanungo (1990) 'Introduction: The Need for Indigenous Management in Developing Countries' in Rabindra N. Kanungo and Alfred M. Jaeger (eds) *Managing in Developing Countries.* London: Routledge.
Lawler, John J. (1996) 'Diversity Issues in Southeast Asia: The Case of Thailand', *International Journal of Manpower*, Vol.17, No.4/5, pp.152–67.
Lawler, John J. and Vinita Atmiyanandana (1995) 'Human Resource Management in Thailand' in Larry F. Moore and P. Devereaux Jennings (eds) *Human Resource Management on the Pacific Rim: Institutions, Practices and Attitudes.* Berlin: de Gruyter, pp.294–318.
Lawler, John J. and Sununta Siengthai (1996) 'Human Resource Management and Strategy in Thailand: A Case Study of the Banking Industry' in Joseph Lee and Anil Verma (eds) *Changing Employment Relations in Asia Pacific Countries.* Taipei: Chung-Hua Institution for Economic Research, pp.317–44.
Lawler, John J., Mahmood A. Zaidi, and Vinita Atmiyanandana (1989) 'Human Resource Strategies in Southeast Asia: The Case of Thailand' in Albert Nedd, Gerald R. Ferris and Kendrith Rowland (eds) *Research In Personnel And Human Resources Management (Supplement 1).* Greenwich, CN: JAI Press, pp.201–22..
Mintzberg, Henry (1989) *Mintzberg on Management: Inside Our Strange World of Organizations.* New York, NY: Free Press.
Nyaw Mee-Kan (1995) 'Human Resource Management in the People's Republic of China' in Larry F. Moore and P. Devereaux Jennings (eds) *Human Resource Management on the Pacific Rim: Institutions, Practices and Attitudes.* Berlin: de Gruyter, pp.187–216.
Oddou, Gary C., Brooklyn Derr and J. Stewart Black (1995) 'Internationalizing Managers: Expatriation and Other Strategies' in Jan Selmer (ed.) *Expatriate Management: New Ideas for International Business.* Westport, CT: Quorum Books, pp.3–16.
Osterman, Paul (1992) 'Internal Labour Markets in a Changing Environment: Models and Evidence' in David Lewin, Olivia Mitchell, and Peter Sherer (eds) *Research Frontiers in Industrial Relations and Human Resources.* Madison, WI: Industrial Relations Research Association, pp.273–308.
Pfeffer, Jeffrey and Gerald Salancik (1978) *The External Control of Organizations: A Resource Dependence Perspective.* New York, NY: Harper and Row.
Schuler, Randall (1988) 'Human Resource Management Choices and Organizational Strategy' in Randall Schuler, Sandra Youngblood and Vandra Huber (eds) *Readings in Personnel and Human Resource Management.* St. Paul, MN: West Publishing, pp.24–39.
Scott, W. Richard, John W. Meyer *et al.* (1994) *Institutional Environments and Organizations: Structural Complexity and Individualism.* Thousand Oaks, CA: SAGE Publications.
Siengthai, Sununta, and Orose Leelakulthanit (1994) 'Women in Management in Thailand' in Nancy Adler and Dafna Izraeli (eds) *Competitive Frontiers: Woman Managers in a Global*

Economy. Cambridge, MA: Blackwell, pp.160–71.

Siengthai, Sununta, and Pakpachong Vadhanasindhu (1991) 'Management in a Buddhist Society – Thailand' in Joseph M. Putti (ed.) *Management: Asian Context*. Singapore: McGraw-Hill, pp.222–39.

Trompenaars, Fons (1994) *Riding the Waves of Culture: Understanding Diversity in Global Business*. Chicago: Irwin.

Walker, James (1992) *Human Resource Strategy*. New York, NY: McGraw-Hill.

Conclusion: Reassessing HRM's Convergence

CHRIS ROWLEY

This collection has analyzed human resource management (HRM) across a diverse spread of locations, sectors and organizations in the Asia Pacific region. This searchlight of inquiry has illustrated some convergence, also some locationally-specific practice due not just to cultural constraints, but also to institutional inhibitors. What is indicated is the key role of external forces on HRM. These include not just types of influence which are organizational (strategies and profitability) and sectoral and product market (simple versus complex products and processes), but also more 'traditional' ones such as labour and the state. While many managers and assorted academics may see these as somewhat 'old fashioned' and even obsolete in their search for nostrums in an era of perceived globalization, their salience remains significant. Despite some changes, HRM often remains, on the one hand diverse and dynamic, and on the other locationally-specific and contradictory, a situation businesses and management gurus need to remember.

At this point it is useful to re-examine the ideas within convergence, culture and institutional approaches, with evidence from the Asia Pacific and the contributors. The key issues of the role of labour, the state, and forms of flexibility are then discussed, followed by some concluding remarks.

BACK TO CONVERGENCE?

A case for convergence can be built upon the foundations of a mix of developments, for example patterns of globalization, economic integration, transnational companies, opening of markets and dominance of free market ideas and privatization. This is combined with two-way investment, both into and out of Asia via multinational enterprises (MNEs) (as into Singapore, Thailand), joint ventures (as into China, Philippines), and transplants (as into West) and searches for 'best practice' solutions to import. Also, there is the belief that the 'borderless world' is emerging under the onslaught of rapid communications and technological change allowing transference. These may produce instances of HRM convergence.

Contributions to this collection[1] lend some support to convergence, or at least overlap, at both intra and international levels. Warner showed some

Chris Rowley, Royal Holloway, University of London

convergence, or at least overlap with more flexibility in labour markets (labour contracts, reward systems) in China between state-owned enterprises (SOEs) and joint ventures. Ng and Poon outlined some convergence of practices between Hong Kong and the West, Japan and other Asian societies. These included Cathy Pacific's 'de-bureaucratization' and labour flexibility, retailers' changes and benchmarked practices. Some convergence of Japanese large firms towards Western notions of HRM was seen by Benson and Debroux, with declining life-time jobs and internal labour markets, more performance-related pay and recruitment and promotion changes. Bae reported some HRM similarities between large Korean firms and smaller US and Japanese firms. Amante noted that by benchmarking HRM practices some Philippine organizations are bringing about convergence, often towards increasing emphasis on human resource development strategies. This is also seen in the combining of company's industrial relations (IR) and HRM functions, and aided by managers educated or trained abroad and by globalization. In Singapore, Yuen reported that US subsidiaries often introduce their 'home country' HRM. Chen indicated some convergence in HRM practices between larger Taiwanese-owned firms and foreign subsidiaries, with SOEs establishing Western practices and no significant differences in most aspects of HRM. In Thailand, Lawler et al. noted some convergence, for example, of human resource strategy between Thai-owned companies and subsidiaries of Western MNEs and employment practices of Thai firms, giving way to HRM methods imported from the West.

However, the evidence supporting convergence in this collection is actually mixed and equivocal, with caveats often used. For Warner, convergence in its strictest sense, even between joint ventures and SOEs within China, was as yet 'far in the distance'. Moves were better seen as more like 'relative convergence' and a more complex, hybrid management model. Ng and Poon viewed convergence as only 'partial', with practices only selectively introduced in Hong Kong. They concluded that there was a hybrid: converging patterns but also divergent practices distinctive to Hong Kong. Benson and Debroux argued that in Japan life-time employment practices actually continue largely intact and regular employees remain protected by traditional, distinctive adjustment measures.[2] Bae reported substantial HRM differences between large and small Korean firms. In Taiwan, Chen noted that small and medium size enterprises (SMEs), which provided the bulk of firms and employment, had distinctive HRM practices. Even in the large firms there were some limits to convergence. For example, performance appraisals and profit-related pay was restricted, especially in SOEs, and seniority-based systems continued. In Thailand, Lawler et al. reported that traditional, family-owned enterprises differed substantially from 'best practice' Western firms, and there was a sectoral distinction: in the private sector most firms began as family-owned and closely tied to the Sino-Thai community and many continue to be managed in that manner with HRM quite distinct from publicly-traded Thai corporations.

Furthermore, when this evidence is contextualized in a broader focus, convergence is again questioned. Indeed, a plethora of relevant, some of it also locationally-related, research amply displays continuing divergence. For example, the varied (sectorally and locationally) contributions to, *inter alia*, Elger and Smith (1994), question the universalizable content and practice of many working practices. Also two seemingly strong examples of single industries presented as open to global competition and common forces are worth repeating – if convergence is constrained here, then it may be even weaker elsewhere. The automobile sector has underpinned much convergence/universalism-type debate in the guise of 'lean production' via work by Womack *et al.* (1990). Yet, research has questioned the transference of production systems (Japanese), and noted considerable sectoral diversity within Japan itself (Deyo, 1996b), and in operations and HRM outcomes, characteristics such as IR continue to shape systems and practices (Graham, 1993; see contributors to Elger and Smith, 1994; Babson, 1995; Green and Yanarella, 1996; Deyo, 1996a; Stewart, 1996). In short, there is continuing divergence, rather than convergence on Japanese production systems, and variety in the meaning and practice of ideas, such as team/group working (Turner and Auer, 1996).

Similarly, comparative research on the telecommunications industry (across ten countries, including Korea and Japan) facing common environmental changes, shows one set of work practices or styles of employment relations to be absent, with variations across and within countries (Katz, 1997). The common tendency was actually towards increased variation and divergence. The limited convergence in the common development of work practices (such as performance-related pay, team systems, direct employee communications), was overwhelmed by variation in specific terms and places where adopted. The reasons for this (and with wider relevance elsewhere) include the growth of: non-union employment with different work practices versus traditional monopolies; and variation of employment practices within both non-union and unionized sectors and across firms in one country, with growing decentralization of authority in firms (ibid.).

More specific examples of locationally-relevant research also 'debunks' convergence. First, evidence of continuing divergence between Asia Pacific locations. Jomo's work (1994) challenges convergence, while Abo's (1996) empirical evidence of Japanese plants in Korea and Taiwan (and the US) shows Japanese production systems adopted differently. Similarly, Japanese television transplants in Malaysia and Taiwan are constrained in transferring elements of Japanese-style management by the strategy and structure of transplants (strongly conditioned by the parent company's global strategy); and local hiring practices resulting in managers unfamiliar with, and not favourable towards, parent practices (Hiramoto, 1995). Hong Kong, Singapore and Taiwan, often clustered in cultural homogeneity and with similar economic development and socio-cultural institutions, vary significantly in performance appraisals (Paik *et al.*, 1996). Similarly, performance appraisals are restricted in Korea due to cultural norms encouraging close relations between work groups (Rodgers, 1996). As Amsden (1989:324) concludes in her magisterial work: 'Of all the characteristics of late industrialization, labor relations show the least consistency across nations', which included Korea, Taiwan and Japan.

Second, evidence of diversity within Asia Pacific locations is available. China's post-1970s division into two economic sectors (state run and urban collective; capitalist and rural collective) produced very different relationships between workers and the state and enterprise management (Chan, 1995). Despite similar environmental 'triggers', Hong Kong's textile and garment making industries diverged significantly in their 'recipes' and processes for restructuring due to institutional features, economic and technological structure, patterns of ownership and management, character of employment systems and IR, which in turn shaped their HRM outcomes (Chiu and Levin, 1995). Capital–labour relations within Malaysia remain diverse, even despite its explicit 'Look East' policy, with its emphasis of labour and Japanese-style work ethics, but which were only partly taken up (Jomo, 1995). Korea operates widely divergent HRM practices among firms in different sectors and categories of employees: while 'elite' firms in advanced industries apply 'sophisticated' HRM policies, it is much more common for firms to adopt practices designed to maximize output through standardized tasks at the lowest possible cost (Rodgers, 1996). Korea witnessed a dualistic growth of flexible and polarized wage formation and sexual division of labour with expansion of labour-intensive products based on female, low wage labour versus higher productivity, capital-intensive industry underpinned by cheap capital and generating a greater degree of technical dynamism (You, 1995). Similarly, HRM's frequent push for flexibility varies not only between, but also within, national sectors. For instance, in Japanese manufacturing: small firms tend to adopt short term, defensive forms of flexibility (maximizing the return on labour and reducing labour costs by wage and numerical flexibility); while large firms maintain a highly skilled, adaptable rather than dispensable, workforce (Benson, 1996). As Elger and Smith (1994) comprehensively show, there is much hype and mythology surrounding de-contextualized 'one best way' ideas as the character, novelty and coherence of practices remain varied, tension-riven, contested, unstable and uneven in their reception, adoption and influence.

It may be argued that these are merely 'snapshots', and that over time convergence will grow, especially with the spread and power of MNEs. Yet, several authors believe that diversity '...is not a transitory phenomenon but an enduring one...' (Turner and Auer, 1996:234), while the lack of a common set of employment relations and variation within and across nations in telecommunications, was likely to persist, and probably expand (Katz, 1997). Also, 'Whether companies internationalise, globalise or transnationalise, HRM will remain largely a national activity, bounded by culture, geography and legislative systems' (Torrington, 1994:251).

In short, the above evidence from the contributors and others indicates constrained support for HRM convergence. Rather, considerable variation remains because even if the driving forces are similar, various routes to work organization and distinctly different HRM outcomes in varied socio-economic and political contexts, remain. Such variation may well be more enduring than is often thought.

CONTINUING CONCERN FOR CULTURE AND INSTITUTIONAL INFLUENCES

Attempts to explain diversity often fall back on cultural and institutional aspects (see Introduction). For Ng and Poon, some of Hong Kong's HRM practices betrayed their Asian traditions and Confucian heritage, with an Eastern–Western 'culture divide' in some of their cases. For Benson and Debroux, Japan's 'gradualism' was firmly and deeply rooted in its context and configuration. Bae's contribution noted that changes were introduced in Korea without much consensus because (unlike Japan) of the family-driven structure and top-down decision making. Amante argued that 'benchmarked' HRM practices still felt the moulding force of Philippine culture, with its entrenched institutional and local work practices. This often produced a style that was a 'blend' of Western and Japanese with local cultural values and sensibilities. In Singapore Yuen noted the importance of local culture, for example, in the reluctance of local employees to accept Western-style performance appraisals, while many Japanese subsidiaries abandoned their HRM systems in favour of wholesale adaption of local systems. This is similar to Taiwan, where Chen reported limits to appraisals, even in large SOEs. For Lawler *et al.*, Thai culture and context had substantial impacts on HRM: some traditional employment practices remained firmly grounded in Thai society, and other HRM practices were changed. Thus, given the system of 'control' rooted in Thai national social fabric, moves to decentralization, worker discretion and work teams were all limited by the hierarchical nature of Thai culture. Also, some Japanese managers in MNEs thought there would be a 'common' culture (yet Thai culture is more individualistic than Japanese) and along with some Western MNEs, imposed HRM systems in an ethnocentric fashion. However, this sort of behaviour generated significant cultural clashes in the workplace.

One way of viewing developments is not as a hard 'either/or' dichotomy but in a more temporally and organizationally complex and nuanced fashion. For instance, in China Warner outlined evolving changes: in the early days of reform there was divergence between SOEs and joint ventures; then relative divergence when Western and Asian management practices became more widely diffused; but relative convergence may follow, in varying degrees (see Ng and Warner, 1998). Likewise, Ng and Poon argued convergence in Asian and managerial practices in Hong Kong has been cyclical: emulation of mainstream practices from the West; followed by departure in pursuit of a culture niche of Asianization or Easternization traditions; then a shift back again, with benchmarking against European/American companies' practices. For Amante, HRM convergence was constrained in the Philippines, producing a 'mixed' style. As we saw in the Introduction, Hasagawa's (1996) findings show the usefulness of moving from simple bipolar convergence or divergence via his more disaggregated model highlighting different aspects: organisations can converge on some areas and practices, but diverge in others.

In short, there are continuing differences in HRM, both between and within the Asia Pacific. For Amante limits on universalism stemmed from the continuing significance of the role of the nation state, particularly its shared cultural norms and values. Yuen made the obvious point that HRM is affected by organizational type and size, head office influence, level of technology, sector, but also constrained by local values/culture and 'realities' of local labour markets. What these mixed, blurred and shifting pictures indicate is the role of not just culture, but also enduring external influences, in particular that of labour and the state, among others (such as organizational economic performance and business strategies, which influence HRM, and are external to at least the HRM function[3]).

THE ROLE OF LABOUR

The role of labour policy in Asian development has been analyzed (see, *inter alia*, Deyo, 1989). Some may argue that it has been over-played as a factor. However, in many explanations of Asian economic success, human resources play a role (see Leggett and Bamber, 1996). Indeed, industrialization strategies and IR policies are seen as closely intertwined and mutually reinforcing in parts of Asia (Kuruvilla, 1995a; Sharma, 1991). This is also indicated in the evocatively labelled 'primitive' (or 'bloody') Taylorization (Lipietz, 1987), of export-oriented industrialization with high rates of labour exploitation and low technological sophistication. Thus, in Korea's early economic development a key to competitiveness included HRM policies designed to minimize labour costs (Rodgers, 1996). However, others view Korean industrialization via authoritarian capital–labour relations, not in the conventional way – giving export-led growth with labour repression to ensure competition based on low wages – but, rather by establishing labour controls and discipline on the shopfloor (You, 1995). Likewise, in the Philippine electronics sector workplace practices mirror the cheap labour focus development policy, producing rigid work rules, strict job classifications, poor health and safety and working conditions, and the use of contracts (Kuruvilla, 1995a). Similar points are made about Malaysia (Kuruvilla, 1995b). Such positioning led Krugman, the famous US economist, to evocatively and succinctly suggest that Asia's 'economic miracle' was based on 'perspiration rather than inspiration' (in Montagnon, 1996).

However, competitive advantage based on cheap, 'sweated' labour often declines. As Ng and Poon note, Hong Kong became less able to compete on low labour costs. Similarly, Singapore continues to shed low skilled, less sophisticated manufacturing to Indonesia and Malaysia, such as Seagate International, the world's largest disc drive manufacturer, which is now considering moving (Kynge, 1997). As even companies in Thailand are discovering, they cannot compete with China (or India) on labour costs alone when they offer wage levels of one quarter (and one fifth) of theirs (Barnes, 1995), and use harsh, military-type labour regimes and long hours to compete, as in the Yu Yuan sports shoe factory in Dongguan City (Chan, 1996).

Thus, trying to maintain initial factors for success may be untenable over the longer term. Furthermore, the picture conjured up by Deyo (1996c:138) is of a 'sandwich trap', as some Asia Pacific countries, such as Thailand, are pushed out of cheap labour export niches from below by the next wave of exporters, while shifts up-market into high-tech, value-added production is impeded by competition from above (Korea, Taiwan, Hong Kong), which began this transition earlier.

The above usefully indicates that the 'type' and 'quality' of human resources has a crucial impact on the type of economic development (see Rowley and Lewis, 1996) and HRM, in terms of routes to competition, forms of production and commensurate employment requirements and practices. An example is the impact of limited skilled human resources but abundant unskilled labour, leading to different trajectories of development, work organization and employment practices. Singapore, for instance, is seen as in an ideal position to continue to develop a sophisticated workforce for complex work (Begin, 1995), and there has been concentration on electronic chip design given the high quality of its labour (Kuruvilla, 1995a), with movement towards a high technology/skill direction for some time (see Yuen). Likewise, there has been Korean recognition of the trap between low labour cost producers and higher quality manufacturers (see Bae). Yet, stimulus for such upgrading may be lacking and is not likely to be created by abundant numerically 'flexible' and unprotected labour. Hong Kong is seen as failing to advance technologically and to upgrade manufacturing to higher value-added activities, exacerbated by problems with employee relations and labour markets suffering from high degrees of flexibility, weak organized labour and large numbers of immigrant workers (Wilkinson, 1994).

Thus, labour is of key importance. There may be a mutually-reinforcing flow of elements: 'quality', skilled employees attracting advanced, sophisticated and value-added production leading to further investment in employees; or vice versa, poor quality human resources attracting simple manufacturing reliant on cheap, unskilled labour leading to less investment. Upgrading in the latter scenario is problematic. China, for example, does not often use (or produce) high technology equipment (Child, 1994). Likewise, Taiwan's SMEs problems include: their suboptimal scale and higher average costs; limited upgrading of production with technical innovation and movement into the highest value research and development intensive sectors; restricted investment in the most advanced capital equipment; and dependence on Japanese technology (Wilkinson, 1994). In short, while management may well make decisions on HRM, these, as well as convergence, are constrained by labour, not least its type and quality. This brings us to the second important variable, external influence on HRM (and labour itself), the state.

THE ROLE OF THE STATE

Another key aspect, and external influence, on HRM in the Asia Pacific concerns the relative role of the state (see more generally, *inter alia*, Amsden, 1989; Wilkinson, 1994; contributors to Sako and Sato, 1997). A traditional model of economic development emphasized the relationship between unions and the state in post-colonial regimes (noted in Verma *et al.*, 1995). Thus, colonial legacies led to politicized roles for unions. While some countries (such as India), appear to have retained a strong political role for labour movements, by the early 1960s several other post-colonial regimes evolved into either a corporatist model in which the state co-opted labour into a subservient role in national policy (Singapore), or an authoritarian model in which labour was excluded from national policy making and suppressed at the workplace (Korea).

The contribution of HRM policies to Asian economic growth, and the appropriate mix for creating higher-value economies, have been analyzed (ibid.). Economic development is outlined in terms of 'critical junctures' when success based on low pay and suppression of workers' rights becomes problematic as over time remuneration rises and employees seek greater 'voice'. States can maintain initial condition advantages (as by wage controls, suppression of unions); or create new factors of competitive advantage at both national and firm levels (for instance, upgrading skills by investing in training and education, wages policies, 'voice' to unions) provided a suitable infrastructure uses HRM as a source of competitive strength, with a shift to practices designed to upgrade their technological capabilities and improve product quality. This evolution is seen in Singapore, Taiwan, Korea and to a lesser extent in Hong Kong. Critically, the state cannot be 'detached' as it needs to ensure firms make commensurate investments (ibid.). Others note Korea's high degree of state intervention and direction (Amsden, 1989) and that public policy supported capital and technology-intensive industries via the emergence of the *chaebol*, thus contributing to upgrading (Rodgers, 1996) with some industries protected from competition via import controls and restrictions on labour disputes and by using scarce resources (skills, physical capital) economically and abundant resources (unskilled labour) lavishly (Bae).[4] Likewise, the Singaporean state not only closely directed education and training, but also deliberately phased-out low skilled, labour-intensive industries and moved to capital intensive, higher-tech and value-added industries and services by increasing labour costs, forcing labour-intensive industries to relocate, while encouraging automation to attract high technology industries (Yuen).

Similar state influences can be seen in the following. State support for education and physical infrastructure and discouragement of cost-cutting labour strategies by establishing minimum wages, benefits and work conditions and investment in the long term, for example, in training, technology development, are all evident during rapid industrial restructuring in Korea and Singapore during the 1970s (Deyo, 1996c). This strikingly contrasts with the relative passivity of the Thai government and failure to encourage human resource development (ibid.). The pro-active Taiwanese state used its vast foreign currency reserves in a high development programme (Wilkinson, 1994). The state helped in developing not only transport, utilities and communications infrastructure, export promotion, investment incentives, market protection, leadership in high technology sectors through public enterprises and a range of government institutions and technological upgrading and enhancement of research and development capacity, but also with capital targeted at human resource development and education (ibid.). Even in Hong Kong, while the state was more minimalist in directing the often fiercely free market capitalism and economy, it still had some 'orchestration' role, such as in infrastructure, education, social welfare, control of supply of labour via immigration controls and business activities (ibid.). The problem with state non-interventionism, as in Hong Kong, is the precarious existence of employees and absence of rights, although the state does provide channels and mechanisms for airing grievances and dispute settlement and welfare benefits, including housing (ibid.; Ng and Poon). Indeed, Hong Kong is an interesting example of the movement from non-intervention to increasing state influence (Poon, 1995).

In short, the absence of state leadership may result in a downward spiral of ever increasing labour casualization and cost-cutting efforts dominating avarice managerial responses to intensified competition. This is seen in examples in the Asia Pacific, for instance, Malaysia (except for a few advanced, core areas) and the Thai textile sector (Deyo, 1995). Such routes to competition are often under the parsimonious drive for flexibility banner.

FLEXIBLE FLEXIBILITIES

The above accounts of the role of labour and the state come together in, for example, drives for, and types of, flexibility.[5] Debate surrounding this topic has become polarized into over-simplified, often visceral, rhetoric of *flexibility* = *'good'*; *inflexibility ('rigidity')* = *'bad'*. Yet, some rigidities (institutional) facilitate internal and external flexibility (Dore, 1987), while numerical flexibility may weaken pressures to develop functional flexibility and its commensurate upgrading of human capital and skills. Thus, this dichotomy is disingenuous and dangerous for long term economic development, productivity and forms of HRM (see Fitzgerald and Rowley, 1997).

As we have seen, such issues are important in many of the locations in this collection, such as Hong Kong, Japan, Korea, the Philippines, and elsewhere (see Locke, 1995). Interestingly, 'dynamic' versus 'static' flexibility provision, each with commensurate HRM implications, such as job security and stability, wages and working conditions, and information sharing, had been explored in Asian contexts (Deyo, 1996b). Such flexibilities are influenced by broader sectoral and national 'governance' systems: institutional environments of economic activity comprising states, associations, bargaining structures, and so on, with the state's role in promoting dynamic type flexibility varying depending on the institutional salience of other elements of governance (ibid.). Thus, in the Thai car industry flexibility took an 'autocratic', low trust form which minimizes and discourages shopfloor participation (Deyo, 1996c). Likewise, in Hong Kong, Cathay Pacific's move to increase labour market flexibility resulted in the collapse of not only its internal labour market, but also commitment, leaving suspicious and demoralized cabin staff (Ng and Poon). Yet, this undermined its competing via 'quality service' strategy.

However, we should not paint too hard a dichotomy between dynamic flexibility that succeeds versus static, autocratic flexibility that fails, at least in the short term. Autocratic flexibility can succeed partly because firms use technology developed and 'de-bugged' elsewhere (Japan), requiring less from the shopfloor, participation, and so on, in product and process innovation, and so allowing low trust, low commitment HRM practices (Deyo, 1996c). Nevertheless, there is a wealth of literature on the more problematic longer term situation for this in terms of dynamic productivity, innovation, and so forth (see Rowley and Lewis, 1996).

In sum, the above points are important and too easily often forgotten. For example, they show that many assertions of the Asia Pacific region as a bastion of *laissez-faire*, free-wheeling, free market neo-liberalist economics are caricatures and too broad. Even where such views are more relevant, they still contain inherent flaws and trade-offs, as between long term, dynamic growth and innovation on the one hand, and 'types' of HRM and commensurate employment practices, on the other. By-passing such ideas leaves an anaemic and one-sided view of HRM.

The contributors' search for HRM in the Asia Pacific region has noted some of its practices. A tentative case for some convergence at intra- and inter- national levels can be made. However, before the convergence case is celebrated, we need to remember its key dimensions. These include time frames, units of analysis and reference points to converge around and direction of changes: Asia Pacific locations moving towards each other or the West; or the West shifting towards the Asia Pacific? Overall, it seems that the relevance of convergence is constrained. This is not to deny that there can be sharing and borrowing of ideas and practices, but that there are very real restraints to convergence and individual HRM policies and practices, let alone as a 'package'.

It may well be that HRM is too institutionally restricted and culturally grounded in Western values (such as individualism, competitiveness, and so on) to be of widespread use in the Asia Pacific region (see Warner, 1996).

HRM is linked to liberal, individualist ideology and deregulation (as in the US), where management authority, autonomy and discretion to introduce initiatives is high. This, and the impact of factors and environments (such as the state, legislation), varies across nations (see Brewster, 1994). HRM's universalistic assumptions, for example, of the ability of managers to exercise 'strategic choice', ignores structures in which these are exercised (Hyman, 1987; Sisson, 1994) due to: the composition/importance of 'types' of management, such as the finance function and the accounting 'logic'; patterns of institutional investment and relations with financial markets; and organizational structures and traditions. HRM is also internally contradictory. Indeed, commonly presented declining state direction and increasing marketization, privatization and organizational autonomy produces paradoxical outcomes: greater freedom to introduce HRM but *also not to*, and to *vary* employment practices by avaricious management. For instance, Ng and Poon note some devolution of HRM in Hong Kong and so they expect divergence. Given this, what then for common HRM and standards and pan-organizational, let pan-national HRM and convergence? As Sisson (1994) reminds us, assertions of increasing management freedom from constraints may produce a low wage/skill/productivity future. Thus, variations in HRM remain shaped by politics, public policy, IR institutions, union and firm strategies, and labour market policies and conditions (Katz, 1997; Turner and Auer, 1996), as institutions and the role of labour and the state retain their relevance.

In conclusion, by casting light across the Asia Pacific in search of HRM and possible convergence, several pictures have emerged in varying levels of relief. There are HRM moves of a 'pick 'n' mix' nature, but also continuing diversity. The particular forms HRM has taken, and the extent to which it has diffused, vary considerably not only across, but also within, locations, industries and organizations with different institutional arrangements and historical traditions (c.f. Warner, 1997). Therefore, convergence, and modern variants – universalism – should be questioned. First, there is not just 'one best way' or magic elixir. While such conclusions may not be welcomed by many parsimonious managers (and, it must be said, some academics), who have become addicted to a diet of simple lists, naive nostrums and pleasing platitudes, such complexity and diversity remains prevalent in the modern, still murky, world of HRM. It remains the case that we are still often 'desperately seeking' HRM as anything approaching a package in many workplaces in the UK, and this is no less so within the Asia Pacific region due to institutions, structure and culture of both domestic locations and owners' home bases. Such perspectives provide a much needed and refreshing tonic to the over-simplistic views of apostles of convergence and universalism. It may be a case of some relative convergence in HRM but more converging relevance concerning the importance of employees to success.

NOTES

1. From now on authors' names without references refer to their works in this volume.
2. However, this may be under threat. This could produce some moves towards Western-style HRM. For example, Benson and Debroux identify that it may not be short term economic recessions driving changes, but shifts in governance structure: companies were insulated from short term demands of shareholders, and so in recessions cut dividends before labour. This is no longer sustainable, with investors beginning to demand higher dividends. From the other side there are falling commitment levels of young employees and the perceived unfairness of management practices is increasing partly because of growing individualistic attitudes and dislike of groupism.
3. Thanks to Rod Martin for this point.
4. However, Rhee (1994) challenges the argument that the state played a vital role in industrial adjustments to direct macro-economic and industrial policy. In the late 1970s and 1980s, these were largely ineffective.
5. The topic of flexibility itself has now produced a heated, but often visceral, debate on its types, newness, trends, and so on, which is beyond the scope of this article. See, *inter alia*, Pollert (1991).

REFERENCES

Abo, Tetsuo (1996) 'The Japanese Production System: The Process Adaptation to National Systems' in Robert Boyer and Daniel Dracke (ed.) *States Against Markets: The Limits of Globalisation*. London: Routledge, pp.136–54.
Amsden, Alice (1989) *Asia's Next Giant: South Korea and Late Industrialization*. Oxford: Oxford University Press.
Babson, Steve (1995) (ed.) *Lean Work: Empowerment and Exploitation in the Global Auto Industry*. Detroit, MI: Wayne State University Press.
Barnes, William (1995) 'Labour: Schooled In Skills Shortage', *Financial Times Survey: Thailand*, 14 December, p.IV.
Begin, James P. (1995) 'Singapore's IR System: Is It Congruent with Its Second Phase of Industrialization?' in Stephen Frenkel and Jeffrey Harrod (eds) (1995) *Industrialization and Labor Relations: Contemporary Research in Seven Countries*. Ithaca, NY: ILR Press. pp.64–87.
Benson, John (1996) 'Management Strategy and Labour Flexibility in Japanese Manufacturing Enterprises', *Human Resource Management Journal*, Vol.6, No.2. pp. 44–57.
Brewster, Chris (1993) 'Human Resource Manangement in Europe: Reflection of, or Challenge to, the American Concept' in Paul Kirkbride (ed.) *HRM in Europe: Perspectives for the 1990s*. London: Routledge, pp.56–89.
Chan, Anita (1995) 'The Emerging Patterns of Industrial Relations in China and the Rise of Two New Labor Movements', *China Information*, Vol.IX, No.4, pp.36–59.
Chan, Anita (1996) 'Boot Camp at the Shoe Factory', *Washington Post (Outlook Section)*, 3 November, pp.1–4.
Child, John (1994), *Management in China During the Age of Reform*. Cambridge: Cambridge University Press.
Chiu, Stephen and David A. Levin (1995) 'The World Economy, State, and Sectors in Industrial Change: Labor Relations in Hong Kong's Textile and Garment-Making Industries' in Stephen Frenkel and Jeffrey Harrod (eds) (1995) *Industrialization and Labor Relations: Contemporary Research in Seven Countries*. Ithaca, NY: ILR Press. pp.144–75.
Deyo, Frederic C. (1989), *Beneath the Miracle: Labor Subordination in the New Asian Industrialism*. Berkeley, CA: University of California Press.
Deyo, Frederic C. (1995) 'Human Resource Strategies and Industrial Restructuring in Thailand' in Stephen Frenkel and Jeffrey Harrod (eds) (1995) *Industrialization and Labor Relations: Contemporary Research in Seven Countries*. Ithaca, NY: ILR Press. pp.23–36.
Deyo, Frederic C. (1996a) (ed.) *Social Reconstructions of the World Automobile Industry*. London: Macmillan.
Deyo, Frederic C. (1996b) 'Introduction': Social Reconstructions of the World Automobile Industry' in Frederic C. Deyo (ed.) *Social Reconstructions of the World Automobile Industry*. London: Macmillan, pp.1–17.
Deyo, Frederic C. (1996c) 'Competition, Flexibility and Industrial Ascent: The Thai Auto

Industry' in Frederic, C. Deyo (ed.) *Social Reconstructions of the World Automobile Industry*. London: Macmillan, pp.136–56.

Dore, Ron (1987) *Flexible Rigidities*. London: Athlone Press.

Elger, Tony and Chris Smith (1994) (eds) *Global Japanisation? The Transnational Transformation of the Labour Process*. London: Routledge.

Fitzgerald, Robert and Chris Rowley (1997) (eds) *Human Resources and the Firm in International Perspective, Volumes I and II*. Cheltenham: Edward Elgar.

Garrahan, Philip and Paul Stewart (1992) *The Nissan Enigma: Flexibility at Work in a Local Economy*. London: Mansell.

Graham, Laurie (1993) 'Inside a Japanese Transplant', *Work and Occupations*, Vol.20, No.2, pp.147–73.

Green, William C. and Ernest J. Yanarella (1996) (eds) *North American Auto Unions in Crisis: Lean Production as Contested Terrain*. Albany, NY: State University of New York Press.

Hasegawa, Harukiyo (1996) *The Steel Industry in Japan: A Comparison with Britain*. London: Routledge.

Hiramoto, Atsushi (1995) 'Overseas Japanese Plants under Global Strategies: TV Transplants' in Stephen Frenkel and Jeffrey Harrod (eds) (1995) *Industrialization and Labor Relations: Contemporary Research in Seven Countries*. Ithaca, NY: ILR Press. pp.236–62.

Hyman, Richard (1987) 'Strategy or Structure? Capital, Labour and Control', *Work, Employment and Society*, Vol.1, No.1, pp.25–55.

Jomo, K.S. (1994) *Japan and Malaysian Government: In the Shadow of the Rising Sun*. London: Routledge.

Jomo, K.S. (1995) 'Capital, the State and Labour in Malaysia' in Juliet Schor and Jong-Il You (eds) *Capital, The State and Labour: A Global Perspective*. Aldershot: Edward Elgar, pp.185–237.

Komata, Satoshi (1982) *Japan in the Passing Lane*. London: Urwin.

Kaple, Deborah (1994) *Dream of a Red Factory: The Legacy of High Stalinism in China*. Oxford: Oxford University Press.

Katz, Harry C. (1997) 'Introduction' in Harry C. Katz (ed.) *Telecommunications: Restructuring Work and Employment Relations Worldwide*. Ithaca, NY: ILR Press.

Kuruvilla, Sarosh C. (1995a) 'Economic Development Strategies, IR Policies and Workplace IR/HR Practices in Southeast Asia', in Kirsten Wever and Lowell Turner (eds) *The Comparative Political Economy Of Industrial Relations*. Ithaca, NY: ILR, pp.115–50.

Kuruvilla, Saroshi (1995b) 'Industrialization Strategy and IR Policy in Malaysia' in Stephen Frenkel and Jeffrey Harrod (eds) (1995) *Industrialization and Labor Relations: Contemporary Research in Seven Countries*. Ithaca, NY: ILR Press. pp.37–63.

Kynge, James (1997) 'Fatigue on the Road to Growth', *Financial Times Survey: Malaysia*, 19 May, p.3

Leggett, Chris and Greg Bamber (1996) 'Asia–Pacific Tiers of Change', *Human Resource Management Journal*, Vol.6, No.2, pp.7–19.

Lipietz, Alain (1987) *Mirage and Miracles: The Crisis of Global Fordism*. London: Verso.

Locke, Richard M. (1995) 'The Transformation of Industrial Relations? A Cross-National Review', in Kirsten Wever and Lowell Turner (eds), *The Comparative Political Economy Of Industrial Relations*. Ithaca, NY: ILR Press, pp.9–31.

Montagnon, P. (1996), 'Both Perspiration and Inspiration', *Financial Times Survey: Singapore*, 8 February, p.II.

Nakamoto, Michiyo (1997) 'Death of the Salaryman', *Financial Times*, 17 May, p.1.

Ng Sek Hong and Malcolm Warner (1998), *China's Trade Unions and Management*. London: Macmillan (in press).

Paik, Yongsuk, Charles Vance and Daniel Stage (1996) 'The Extent of Divergence in Human Resource Practice across Three Chinese National Cultures, Hong Kong, Taiwan and Singapore', *Human Resource Management Journal*, Vol.6, No.2, pp.20–31.

Pollert, Anna (1991) (ed.) *Farewell to Flexibility?* Oxford: Blackwell.

Poon Wai Keung (1995) 'Human Resource Management in Hong Kong', in Larry F. Moore and P. Devereaux Jennings (eds), *Human Resource Management on the Pacific Rim: Institutions, Practices and Attitudes*. Berlin: de Gruyter, pp.91–117.

Rhee, Johg-Chan (1994) *The State and Industry in Korea: The Limits of the Authoritarian State* London: Routledge.

Rodgers, Ronald A. (1996) 'Industrial Relations in the Korean Auto Industry: The Implications of Industrial Sector Requirements and Societal Effects for International Competitiveness' in Frederic C. Deyo (ed.) *Social Reconstructions of the World Automobile Industry*. London:

Macmillan, pp.87–135.

Rowley, Chris and Mark Lewis (1996) 'Greater China at the Crossroads? Convergence, Culture and Competitiveness', *Asia Pacific Business Review*, Vol.3, No.3, pp.1–22.

Sako, Mari and Hiroki Sato (1997) (eds) *Japanese Labour and Management in Transition: Diversity, Flexibility and Participation*. London: Routledge.

Sharma, Basu (1991) 'Industrialisation and Strategy Shifts in Industrial Relations: A Comparative Study of South Korea and Singapore' in Chris Brewster and Shaun Tyson (eds) *International Comparisons in Human Resource Management*. London: Pitman, pp.92–109.

Sisson, Keith (1994) 'Personnel Management: Paradigms, Practice and Prospects' in Keith Sisson (ed.) *Personnel Management: A Comprehensive Guide to Theory and Practice in Britain*. Oxford: Blackwell, pp.3–50.

Stewart, Paul (1996) (ed.) *Beyond Japanese Management: The End of Modern Times?* Frank Cass: London.

Turner, Lowell and Peter Auer (1996) 'A Diversity of New Work Organization: Human-Centred, Lean and In-between' in Frederic C. Deyo (ed.) *Social Reconstructions of the World Automobile Industry*. London: Macmillan, pp.233–57.

Torrington, Derek (1994) *International Human Resource Management: Think Globally, Act Locally*. Hemel Hempstead: Prentice Hall.

Verma, Anil, Thomas A. Kochan, and Richard D. Lansbury (1995) 'Employment Relations in an Era of Global Markets: A Conceptual Framework Chapter' in Anil Verma, Thomas A. Kochan and Richard D. Lansbury (eds) (1995) *Employment Relations in the Growing Asian Economies*. London: Routledge, pp.1–26.

Warner, Malcolm (1996) 'Culture, Organisations and Human Resources: Global Versus Less Global HRM Decision Making Models' in Pieter J. D. Drenth, Paul L. Koopman and Bernhard Wilpert (eds) *Organizational Decision-Making under Different Economic and Political Conditions*. Amsterdam: North-Holland, pp.189–95.

Warner, Malcolm (1997) 'Introduction: HRM in Greater China', *International Journal of Human Resource Management*, Vol.8, No.5, pp.565–8.

Wilkinson, Barry (1994) *Labour and Industry in the Asia–Pacific: Lessons from Newly-Industrialized Countries*. Berlin: de Gruyter.

Womack, James, Daniel Jones and Daniel Roos (1990) *The Machine That Changed the World*. New York: Rawson Associates.

You Jong-Il (1995) 'Changing Capital–Labour Relations in South Korea' in Juliet Schor and Jong-Il You (eds) *Capital, the State and Labour: A Global Perspective*. Aldershot: Edward Elgar, pp.111–51.

Abstracts

Introduction: Comparisons and Perspectives on HRM *by Chris Rowley*

The management of human resources in different countries has become an area of increasing interest for academics and business, one that has taken on Asian aspects. Contributing to this fascination are various views of economic development and the key ingredients of employees, 'the human touch' and people management. Various contributions to the field are outlined, including such perennially popular siren songs as convergence and 'one best way', concluding that ideas of universalism and nostrums of best practice remain far too simplistic in the dynamic and diverse world of HRM.

China's HRM in Transition: Towards Relative Convergence? *by Malcolm Warner*

In this contribution, the author reviews the current trends in HRM in the People's Republic of China. He then traces the impact of the post-1992 and 1995 economic reforms on Chinese personnel and industrial relations systems in both joint ventures and state-owned enterprises. Next, data from a recent field-investigation is reported *vis-à-vis* dimensions of HRM in these enterprises. The contribution particularly focuses on the problems of dimensionalizing HRM practices in such contexts. The author concludes that there may now be a growing but still limited overlap between joint ventures and state-owned enterprises in terms of their human resource policies and practices.

Economic Restructuring and HRM in Hong Kong *by Ng Sek Hong and Carolyn Poon*

This article discusses the human resource implications of business readjustment and advances in Hong Kong as its economy is restructured into a post-industrial centre of tertiary service industries. Corporate reforms are benchmarked against Western practices of exploring flexibilities and competitiveness which emphasize labour performance and cost savings. However, job security does not appear to have been eroded, possibly betraying an Oriental importance placed upon trust and commitment between employer and employee. As a meeting-place where Eastern and Western cultural practices interface, Hong Kong probably remains economically resilient by keeping its normative and institutional permissiveness in a hybrid mix of Western and Oriental practices.

HRM in Japanese Enterprises: Trends and Challenges *by John Benson and Philippe Debroux*

The rise in the Western concept of HRM parallels the global success of

Japanese manufacturing enterprises. HRM in these firms emphasized an internal labour market and stable relationships between all stakeholders. The global environment may now require firms to shift to a more market-oriented approach. The evidence points to peripheral changes taking place but within the overall structure of traditional Japanese management. This gradualism has important implications for Western firms adopting the HRM paradigm. The context and configuration of HRM is the essence of Japanese managerial strategy. Failure of Western firms to recognize this will mean that HRM will lack a strategic focus and be unable to produce the desired outcomes.

Beyond Seniority-Based Systems: A Paradigm Shift in Korean HRM? *by Johngseok Bae*

This contribution delineates human resource management in Korea in the context of macro environments, recent trends, and an international and comparative framework. Traditional seniority-based HRM systems with job stability, which worked well until the mid-1980s, have been recently challenged by global competition, in turn pushing towards ability and performance based systems with more flexibility. Therefore, two major issues of the recent trends are a 'seniority versus ability/performance' dimension and a 'job stability versus flexibility' dimension. Results from case studies and field data show that foreign firms from different countries had somewhat different employment policies. Finally, some implications of the results are discussed.

Converging and Diverging Trends in HRM: The Philippine 'Halo-Halo' Approach *by Maragtas S.V. Amante*

The article is an analysis of case studies of human resources in seven large, industry-leader and influential companies in the Philippines. The author analyzes the trends, and the motives for convergence and divergence of practices, in the workplace arising from openness to foreign investment and global/regional competition. Benchmark practices in human resource development bring about convergence, but innovations with entrenched local work practices and sensitivity to local cultural values ensure that Philippine HRM has its own characteristics. These practices could be called the Philippine *meztizo* or *halo-halo* (mixed) approach – most appropriate in the Philippine workplace, but which may not work in other foreign contexts.

HRM Under Guided Economic Development: The Singapore Experience *by Yuen Chi-Ching*

The article begins with the three stages of Singapore's economic development as the context from which the local labour-management relations system emerged. This is followed by a discussion of the institutional framework under which the government managed to attract multi-national enterprises to provide the necessary capital, technology, management expertise, and access to international markets – conditions required for the attainment of its economic goals. However, while the government did deliver a disciplined, hard-working and trained labour force, it also ensured that workers received a share of the wealth generated in the labour process. In the second part of the article, local employment practices, as well as the trends for future development are discussed.

The Development of HRM: Practices in Taiwan *by Shyh-jer Chen*

Small and medium-sized, mostly family-owned, enterprises employ more than 60 per cent of paid employees in Taiwan; however, these enterprises traditionally do not have distinct human resource management functions. In contrast, state-owned and large-sized private enterprises have gradually established their human resource systems and learned HRM techniques from foreign-owned companies. The article first examines employment structure and labour market development in Taiwan, then evaluates employment legislation and the development of HRM functions, and finally identifies several major future challenges, such as employee participation and employment security.

HRM in Thailand: Eroding Traditions *by John J. Lawler, Sununta Siengthai and Vinita Atmiyanandana*

This study explores the changing HRM practices in Thailand, especially over the past decade, during which the country has undergone substantial economic growth. It begins by examining the employment practices of traditional family-owned enterprises, which differ substantially from what have become thought of as 'best practice' in Western firms. It then analyzes the professionalization of employment practices in large-scale, publicly held Thai corporations. The final sections of the consider the nature of employment practices in the subsidiaries of multinational firms, which play a major role in the Thai economy.

Conclusion: Reassessing HRM's Convergence *by Chris Rowley*

This piece re-examines perspectives and evidence on the management of human resources and raises key issues, such as the role of labour, the state, and forms of flexibility. It seems that rather than simply being business-driven and introduced, the management of human resources remains influenced and constrained by key external influences. Despite some change, HRM often continues to be, on the one hand, diverse and dynamic while on the other, locationally-specific and contradictory, a situation many businesses and management gurus need to remember.

Index

Printed in the United States
by Baker & Taylor Publisher Services